Music in Christian Worship
At the Service of the Liturgy

Wilma Ann Bailey
Frank Burch Brown
Linda J. Clark and Joanne M. Swenson
Michael Driscoll
C. Michael Hawn
Michael Joncas
Charlotte Kroeker
Mary K. Oyer
Bert F. Polman
Don Saliers
John Witvliet
Nicholas P. Wolterstorff

Edited by
Charlotte Kroeker

LITURGICAL PRESS
Collegeville, Minnesota

www.litpress.org

Dedicated to
Kenneth Wayne Shipps
(1942–1996)

Cover design by Joachim Rhoades, O.S.B. Cover illustration: *The angel blowing the trumpet, the seven stars, and the eagle of Saint John. Apocalypse of Saint Jean de Lorvao.* Portuguese, 12th c., Arquivo Nacional da Torre do Tombe, Lisbon, Portugal. Giraudon/Art Resource, NY.

1   2   3   4   5   6   7   8

Library of Congress Cataloging-in-Publication Data

Music in Christian worship : at the service of the liturgy / Wilma Ann Bailey . . . [et al.].
    p. cm.
    Summary: "A collection of essays from experts (in music, philosophy, theology, and history) who write from the perspective that music for liturgical worship must be approached in an interdisciplinary manner, with attention to faithful theology, musical quality, accessibility to worshipers, and pastoral sensitivity"—Provided by publisher.
    Includes bibliographical references and index.
    ISBN 13: 978-0-8146-3021-1 (pbk. : alk. paper)
    ISBN 10: 0-8146-3021-9 (pbk. : alk. paper)
    1. Church music.   2. Music—Religious aspects—Christianity.   3. Public worship.   4. Music—Philosophy and aesthetics.   I. Bailey, Wilma A.
BV290.M88 2005
264'.2—dc22
                                                    2004020892

Permissions

Liturgical Press is grateful for the subvention from The Louisville Institute toward the publication of this volume.

Chapter 11: "Using Music from Other Cultures in Worship.
A Conversation with Mary K. Oyer"

"O Worship the King," pp. 161–2

"O Worship the King" from *Sound the Bamboo,* © 1990, 2000, Taiwan Presbyterian Church Press. All rights reserved. Reprinted by permission.

"He Is the Way," pp. 163–4

"He Is the Way" © Westminster Press & Faber & Faber
Words: W. H. Auden.
Music: Richard Wetzel. Used by permission of Westminster John Knox Press.

"Christ Burning Past All Suns," pp. 166–7

"Christ Burning Past All Suns." Words © 1972, Stainer & Bell Ltd. Admin. by Hope Publishing Co., Carol Stream, IL 60188. All rights reserved. Used by permission.
Words: Ian Fraser

"Lord, We Are Blind," pp. 167–8

"Lord, We Are Blind." Music © Hope Publishing Co., Carol Stream, IL 60188. All rights reserved. Used by permission.
Words: David Edge via Mrs. Barbara Edge (David Edge is deceased.)
Music: Peter Cutts

"All Who Love and Serve Your City," p. 168

"All Who Love and Serve Your City." Words © 1969 Stainer & Bell Ltd. Admin. by Hope Publishing Co. Music © 1969 Hope Publishing Co., Carol Stream, IL 60188. All rights reserved. Used by permission.
Words: Erik Routley
Music: Peter Cutts

"God Came, Body and Blood," p. 169

"God Came, Body and Blood" © 1969 Stainer & Bell Ltd. Admin. by Hope Publishing Co., Carol Stream, IL 60188. All rights reserved. Used by permission.
Words and Music: Peter Youngson

"O Come O Come, Emmanuel," p. 172

Risk: New Hymns for a New Day, Vol. II, No. 3 (Geneva, Switzerland: Youth Departments of the World Council of Churches and World Council of Christian Education, 1966). All rights reserved. Used with permission.
Music: Fr. James Minchin. Used with permission.

Diagram, p. 173
From: *Trouble at the Table: Gathering the Tribes for Worship* by Carol Doran and Thomas H. Troeger, Nashville, Tennessee, Abingdon Press, 1992. Used by permission.

***Kyrie eleison*, p. 183**
From *Hymnal: A Worship Book*, copyright 1992 by Brethren Press, Faith and Life Press, and Mennonite Publishing House. Used by permission.
Psalm 51, Kyrie Eleison, in *Sing! A New Creation*, #50. © CRC Publications, Grand Rapids, Michigan, 2001. Used by permission.
Music: Dinah Reindorf

"Have Mercy on Us Lord," pp. 183–4
From *Sound the Bamboo* © 1990, 2000, Taiwan Presbyterian Church Press. All rights reserved. Reprinted by permission.

"Come, Lord Jesus Christ," p. 185
From *Sound the Bamboo,* © 1990, 2000, Taiwan Presbyterian Church Press. All rights reserved. Reprinted by permission.
Words and Music: Bart Shaha

"Jesus, We Want to Meet," p. 186
From *Hymnal: A Worship Book*, copyright 1992 by Brethren Press, Faith and Life Press, and Mennonite Publishing House. Used by permission.
Words: Abingdon Press, © 1964 Abingdon Press (administered by The Copyright Company, Nashville, Tennessee). All rights reserved. International copyright secured. Used by permission.
Music: Nigerian Melody; adapted by A. T. Olajide Olude

Chapter 12: "Choosing Music for Worship"—Charlotte Kroeker

The Holy Eucharist I, Fraction Anthem: O Lamb of God *(Agnus Dei)*, p. 195
From The Hymnal, © 1982, by The Church Pension Fund. All rights reserved. Used by permission of Church Publishing, Inc., New York, N.Y.

Bach's B-Minor Mass *Agnus Dei* (Bärenreiter edition), p. 196
From the Bärenreiter edition (BA 5102a) of Johann Sebastian Bach's *Mass in B-Minor* "Agnus Dei" © Bärenreiter Music Corporation, Englewood, New Jersey. All rights reserved. Reprinted by permission.

Lamb of God, Setting 4, Augsburg Fortress, Publishers, p. 197
Lamb of God, Setting 4. From *With One Voice*, © 1995, Augsburg Fortress. All rights reserved. Used by permission.

***Agnus Dei* from "A Community Mass," by Richard Proulx, 1970, p. 198**
From "A Community Mass," Richard Proulx, © 1970, GIA Publications. All rights reserved. Used by permission.

Contents

Part III: Contemporary Cultural Considerations in the Light of Biblical Mandates

Part IV: Practical Considerations in the Light of Biblical Mandates

Acknowledgments

Thanks are due to many: Liturgical Press, especially Peter Dwyer and Aaron Raverty, O.S.B., who have shepherded this book from its beginnings to publication; The Louisville Institute and its director, James Lewis, who funded the conference that yielded the first of these essays, and who provided the subvention for the publication of this book; The Lilly Endowment and Craig Dykstra for providing funding for conversations of musicians, clergy, and academics, and for research with academic musicians across the United States and churches in Indiana; John Witvliet, of the Calvin Institute for Christian Worship, who helped conceive the first conference at the Boyer Center at Messiah College; Richard W. Conklin, who copyedited so that the text could be read across disciplines; John Roche, who helped to develop a coherent framework for seemingly disparate essays; John Cavadini, who provided support as director of the Institute for Church Life; Ernan McMullin and John Roche, who, with their unfailing logic and good questions, encouraged, challenged, and helped to develop the unarticulated intuitions of a musician; Notre Dame colleagues Calvin Bower, Craig Cramer, Michael Driscoll, Mary Frandsen, Michael Joncas and Gail Walton who make daily contributions to further our common commitments to the music of the church; Carol Doran and members of the Wolterstorff Seminar in Liturgy and the Arts whose suggestions yielded a much improved text; Goshen College for hosting initial stages of the project; the authors of the essays who have given countless hours in discussion of these topics beyond the time spent writing the subsequent essays.

Special thanks to Kenneth Shipps, husband, friend, mentor, soulmate, who taught me how faith informs academic vocation; Dolores Kroeker (1922–1989), mother, friend, encourager, who taught me that prayer and music can be one; Wesley Kroeker, father, who taught me the benefits of persistent work, that church is always a good place to go, and who brought Dorothy into our lives; siblings and their spouses, Bryan and Lavonne, Annette and Gary, Marcia and Steve, who understood when family time was sometimes difficult to find.

Introduction

If [the clergy] say that the hymns (words and music) which keep me
away from church draw others thither, and excite useful religious emotions, then they must take the responsibility wholly on themselves. I
would not choose for them. All I can urge is that they should have at
least *one* service a week where people like myself can attend without
being offended or moved to laughter. Robert Bridges, Poet Laureate of
England, October 1911.

Each of us has a repertoire of music familiar to us that prompts our
responses to any new music we hear. We are not only surrounded
by music of our choice, as when we play a musical instrument or a
recording, or choose to attend a concert. We are also affected by music
we have not chosen for itself, such as that music accompanying a
movie or television documentary, for example. When we come to
church, like the poet Robert Bridges, we experience the music of worship through ears that have heard a vast body of music, collected over
a lifetime.

Historically, music has been linked almost inseparably with the
practices of Christianity. Augustine, Martin Luther, and Simone Weil,
and many others, make a strong case for linking the arts with worship.
Ernest Boyer argued that the arts are necessary for achieving whole-
ness, that they provide a way of knowing crucial to the human spirit.
In particular, music in worship deserves our special thought and care
because it is so powerful. It invites our involvement on many levels; it
provokes and creates lasting memories; it taps into our emotional
being, and it has the capacity to link us with our spiritual core.

Whether or not the theological role of music in the church was well
understood, its practice has been commonplace in the life of the Christian church. A culture borrowed from Europe supported singing schools

that taught parishioners to read music. Children's choir programs in both church and school assumed all children needed to learn to sing. Pianos and pump organs crossed the prairies in covered wagons and provided the accompaniment for worship. Today, however, our culture has produced several generations who have not been universally educated in the arts and whose musical repertoire may largely originate in a passive experience of the music of popular culture rather than as part of an educational curriculum where music skills are taught and where an appreciation for art music is honed. While concert halls and museums still make substantial contributions to the cultural life of our society, the exchange between high art and everyday life is often missing. One result is that the quality of our worship is threatened by the general lack of understanding of the nature of the arts, and of their relation to theology and religious practice. We can no longer rely on background culture to cultivate an appreciation of education in the fine arts or to support their natural integration into congregational worship life.

Fortunately, it is still generally recognized that music is important in the life of the church. Religious and denominational publications are filled with articles and essays on the topic of church music and worship styles. Difficulties with musical decisions in local congregations are commonplace, even to the point of dividing congregations when differences cannot be reconciled, which shows, at least, that church music remains important. Rarely, however, do these writings and discussions address the more basic questions or issues. How, for example, can an understanding of how music historically has contributed to liturgy, together with a coherent theological context for the arts, lead to ways of creating more meaningful worship?

Most current discussion can become shortsighted when it is not grounded in reflection on the Christian tradition or in anything deeper than personal preferences. When solutions are found, they frequently take the form of alternative services for differing musical tastes in the congregation, or "blended" services that include the various styles of music preferred by different elements of the congregation. Such approaches can tend to be practically or politically grounded rather than to be derived from thoughtful reflection on knowledge of the liturgy. The broad historical range of the music of the church and coherence of liturgical flow are often lost. *Why might this be so?*

The content of this book acknowledges that the nature of church music is interdisciplinary. While it may be based in the field of music, the standards and practices of music alone are not adequate foundations for church music. Church music is in the service of the liturgy, so liturgy matters. Church music at its best is a way to understand theology, so theology matters. When worship is crafted well it ministers, so the ministry and pastoral aspects of church music matter. Music in Christian worship is participatory, so the knowledge and experience of the congregation matter. All of these dimensions of church music are represented here. The contributors to this volume are experts in at least one of the disciplines relevant to church music. They are committed Christians from a variety of faith traditions. They have thought deeply about what their expertise might contribute to a vision for the music of the church in the twenty-first century.

This book is intended for those persons who are responsible for church music, and who may have found themselves, even to their own surprise, ill prepared to work in this complex field. Pastors, who are theologically trained and have the most say in creating worship, often do not have training in music or in the historical repertoire or traditions of church music. Church musicians, who are primarily responsible for music-making, only rarely are trained theologically or in church music history. Academic musicians, who may be working in church-related colleges or universities, and have access to the traditions and to scholarly advances in the subject, often do not interact regularly with pastors and church musicians. (These same academic musicians, however, have the responsibility for training new generations of professional and lay musicians, many of whom will serve the church. The perspective of the clergy and local congregation is needed.) Performers and composers who create and transmit the music of the church frequently must rely on secular models for an ordering of values and performance ethos. Congregations, who may lack knowledge of theology, music, or historical traditions of music in worship, may find themselves caught in the role of consumers, for whom the music of the church is interpreted as a product for their consumption. If these same congregations and their musical leaders had more options to pursue, it is likely they could enrich their musical worship experience.

In June 1999, 152 pastors, academic musicians, church musicians, and laypersons concerned about church music gathered at the Boyer Center at Messiah College in Pennsylvania with the purpose of thinking about church music. The conference was titled "Church Music: Looking Back into the Future." It was funded by the Louisville Institute in cooperation with the Calvin Institute for Christian Worship. Conferees represented twenty-one denominations and spanned the continent from British Columbia to Puerto Rico. They were thoughtful, open to discussion, and appreciative of the opportunity to think about foundational issues in church music. Evaluations indicated that the conference accomplished its goal: to ground discussions of current issues in church music on historical Christian traditions. Several recurring themes were apparent from this conference and subsequent gatherings:

1. It is rare to address basic issues of church music in worship in contrast to the more common implementation ("how to") conferences offered within professional disciplines or specific denominations.
2. It is important to address the interdisciplinary and ecumenical nature of the issues.
3. The absence of a music of lament is evident in much contemporary liturgical music, even though the element of lament has always been present in the history of church music.
4. Addressing issues of church music through dialogue—among pastors, church musicians, academic musicians, composers, performers—rather than in individual professional societies, was affirmed.
5. Effective worship requires that the power and ego struggles over music style be recognized for what they are, and give way, in love, to focusing on the worship of God.
6. There is concern over the considerable influence our market-driven culture has on so many decisions in worship.
7. There is a need for the education of pastors, musicians, and congregations in liturgy and music.
8. There is a concern for the loss of the song of the church for younger generations.
9. There is a need to find ways to bring effective music ministry to diverse congregations.
10. Materials and resources that focus on the basic issues of worship are needed for pastors, musicians, congregations, and faculty members at colleges, universities, and seminaries.

Many of the contributors to this book spoke at the conference. We were amazed to find so much interest in a conference that was clearly interdisciplinary in nature and presented outside the confines of any one professional organization or denomination. We have had many requests for copies of papers from the conference, and this book is an answer to those requests, as well as an opportunity to continue, through a grant from the Lilly Endowment, the line of inquiry started by the conference. Though the book may have begun as a collection of conference papers, it has evolved to include the writings of others who have thought insightfully about the interdisciplinary understanding of church music.

Part I. Theological and Philosophical Considerations: How can understanding the intersection of worship and art affect its integral contribution to Christian worship?

In "Thinking about Church Music," Nicholas P. Wolterstorff, recently retired, and formerly the Noah Porter Professor of Philosophical Theology at Yale University, provides a philosophical basis for music in the church, probing ways we can *think* about how music functions in liturgy. While most of us might easily identify the particular music we like to accompany religious practice, and can identify a local church with the "best" music, it is more difficult to identify the differences in how music functions, for example, in the concert hall, in the liturgy, and in specific parts of the liturgy. He also addresses issues of style, coining the term "fittingness" to help us think about what music belongs where. In short, this chapter functions as a foundation for the chapters that follow, helping to establish the conceptual framework and terminology that will help us understand and reflect wisely on subsequent ideas.

"Sounding the Symbols of Faith: Exploring the Nonverbal Languages of Christian Worship," is an essay by Don Saliers of Emory University, Candler School of Theology. Professor Saliers probes the use of metaphor and symbol in the arts as vital, nonverbal contributions to worship. He demonstrates how little of our worship is merely the passing of information, and how much of communal praise and prayer depends upon nonverbal, symbolic means in order to be accomplished. We need and want to go somewhere other than the known and familiar. The arts provide the means to take us to another place, give us a vehicle for carrying that which words cannot express.

"Musical Mystagogy: Catechizing through the Sacred Arts," is written by Michael Driscoll, associate professor of liturgy and sacramental theology at the University of Notre Dame. Father Driscoll, drawing on the initiatory practices of the early church, suggests that today mystagogical catechesis includes the sacred arts, particularly sacred music. One way that mystagogy, or the teaching of mystery, can be accomplished is through perhaps the most natural and personal of means, that of using the voice in song. Though we will never fully comprehend the mystery of God, we will understand it best through a language familiar to us, that of music and the other sacred arts.

Part II. Historical Perspectives: What does the history of music in the church have to teach us about current and future practice of music in worship?

Jan Michael Joncas, professor of Catholic studies at the University of St. Thomas, wrote a definitive book in 1997, *From Sacred Song to Ritual Music*, an analysis of nine major documents of the Roman Catholic Church on music from papal, conciliar, curial, bishops' conference, and scholarly sources. In "An Anniversary Song: Pope John Paul II's 2003 Chirograph for the Centenary of *Tra le Sollecitudini*," Father Joncas uses Pope John Paul II's reflection on this one-hundred-year-old document to extend our understanding of the role of music in the church. Then, given the intellectual foundations of this and earlier documents, he brings their pastoral implications into the present, providing useful understandings for all Christian faith traditions.

Joncas aptly questions the definition of the various terms to precede "music" in referring to the music that accompanies worship, i.e., "sacred," "religious," "church," "liturgical," "worship," or "devotional" music. Indeed, there seems to be no consensus for meanings of these terms. *The New Harvard Dictionary of Music* [1986] chooses "Church Music" as the heading for a long entry on the history of music associated with the church. *The New Oxford Companion to Music* [1983] chooses likewise. Neither the Harvard or Oxford volumes have entries under "liturgical music." *The New Grove Dictionary of Music and Musicians* [2nd ed., 2001] chooses to ignore such terms, preferring articles on more specific topics. *Worship Music: A Concise Dictionary* [Foley, ed., Liturgical Press, 2000] suggests "church music" and "liturgical music" are often used interchangeably, but that "liturgical music" sometimes refers to that music written post-Vatican II which accompanies the liturgy. It will be helpful for the reader of this book to acknowledge the varied academic and denominational backgrounds of the contributors, and to consider the context in which such terms are used.

In "Forward Steps and Side Steps in a Walk-Through of Christian Hymnody," Bert F. Polman, musicologist and professor of music at Redeemer College in Ancaster, Ontario, provides us with a concise history of hymnody. Professor Polman describes the ebb and flow in the song of the people throughout the history of the church, placing current issues in context of the long journey through hymnody. Such issues can look quite different when viewed through the lens of historical patterns and practices. Professor Polman reminds us that we are a part of a continuum rather than a discrete entity in our music-making and that a longer view is necessary to give perspective to the present.

Part III. Contemporary Cultural Considerations in the Light of Biblical Mandates: What issues in our current environment must be addressed in order for faithful music-making to occur?

"The Sorrow Songs: Laments from the Old Testament and African American Experience," compares expressions of lament in Lamentations and the Psalms with the lament in African American spirituals. Wilma Ann Bailey, Old Testament scholar at Christian Theological Seminary in Indianapolis, demonstrates how the nature of lament from two chronologically distant times is very similar, and how the music of lament can "function as an aid to grief, to help people to grieve, to encourage them to grieve." Instead of always serving as a balm for pain, a number of the laments lack closure, allowing sufficient time for the grieving process to complete its task. In an era where much recently written sacred music avoids pain and darkness, we are reminded of how music in the Christian tradition has addressed all aspects of what it means to be human.

In "The Virtue of Discernment and the Present State of Crisis in Church Music," John Witvliet, director of the Calvin Institute for Christian Worship, develops models for a rhetoric of discernment necessary for making good decisions about music for worship. He quotes Augustine in advocating for discernment and prudence as "love distinguishing with sagacity between what hinders it and what helps it . . . prudence is love making a right distinction between what helps it towards God and what might hinder it."

"Reverse Missions: Global Singing for Local Congregations," is written by C. Michael Hawn, ethnomusicologist and professor of church music at Perkins School of Theology, Southern Methodist University. At a time when Pope John Paul II is searching for ways to define culture, when ethnic cultures collide with disastrous results, and when popular culture in the United States is a dominant force, Professor Hawn gives examples of how using music from a variety of cultures and Christian traditions can enrich both liturgical prayer and the understanding of the larger family of God. He reminds us that "we need to experience 'reverse missions' to keep us mindful that western (or northern) church is not the center of God's realm and the incarnation was a gift for all humanity."

"The Altar-Aesthetic as 'Work of the People'" gives us insights of two scholars and professors of church music at Boston University, Linda J. Clark and Joanne M. Swenson, who have extensive experience in congregational research. Professors Clark and Swenson help us to understand the importance of how space, objects, movement, and music function in individual congregations, and how these take on aesthetic and spiritual meaning. Clark and Swenson coin the term "altar-aesthetic" to describe that set of characteristics unique to any particular congregation. The meaning and nature of the altar aesthetic may differ significantly from congregation to congregation, yet is very important within any discrete group of worshiping Christians.

Part IV. Practical Considerations in the Light of Biblical Mandates: How do we go about choosing music faithfully for worship?

"Religious Meanings and Musical Styles: A Matter of Taste?" draws from an article in *Christian Century,* and his book, *Good Taste, Bad Taste, Christian Taste* by Frank Burch Brown, professor of religion and the arts at Christian Theological Seminary in Indianapolis. Professor Brown explores musical "taste" by helping us to understand the way that aesthetics, religious meaning, and artistic style function in a choice of music for worship setting. He points out pitfalls that can erode the quality of religious experience, and uncovers core truths that, when considered carefully, can lead to heightened awareness of God through the arts. In his own inimitable way, Professor Brown opens exceedingly abstract concepts in understandable and accessible language.

"Using Music from Other Cultures in Worship" is an interview with Mary Oyer, professor emeritus, Associated Mennonite Biblical Seminary and Goshen College. Building upon her considerable experience with Christian music-making in many settings, Professor Oyer helps us understand how music can cross cultural lines to inform and enhance worship. The description of the Dunblane gatherings recalls an intensely creative period of hymn writing, and reveals some of the complexities involved in introducing new music into worship. From her experience both as a college professor and a church musician in diverse cultures, she reflects on the relationship, both differences and similarities, between academic and congregational approaches to the music of the church. She also demonstrates how experiencing the music of ethnic cultures other than our own can help us use our own music in more meaningful ways. Her insights about ethnic music can help us understand the larger church to which all Christians belong, as well as the many "cultures" that may be found in any one congregation.

"Choosing Music for Worship: Contextual Considerations," my own article, was begun as part of the Calvin Summer Seminar in Liturgy and the Arts led by Nicholas Wolterstorff in 2002. After addressing theological, musical, and congregational concerns, I suggest contextual questions that must be raised to choose music wisely for a particular group of people, faith tradition, and location. Rather than giving absolutes for choices, I offer questions that, when answered thoughtfully, may lead to musical choices that will be meaningful to individual congregations and specific occasions.

Why this particular collection of essays, and why are they important now? Perhaps for the first time in history, the amount of religious music available has never been greater, requiring a level of discernment not always demanded of prior generations. Where music was formerly screened by denominational publishing houses and churches could be counted on to use the hymnal and other music provided by the denomination, now nondenominational, commercial publishers fill this role. A mobile society and technology have given us access to more religious music than ever. We share a repertoire across Christian denominations in ways unheard of in prior generations. Yet the means for sorting all this music thoughtfully has not developed along with the quantity of the music available. Where more discernment is required, we are less able to discern. Careful scholarship in liturgical studies since Vatican II has not been matched with careful scholarship in liturgical music.

This small collection is only one effort in the quest for deeper musical experience in worship, but it is that. I thank the writers profoundly for applying their expertise in ways that for some is a stretch beyond their academic comfort zone. Yet they have chosen to stretch because they care deeply about the music that accompanies worship. Their faith is that strong. And so our essays are here for you, our readers, for your own thought and reflection, as together we seek to offer music worthy of the God we love and serve.

Charlotte Kroeker, PH.D.
University of Notre Dame
February 2005

Part I

Theological and Philosophical Considerations

1

Thinking about Church Music

Nicholas P. Wolterstorff

I

Throughout the ages, the music of the church has been mingled with tears. Sometimes tears of gladness. A new arrival at Calvin's church in Strasbourg in the early 1540s wrote about his experience of first hearing the entire congregation singing psalms to some of the earliest Calvinist tunes, that

> for five or six days at the beginning, when I looked on this little company of exiles from all countries, I wept, not for sadness, but for joy to hear them all singing so heartily and as they sang giving thanks to God that He had led them to a place where His name is glorified. No one could believe what joy there is in singing the praises and wonders of the Lord in the mother tongue as they are sung here.[1]

And in the *Confessions,* his eloquent and endlessly fascinating address to God, Augustine similarly recalls weeping in response to the music of the church at the funeral of his seventeen-year-old son Adeodatus: "[T]he tears flowed from me when I heard your hymns and canticles, for the sweet singing of your Church moved me deeply. The music surged in my ears, truth seeped into my heart, and my feelings of devotion overflowed, so that the tears streamed down. They were tears of gladness" (IX, 6). Augustine checked himself from weeping tears of grief over the death of his son—such tears, he believed, were wrong; but he freely allowed himself tears of joy over the music of the church sung upon the death of his son. Of course, I need not cite historical examples to make the point: many of those reading this essay will have had the experience of being moved to tears of joy by the music of the church.

The music of the church has also been mingled with tears of grief. When fifty-seven Huguenots from Meaux were led off to the dungeon, they sang the opening of Psalm 79 to the Genevan tune:

> O God, the heathen have come into thy inheritance
>   they have defiled thy holy temple;
>   they have laid Jerusalem in ruins.
> They have given the bodies of thy servants
>   to the birds of the air for food,
>   the flesh of thy saints to the beasts of the earth.

And when fourteen of them were later led out to execution, they sang on from the same psalm until their tongues were cut out to silence them:

> Why should the nations say,
> "Where is their God?"
> Let the avenging of the outpoured blood of thy servants
> be known among the nations before our eyes!
> Let the groans of the prisoners come before thee;
> according to thy great power preserve those doomed to die![2]

The music of the church has obviously not been mingled with the tears of the martyrdom of any of us. Yet for many of us it will have been mingled with tears of grief. Recently a graduate student of mine asked if he could take me out for lunch. We talked for a bit about how his dissertation was going. Then it all came out. A few years back he and his wife had found a lively, committed church where they felt at home. They had become active; and young though he was, he had been elected to the council. Now the church was being split apart, and he and his wife were in deep grief. What was the problem? Music. A deep conflict had arisen between the pastor and a number of his supporters on the one hand, and a sizeable group of protesters on the other, over the music of the church, and my student was hurt and bewildered by the whole experience. Bright and reflective though he was, he had never thought about church music; he had just experienced it. Now his position of responsibility within the group embroiled in controversy was forcing him to think about it. But he had no idea what to think—no idea even how to go about thinking. How should we think about church music, he asked me, tears in his eyes.

I do not doubt that now and then it is tears of joy that evoke reflection on church music. That young person experiencing for the first time the congregational singing within the early Protestant liturgy in Strasbourg might well have been provoked by his tears of joy into reflecting on this new use of music in the liturgy. More often it is tears of anger, frustration, or grief that provoke the reflection. Either way, we are dealing with passions. I have yet to come across the church member for whom the music of the church is a matter of sheer indifference.

My question for today is the question posed by my student: How should we think about church music? My answer is simple: we should think of church music as serving the liturgy. I admit there is a bit more to be said than just that. So let me insert the qualifier: we should *primarily* think of church music as serving the liturgy.

A few years back, when we at Yale were looking for someone to fill our position of church music, one of our candidates, a well-known teacher of church musicians, argued that the governing principle of church music should be that God wants the best—by which he meant the *aesthetic* best. In the question period after his lecture it became clear that he did in fact draw the obvious implication, that congregations should be allowed a relatively small role in church music; if one had to let them sing, best to drown them out with powerful organ playing. At the time, I happened to be teaching a seminar on the issue of divine impassibility: does God suffer, does God experience grief? I remember thinking the mischievous thought that if what God wants out of church music is the aesthetic best, then, given the state of church music, one has to conclude that God suffers—every Sunday anew! I cite this example to make clear that there are alternatives to the principle I will defend, that we should primarily think of church music as serving the liturgy.

II

As my opening point, I wish to argue that all music, with the rarest of exceptions, is composed or used for the service of something or other. By this I do not mean all music is produced for some reason or other. That is obviously true. Works of music are not objects of nature produced by one and another natural process. They are human artifacts—the outcome of intentional action on the part of human beings. That, I say, is obvious. What I have in mind when I say almost all music is composed or used for the service of something or other is that almost all of it is composed or used for some social function.

The reason I emphasize the point is, of course, that this is not how the situation is customarily seen. Ever since the eighteenth century it has been customary for theorists to work with the distinction between music composed and used for the service of something external to itself, and music not so composed and used—between so-called functional music and so-called absolute music. Almost invariably, when this distinction is employed, a comparative evaluation is lurking in the wings: absolute music is higher on the scale of worth than functional music. For when music is freed from the need to be in the service of something outside itself, it is free to follow out its own inherent laws of development rather than having its development shaped and stunted by the requirements of liturgy, the requirements of entertainment, the requirements of national celebrations, or whatever.

This is not the occasion to dig into the ideological and historical origins of this way of thinking about music—and about the arts generally. Let me content myself with observing that by the end of the eighteenth century, the concept and celebration of supposedly absolute music had become intertwined with the emergence of a new cultural paradigm. It was said that if one wants to be a person of culture, of *Bildung*, as the Germans called it, you must engage yourself with nonfunctional art: attend concerts, visit galleries, read novels and poetry, admire architecture. The connection established between supposedly nonfunctional art and the cultural elite remains intact to this day. If I confessed in public that I never went to concerts, that hymns and birthday songs were good enough for me, that I never visited museums, that a few mountain scenes on my walls at home are quite sufficient, that I never read novels, that the stories I share with the guys on the job are quite enough, I would immediately be judged as embarrassingly uncultured. No doubt many of those in the hordes who crowd our present-day museum blockbusters genuinely take delight in what they see; it is safe to say, however, that all of them, without exception, are aware of the fact that by attending the Van Gogh exhibition, they are acquiring culture, and that that is seen by our society as a really good thing.

My own judgment on this line of thought is that it is a thicket of theoretical confusion and indefensible elitism. At the heart of it is the claim or assumption that concert hall music, museum painting and sculpture, reading room poetry and fiction, represent *art come into its own*, since the works are presumed no longer to serve a function outside themselves. To get started in thinking about this, consider something not an example of any of the fine arts—a chair, say. The concept of a chair is of something meant to be regularly used for sitting. Chairs can serve other functions than being used to sit on; and things other than chairs can be sat on. Furthermore, chair-like objects can be produced with the intention that they shall never be sat on. Yet it remains the case that the concept of a chair is of something meant for sitting. The concept of a chair is thus a *functional* concept. And when a chair is used as it is meant to be used, one might appropriately say it has then "come into its own"—that is to say, it has then come into its own intended function. A chair used to prop a door open, or to provide aesthetic delight in a museum, has not "come into its own."

Compare, now, the concept of a chair to the concept of a work of music. The latter, admittedly, is not a functional concept. If one asks what chairs are for, the answer is clear: chairs are for sitting. But if one asks what works of music are for, no similarly clear and unambiguous answer is forthcoming. The concept of a work of music, instead of being a functional concept, is of a sequence of sounds of a certain kind. But— and this is the important point—it does not follow that works of music are not meant to serve some social function. With rare exceptions they surely are. Where they differ from chairs is that they are meant to serve a wide variety of different social functions. The concept of a work of music is thus more like the concept of an item of furniture than like the concept of a chair. Music is *multi*functional: some works are meant for one function, some, for another. And as with chairs, they can be used to serve functions for which they were not meant. A Bach cantata can be performed in the concert hall; a Bach fugue, as postlude to the liturgy.

One may say that music performed and listened to in the concert hall nonetheless represents music freed from function. My response is that it represents nothing of the sort. Music in the concert hall is caught up into the social function of contemplative listening for the sake of delight, inspiration, and so forth. Listening carefully to music is doing something with it, putting it to a use. So-called absolute music is just as functional as liturgical music; what makes it different is that it is meant for serving a different function.

Music meant for the liturgy comes into its own when it functions in the liturgy. It is not waiting, longing, to be allowed to come into its own by being freed from service to the liturgy. It is doing what it was meant to do; it has come into its own. By the same lights, music meant for contemplative listening in the concert hall comes into its own when it is listened to contemplatively in the concert hall. It comes into its own when it is put to that use, when it serves that function—not when it serves *no* function, but when it serves *that* function.

That's my case for the conclusion that the distinction between functional and absolute music is a piece of confusion, as is the claim that absolute music represents music come into its own. What remains to consider is the elitism interwoven with this way of thinking. The central issue is now clear. Is contemplative listening a nobler action than all the other things done with works of music—nobler, for example, than any of the things done with music when it functions in the liturgy? I refuse to accept such Platonism. I do indeed want to defend the worth of contemplative listening to those who are dismissive of it. But I reject emphatically the suggestion that the use of music as an object of contemplative listening is nobler than its use for praising God. I would in fact contend the opposite.

III

My thesis, again, is that we should primarily think about church music in terms of its service to the liturgy. I have argued that there is nothing distinctive about church music in its being of service to some social function; that is true of virtually all music, concert hall music included. What is, or ought to be, distinctive about church music is what it is in service to, namely, the liturgy.

But is church music not best thought of as *religious* music, some might ask? I think not. A great deal of the music meant for the concert hall—hence meant to serve the function of contemplative listening—is religious music: Beethoven's *Missa Solemnis*, Brahms' *German Requiem*, and Penderecki's *Utrenja* come to mind. Not only is each of these masterpieces a work of religious music meant for the concert hall rather than for the liturgy; none of them would function at all well within a liturgy. They are too powerful, too overwhelming. Church music and religious music are distinct categories—overlapping, of course, but not coinciding.

To advance our discussion I must now say a word about how I understand liturgy. First, the word itself. To some, the word will evoke thoughts of Orthodoxy, high-church Anglicanism, and pre-Vatican II Catholicism. Those for whom the word has these connotations will think of some traditions as liturgical and of others as nonliturgical, perhaps even of some as *anti*liturgical.

That is not how I use the word—nor, to the best of my knowledge, how any contemporary liturgical scholar uses it. In my tradition, an Americanized version of the Dutch Reformed tradition, we customarily spoke when I was growing up of what transpired in church on Sunday as "the service"—sometimes, more elaborately, as "the worship service," but usually just as "the service." We spoke of when the service began, of when the service was over, of the language of the service as either Dutch or English, and so forth. That is what I mean when I speak of the liturgy: the liturgy is the service. If the word "liturgy" evokes for you connotations of elaborate rites and rituals, replace it with the word "service."

What we in my childhood meant by "the service" is exactly what the Orthodox mean when they speak of "the divine liturgy." In fact the Greek word *leitourgia*, of which our English word "liturgy" is merely the transliteration, just meant, in classical Greek, a service to the public rendered by a well-to-do individual. Liturgy is public service. The word "service," as used in my childhood to refer to what transpires in church on Sunday, was a precise translation into English of the Greek word *leitourgia*.

It follows that all traditions of Christianity have liturgies. For they all have services. And it makes no sense to speak of some of them as more liturgical than others. They either have a service or they do not; in fact, all of them do.

The question of substance is how we should understand what goes on in these services. A near consensus has emerged among contemporary liturgical scholars on the basic answer to this question. It's a consensus I gladly affirm: *Liturgy is action.* I once had a pastor who insisted to me—"argued with me" would better describe the character of our discussions—that the liturgy, that is, the service, is a sequence of happenings meant to produce a religious experience that he called "edification." For each Sunday, he would design a somewhat different liturgy depending on what he judged would prove edifying for the bulk of the congregation on that day. I think I can safely say no liturgical scholar writing today would accept that way of thinking of the liturgy. Liturgy, to say it again, is action. On that there is now, to the best of my knowledge, universal agreement among scholars.

As to the sort of actions that comprise the liturgy, there is considerably less agreement; on this occasion I must present my own view without doing much to defend it against alternatives. One can see in those from the Lutheran tradition a strong tendency to fit all the actions of the liturgy under the rubric of proclamation; one can see in those from the Orthodox and Catholic traditions a similarly strong tendency to fit all the actions of the liturgy under the rubric of prayer, or more broadly, worship. My own view is that the liturgy properly incorporates actions both of proclamation and of worship; and not only does it properly do so, but every actual liturgy does in fact include elements of both, albeit in different proportions. In Lutheran liturgies one finds elements of worship; in Orthodox and Catholic liturgies, one finds elements of proclamation.

Whatever one's answer, proclamation, worship, or both, a question one must soon consider is who is the agent of the liturgical actions—or who are the agents? There is a strong impulse in most contemporary Christians in the West to say the agents of the liturgical actions are the individual human beings assembled—the preacher is the agent of acts of proclamation, the individual congregants are the agents of the acts of worship. Thus, for example, in my own church recently, the layperson leading the prayers introduced them by saying, "Will you join me in prayer?"

I think I can safely say that on this point too there is today a consensus among liturgical scholars: none would accept this individualistic answer to the question as to who is the agent, or who are the agents, of the liturgy. The Lutheran inclined to fit the actions of the liturgy under the rubric of proclamation will correspondingly be inclined to say God is the agent, and/or Christ; it is not the preacher who proclaims the gospel but God by way of the preacher. And the Orthodox and Catholic inclined to fit the actions of the liturgy under the rubric of worship will be correspondingly inclined to say the people is the agent, the people being understood not as a collection of individual persons but as *a people*. The person leading the prayers does not invite the assembled individuals to join in on *her* prayer; instead, she leads the congregation in *its* prayer. It is neither *her* prayer that is prayed nor *their* individual prayers but *its* prayer, that is, the people's prayer.

As expected, my own view is that the liturgical agent is both of these—both God and the people. I concede that in most liturgies there are a few actions that are the actions of individual congregants—as, for example, when the peace is passed, or, more casually, when people are invited to greet each other. But for the most part, liturgy is a dialogue between God and God's people. In the assembly, the people of God address God and God addresses the people, back and forth.

Liturgies vary from each other in the specific actions of proclamation and worship they incorporate; they vary even more in the sequence of such actions; they vary yet more in the words and gestures used to accomplish such actions. But we must be careful not to exaggerate the differences: any outsider to Christianity would discern, beneath the differences in specific actions, sequences, words, and gestures, a remarkable similarity. It is in the Eucharist—the Lord's Supper—that both the actions and the official understanding of the actions diverge most widely.

IV

Suppose you are willing to go along with my suggestion that the primary way to think of church music is as music in service of the liturgy. And suppose you are also willing to think of liturgy as a sequence of actions—actions on the part of God addressed to the people interwoven with actions on the part of the people addressed to God. Then quite obviously what we want to consider, when we get down to details, is how music can best serve the diverse actions of the liturgy. I think I can best proceed by stating, and all-too-briefly developing, a few relevant principles.

(1) My first principle is Christian liturgy *calls for* music. The testimony of history speaks so loudly here that belaboring it would be pointless and tedious. It is true that the actions of the liturgy can be performed without the service of music. In some traditions, they are so performed during Lent. So it cannot be said that Christian liturgy *needs* music. It does not. Nonetheless, the testimony of history is that the liturgy cries out for, calls out for, music. The church has always felt that, in ways too mysterious to describe, music profoundly enhances its liturgy. The way to put the point is perhaps this: in its assemblies the church has always found itself *breaking out* into music, especially into song.

Given the pervasiveness of background music in our culture, I think it worth adding that at some points in the liturgy silence is appropriate: neither words nor music. In the liturgy of my own congregation silence occurs at two points: for a few minutes after the sermon, and during the offertory. We conduct the offertory as did the ancient church, by people getting out of their seats and bringing their gifts forward. When we first adopted this practice, the musicians provided some background instrumental music. After a few weeks, we asked ourselves why we were doing that; finding no good answer, we stopped. Now there is just the rustle of people moving forward and returning.

(2) A second, more specific, principle is that any action of the liturgy can be enhanced by the use of music. Though this enhancement can consist of background music, what I really have in mind is song and

chant: any liturgical action can be enhanced by song or chant. No liturgical actions permit one to dismiss music out of hand as inappropriate. What this implies is that discerning judgment is needed about when to use or not to use music.

Most Protestants operate with the tacit principle that only acts of the people are appropriately served by music, not acts of God. Hence there is no chanting of Scripture or sermon. And today even the Orthodox and Catholics do not chant their sermons. My own view is that most of the time Scripture and sermon are best not chanted; chanting, in my experience, makes them too much an artifact to be admired rather than a message to be received. But what makes me resist saying "never," even about the sermon is a recording of the Easter liturgy celebrated in one of the monasteries on Mount Athos. In the liturgy, an Easter sermon of John Chrysostom is chanted by the presider. I find the chanting in this case grippingly celebrative. And Easter, need I say, ought to be celebrative!

(3) My third principle for your consideration is that all the music occurring during the liturgy should be in the service of one and another liturgical action, and that it should be relatively clear to the congregation what that action is. At no point should the liturgy be halted to enable the choir to sing an anthem, or a soloist to render "special music." Mind you, I have no objection to concerts of religious music; my own life has been wonderfully enriched by attendance at such concerts. But the Sunday service, the divine liturgy, is not the occasion for concerts of religious music.

I admit that the application of this principle can get a little sticky. I think if some action of the people is going to be accomplished by song, then most of the time all the people together should be the singers. My own view, in contrast to the candidate I mentioned for our position in church music, is that the sound of the monotone trying to sing is far sweeter in God's ear than the sound of the professional choir singing religious music with the congregation all listening with aesthetic delight. But I readily concede the people can normally use some assistance in the form of instruments or choir. Let us be sure, though, the instruments really do assist the song of the people, rather than the song of the people being turned into a *sotto voce* accompaniment to the organ; and let us be sure the choir really assists the song of the people, rather than the song of the people being turned into a murmuring continuo to the song of the choir.

Not only do I think it appropriate for instruments and choir to assist the singing of the congregation; just as I think it appropriate sometimes for someone to *lead* the people in its intercessory prayer, the leader alone speaking and the people being silent, so I think it appropriate sometimes for a choir to lead the people in its confession, its praise, its thanksgiving, and so forth, the choir singing and the people being silent. What I insist on, however, is that this be practiced and understood as I have just described it. We are not listening in on the choir's praise of God. The choir is not praising God in place of our doing so; not even, strictly speaking, is the choir praising God *on our behalf*. Rather, we as a people are praising God, being led in our praise, on this occasion, by the singing of the choir.

(4) My fourth principle for your consideration—one I regard as extremely important—is that the character of the music *fit* the liturgical action it serves—and fit the theologically correct understanding of that action.

In my book *Art in Action* I develop at length the concept of *fittingness* I use here; in this essay I will have to be content with offering no more than hints of what I mean. It is probably best to do so by way of examples. Everybody ever asked has agreed with me that an undulating line fits better with tranquility and a jagged line better with agitation; a straight horizontal line fits better with green and a straight vertical line better with red; the interval of a seventh or a second fits better with tension and the interval of an octave or a fifth better with rest; the tritone fits nicely with, say, the demonic—and so forth.

These examples are, of course, abstract: actual paintings come with a thick complex of lines and colors; actual passages of music with a thick complex of melodic lines, harmonies, rhythms, and volumes. But I submit that fittingness applies as much to such complexes of qualities as to the simple abstracted qualities I invited you to consider. If someone who does not know the title listens to Chopin's Funeral March, it might not occur to him to think of it as funereal in character; nonetheless, he would surely think of its character as somewhere in the region of the funereal. No one would think of it as light, gay, and skipping. Though someone who listens to the section called "The Angels" from Messiaen's Nativity Suite might not, in the absence of the title, think of angels, nonetheless, anyone to whom the choice is presented will think it fits archangels much better than cherubim. My view, in fact, is that if you want to know what archangels are like, listen to Messiaen's piece; then you will know.

Back to the issue at hand: just as the character of a piece of music will typically be more fitting to one emotion than another, so too it will typically be more fitting to one liturgical action than another, and to one way of understanding that action than another way. Some music better befits the liturgical action of confession than the action of praise; and some music better befits a worried, anxious way of understanding confession than a humble but confident way of understanding it. Of course, I concede that distinct ways of performing a passage of music can give it a quite different character—and even that different words connected with the same passage can lend it a quite different character. Witness the difference in how the tune sounds when the words sung are "Baa, baa, black sheep" from how it sounds when the words sung are "Twinkle, twinkle, little star."

I am not an aficionado of contemporary Christian praise music. But on those occasions on which I have been confronted with it, I have found those who use it bafflingly insensitive on this point of fittingness. I also find the words painfully prosaic and sometimes even shudderingly inappropriate. I will not soon forget being confronted, in the service in the Anglican church in Amsterdam my wife and I attended last June, with a song on the overhead projector whose first line was, "Oh how I appreciate you, Jesus." But on the issue of fittingness, my most unnerving experience occurred at a Christian school convention in Sydney, Australia, where we confessed our sins to a rollicking tune accompanied by a rock band. The only conclusion I could come to is that those who had put these words to that music had never asked the question of fittingness. They thought we ought to confess our sins, they had this tune in their repertoire, so off we went on our clangorous, hard-driving, rollicking confession.

(5) Let me finish with a word about style. I think fittingness, not style, is the basic consideration to be introduced when thinking about music in the liturgy; but once the requirements of fittingness are satisfied, then certain considerations of style do become relevant. Perhaps I should first articulate my assumption that music in many different styles can be equally fitting to a certain action in the liturgy. I have never heard any rock music that struck me as fitting the action of confession; possibly that indicates a deficiency in either my experience or imagination. But certainly music in the style of Gregorian chant, of Genevan psalm tunes, of Lutheran chorales, and of African American spirituals—to mention only a few—can all be used to set fittingly Psalm 51.

When it does come to choosing style, I think it desirable that the music of the liturgy fit comfortably the ears of participants in the liturgy. Let me explain what I mean by "ears." Any musical culture whatsoever has two sides to it: the objective and the subjective. The objective side consists of the works available for performance within that culture; the subjective side consists of the habits acquired for listening to the music performed. Genuinely listening to music requires more than just the ability to hear; it requires those habits that consist in highlighting some elements and allowing others to recede into the background, recognizing repetitions, noticing harmonic contrasts, being able to pick out melodies, and so forth. Only a very few highly trained specialists will have acquired the ears appropriate for every style of music; most of us in the modern world will have acquired the ears appropriate for a few distinct styles, though only a few.

Back to the principle I propose: it is desirable that the music of the liturgy fit comfortably the ears of participants in the liturgy. I do not mean to imply that the congregation should never be invited to sing or listen to music for which it has not acquired the ears; but it should then be taught how to listen. It should be assisted in acquiring the ears. The liturgy, after all, belongs to the people; it is the dialogue of the people with God, not the performance of some specialists to which the people are invited to listen.

You see the implications. No matter how fond you, the music director, may be of Palestrina and Bach, if your congregation has not acquired the ears for listening to Palestrina and Bach, I do not think it appropriate for you to impose Palestrina and Bach upon them. Wherever the congregation does have the appropriate ears, then by all means do what you can to keep alive the richness of the Christian tradition of church music as well as honoring what is good in the here and now; but if those ears are absent, then it would be wrong for you to alienate the congregation from its liturgy on some such ground as that God wants the best and that Palestrina and Bach are the best. Of course there might be some congregations that have acquired the ears for Palestrina and Bach but not for any music beyond, say, 1900; then give those people Palestrina and Bach.

These last comments of mine describe an idealized situation. I have been talking as if the members of the congregation have all acquired the same ears—not to mention the same preferences. In most of our congregations, that is far from the situation. I will never forget the time a friend took me to visit his home congregation in the village of Karatina, in the Great Rift Valley above Nairobi, Kenya. The congregation was Catholic; the language used was Kikuyu, so I understood not a word of it. When the priest said something, the congregation chanted in response. And when it was time for a hymn, a small percussion band up front set the rhythm and shortly the people joined in. The music was completely unfamiliar to me. The week before I had visited, with the same friend, the Anglican cathedral in Nairobi. There too, when the people began singing, I found it unfamiliar; but invariably, after about five seconds, I recognized a familiar tune, sung, however, in a most unfamiliar way. Not so for this village church in Karatina.

Afterward I asked the priest where the music came from. He said when first the new Vatican II liturgy was translated into Kikuyu, the people spoke their responses, but gradually the congregation fell into chanting them. As to the hymn tunes, these, he said, were tunes used at weddings, birthdays, and so forth. I felt a profound nostalgia for a musically unified culture.

That day is past for us. Given the ready availability of radio and CDs, and the diversity of musical styles heard on these, the members of virtually every congregation in North America come to church with significantly different ears and significantly different tastes. What is one to do when choosing a style—or styles—for the music of the church? I have no other answer to this difficult question than the answer of charity: I will sing hymns in the style that fits comfortably with your ears and suits your tastes, and I will ask and hope that you treat me likewise.

V

I close by returning to my beginning. When those of you who occupy positions of leadership in church music grow weary—I do not say "if" but "when"—when you grow weary, just remember the music of the church sinks so deeply into our identity as Christian human beings it brings tears to our eyes. Tears of grief, sometimes; more often, tears of joy. Our tears are existential testimony to how important the music of the church is. When you grow weary, remember the tears. Your work contributes to our shalom, our flourishing. Yes, the liturgy can be performed without music. But if the liturgy is to be caught up into our shalom, there has to be music. In the new age of God, we will not be reciting the *Sanctus*, we will be singing it—most of the time, I would guess, to its hair-raising setting in Bach's B minor Mass.

Notes

1. Quoted in James Hastings Nichols, *Corporate Worship in the Reformed Tradition* (Philadelphia: Westminster Press, 1958) 35.
   2. Ibid., 39.

2

Sounding the Symbols of Faith
Exploring the Nonverbal Languages of Christian Worship

Don E. Saliers

In this discussion of the nonverbal languages of Christian worship, I begin with four substantive points and then proceed to what C. S. Lewis called "festooning." I'll put the points in the form of propositions or theses, and then we'll discuss them in detail.

First, the words we use in worship depend radically on that which is not verbal language. The meaning and point of words we use in worship depend radically on the nonverbal. You could call them "languages" if you wanted to be metaphorical, but such symbolic forms animate the verbal or the textual dimensions of liturgical assemblies.

Second, the language we use in prayer, proclamation, sacramental celebration, and blessing, is itself, to use a visual image, a prism, a prism of nonverbal symbolism. Human utterance in the worship of God is multivalent, opening a spectrum of meaning beyond the literal. If you wish to change the metaphor, change it to "crucible" because it is also a crucible—a place where things are heated to intensity, brought together, melded.

Third, we do things with the words we use in worship. Words are, as we have been taught by some philosophers, "performative." We don't use words in worship primarily to state facts or information or ideas. Nor do we use words merely to express immediacy of feeling. Rather, in worship, we are *acting* with words. We pray, we bless, we cry, we hope, we are grateful. Those are performances with words. The words are not just there to give us information. Worship is not info-serve. The language is more like gesture, like music.

Fourth, in worship the senses cross over. "O taste and see the good-ness of the Lord." Has that not captured your imagination at one time? Have you not come to a place where in tasting the bread you come to see something, but not just visually? You see a virtue, the very virtue of God, the grace of God—"O taste and see"? It is no accident that persons working in the worship environment where things are alive to God sense that the eye can hear, or the ear can see, or sometimes the body speaks, the gesture is blessed, the gestalt of worship is accomplished.

These are four points we can think about, but I'd rather have you think *with* them than *about* them. So I want you to hold those proposals as avenues of possible insight. And now, go with me to a different kind of rhetoric—nonpropositional and narrative.

Let's start with a story dear to me. I think it illustrates so much of what you and I work for in our ministries and theological reflection. For several years, in the inner city in the late '60s and early '70s, my family and I lived in 221 D Housing. It was a wonderful project those days, an idealistic project in inner-city living, integrated housing. And our children, then quite young, learned to sing a set of ritual songs while skipping rope. The skipping ropes would start turning, and the children would dance in and out, singing "Mary Mac—Mac—Mac/All dressed in black—black—black/With silver buttons—buttons—but-tons/All down her back—back—back" rhyme. The children learned these ritual songs, this skipping rope, with its particular ethnic origins. I hold that image of the vitality of my daughters skipping in and out to the singing, and the action, and the admonitions. And if they missed a step: "It's all right, honey. It's all right. Try it again." That vibrant image of the skipping rope and the ritual song has been for me, over these many years, what good liturgy is all about. That is to say, that cir-cling song and movement where the rules were clear, the catechesis re-quired, but improvisation was allowed. "Don't miss the skips, or you have to start over. Sing the song in the right accent as well." The de-light and the physical energy were also marked by surprises. These, I think, are the characteristics we work with and must encourage. These are features of deep worship where language and the nonverbal work together. It's an image of doxology. If you will, those children were practicing a natural language of praise.

So shared music-making in the gathered assembly is about the book of our memories; about the font of our baptism, or death and resur-rection; about the table where we "taste and see" the goodness of the Lord. In this gathered community, shared music-making helps the human body remember long after the mind has forgotten. Those children knew what we adults so often forget: that there exists a natural, communal way in which we come to vitality in life. Thus, human beings have always ritualized life and sung it in our work, in our festivals, in our solemn occasions of grief and joy. Whether around campfires or in recital halls, on the playground, or in synagogue and church, the act of singing has brought together a kind of acoustical gathering of life. Singing has released for us, through a natural language of doxology, what the human soul longs for, what signals the transcendent. For the dance of the children is more than their dancing, and their song more than their singing, and their mutuality more than just friendship. It's a sign of what we're meant for: a God-given liturgy on earth.

It's a sign of that same image many of you know from the apocryphal acts of St. John written toward the end of the second century. There are a lot of wild things in the text, but there's one thing lovely and to the point, the image of Jesus and the disciples singing a hymn, as Scripture says, before they went out. And this is the description found in the text. "Jesus asked us to form a circle, make a ring. And joining hands and standing in the middle of us, he said, 'Answer amen to me,' and we began to sing and say, 'Glory be to thee.' And we, going round in a ring, sang amen, amen." And then the account goes on to this responsorial ending. "I would pipe, dance all of you. Amen. I would mourn, all of you lament. Amen. The eight signs praise on high with us. Amen. The twelve dance on high. Amen. Everything on high takes part in our dancing. Amen. Whoever does not dance does not know what is coming to pass. Amen." Suddenly, there it is: another illumination of that liturgy, in that gathering that requires word, and gesture, and sight, and sound, and movement. We receive back the gift of what we are created and redeemed to be.

Think with me on those two images as well as about the relationship between words, music, and the whole range of the nonverbal that constitute the idioms, if you will, of our common worship.

When we gather in community to sing and make music to praise God, or perhaps to lament our grief, deep memory is required. Any musical act of prayer itself must go beyond the surface of the words, beyond the musical score. The memory of God becomes incarnate in the gathering beyond our own personal memories, something going on for many centuries. We are more than we can think; we are more than we can feel. So singing and making music together that expresses our life before God is, in this way, identity confirming and future open-ing—duty and delight. Something about being human requires this. Something about the way we come to know and understand our des-tiny and our world through the senses is provided for us; things God holds out for us in the gathered assembly. One thinks of Gerard Man-ley Hopkins' slightly paraphrased poem here: "The beauty was there but the beholder wanting, which two, once they meet, the heart rears wings and hurls earth off from under our feet." Something is there waiting for us, waiting to be released.

It is no accident that worship requires seeing, hearing, gesturing, moving, inhabiting space through time, and doing things with words. Above all, it requires the human heart at full stretch in the senses, in and through the language. A first starting place might well be that we need this beauty. We start with creaturely things. The sudden graceful gesture of a child fresh home from a ballet lesson, or an innocent child's hand waving, wherein everything is contained. A graceful daf-fodil in a simple vase. The unprompted thank-you. A passage of music that captures your attention and haunts you, perhaps your whole life. A piece of poetry. A scene from a play that gives you language to say what you've always wanted to say. And for us, in the Christian assem-bly, the language of Scripture made real. We have been so fashioned that, indeed, our hearts are restless until they find places where we know again the deepest language of the heart. Whatever is it about us that responds to this range of beauties in our creaturehood? I suppose we can offer only what T. S. Eliot once observed, "hints and guesses," and the rest is the discipline and perhaps the improvisation.

At the heart of the gathered community for worship, we should come alive to see, to hear, to taste, to touch, to dance, to move. All the arenas of our life, what we touch, what we taste, what we see and don't see, what we hear and don't hear, can be charged in the gather-ing for worship, charged, as Gerard Manley Hopkins would say, with the grandeur of God. This is the beauty drawing us beyond ourselves, giving us the knowledge not merely rational, certainly not contained in the verbal, but rather in a knowing deeply implanted in the heart of being a community, and hence, creatures of grace.

But, of course, we face a minor problem with this kind of beauty in our culture, a culture that uses the very senses I've named to sell some-thing. Our culture is a culture of hype. Our culture is a culture of im-mediacy. Are we feeling it now? Are we having fun now? Are you having fun now? Are you buying it now? The modes of cultural communication so indigenous to Christian assembly can become signs of market forces, signs of a consumerist situation. Art becomes a sign of elite interest and financial prestige. Art as financial investment, a status symbol, or as elevator music, form of ornamentation, a background for shopping. All this becomes a means for assuring certain "artistic" things are disconnected from the deeper human sources of joy, from the transcendent elements of which music and verbal text together are capable.

I do not want to continue this invective against our society's consumerist framework. We live in this house of glass, and no one here can cast the first stone. But what we need is the recapturing of arresting beauty when language, music, and taste, and touch, and sight work together to take us toward the transcendent. This is about language and music shining with a grandeur we cannot see until we view it through the lens of praise, lamentation, confession, hope, and prayer.

Worship in that sense has everything to do with the deepest aspects of our yearning, and hence with beauty, sound, shape, and form. But this is a beauty that takes us beyond what is immediately present, what is consumable. We speak too quickly about beauty because we also know aesthetic appreciation has been subject to demonic forces, not just to the consumerist banalities. Think of Theresienstadt, a Nazi concentration camp disguised as a model ghetto where Jews were forced to play Beethoven and Bach. So in our century the preoccupation with the aesthetic and beautiful had better have a prophet, that is, a reminder that this beauty can be abused; in fact, the beautiful can be made to serve something perverse.

The church's musical traditions do have something to offer us if we keep the tension between what the beauty is we seek and the social orders and the preoccupations of the time. Elevator and grocery store music are not offered in praise of God, but rather in praise of us or what we might yet be if we buy the right things. Let our music, then, and our language not be a luxury but something like breathing, like heartbeat, like manna in the desert. Let it not be so much a public status symbol, not so much an aesthetic treat, but an instrument whereby our loves, our hopes, our anguish, our delights, yes even our untruths may be, as it were, refined. That whatever purity of heart may remain in the human scene can be sounded and tasted there, and hence, bring life.

So the point, specifically, of our music-making and offering is to nurture and sustain the capacity to see and hear and receive all things as God's, as God's gift and work. Music and worship can, I do believe, deepen our capability of referring all things to God by sound and sight, by gesture and ritual action. The poet Shelley once observed that we should celebrate "whatever strengthens and purifies the affections, enlarges the imagination, and adds to the spirit or sense of becoming human." What he said about poetry needs to be said now, once again, in this culture of hype, immediacy, forgetfulness, and the violent. There is still a beauty in the service of God, a fountain overflowing with waters of wisdom and illumination, when the arts meet the worship of God. The love of the beautiful, the delighting, and the truthful, and the love and praise of God, are to meet, even on Sundays when the choir is not up to par, and the altos are on their wide vibrato trek again, or the tenors didn't show up, or the sermon is a flat EKG, and things go wrong, and the great liturgical gestures (folded arms) issue from the back of the congregation when it's 12:02. This is still a place where you may be surprised that the innocent gesture, the one word you spoke in your sermon that was truthful—that is to say, not filled with you, but transcendent and open—surface people who encounter God and are willing to share it. A place where the beauty of seeing, tasting, touching, hearing meets the vision and the reality of God.

Several years ago I had occasion to teach a new setting of Psalm 95, a psalm for Morning Prayer found in many of our traditions. And the antiphon for the day was: "Listen today for God's voice, harden no heart. Harden no heart." This is a setting some of you may know by Christopher Willcock, s.j., the wonderful Australian composer. The congregation sings a kind of Taizé ostinato while the cantors and the assembly are invited to the text of the psalm. I was struck by a question once asked by Frank Burch Brown, a friend of many of us, in a paper dealing with Mozart. The question was: Can music voice what God wants us to hear? And that's the question for us. The mystery is how music could reveal to us and make our heart more deeply attuned to what God wishes to speak to us. But in speaking, God does not simply utter words. In speaking, the psalm reminds us, God does many things— brings things into being, molding the sea and dry land, gives us the sounds of heaven and earth. In speaking, God also gives everything needed to a trembling hand reaching out for a piece of bread. So could music voice what God wishes us to hear—what God wishes to receive? The question is about the very conditions for how worship itself can be a sounding, a receiving. There has recently been much attention paid to participation, of getting people involved. There are the questions of the strategies for preparing the assembly. Not just planning good liturgies, but preparing the people. But for all our concern about that, I wonder if we haven't missed certain things about participation in and through the language and the nonverbal symbolism of worship.

Let me propose there are three levels of participation. The first, in a way, is the one we've been most preoccupied with, as pastors, as musicians, and worshipers Sunday after Sunday. That is the level of participation *in the phenomena*, in the actual singing, in the reading, in the praying, whether reading off text or spontaneously, and so on. The actual doing, as it were, the rites themselves. Participation in the phenomena of the rites. We need a lot more work there because, as you well know, there is a question of trying to listen to one another, and how people actually bring themselves to participate. Qualities of participation in the rites are so different. For example, Fanny Crosby's hymn texts are deeply moving to some but ironic to another. But the first level is, I think, required of us. Participation in and through the communicative power of the visual, the acoustical, and the oral— which, of course, includes silence—the tactile, the gestural, the movement, the dance. We can and must work on how people can be formed in and through those languages so they hear more than words say.

But there is a second level, neglected in a culture of radical individualism. This second level is participation in the singing, praying, reading, listening, *as church*. It involves participating as a solidarity, as belonging to one another, not just as accumulation of interested sensorium seekers who want bigger and better, and more dramatic this week than it was last (because it's better on television than it is here, anyway). The second level is participating in and through these means as church. In worship of God we belong to one another over time. We are in solidarity with the people who lamented the psalms from Moses to David and on; we were in solidarity with those Huguenots who sang Psalm 79 into their execution. We are in solidarity with all God's people. In our society, we often can participate well with like-minded folk, but the sense of solidarity with all who suffer and all who delight, with the strong and the weak, the rich and the poor, is another matter. Our natural bent is to stick with those we know and the comfort zone, as it were. But the Gospel calls us to be a community of people in continuity with all who have gone before, and in continuity with those yet unborn, and in continuity with the poor and the unlike. We are so connected with the suffering of the world that most of us cannot pray without mentioning the refugees and the children caught in the crossfire, whether in Columbine or Kosovo or Iraq or Afghanistan. That's prayer as church. It isn't just being friendly, as in "We're the friendliest church in town," or "We're the vibrant seven-day-a-week church in town," or "We're a 7-24 church." It's because we're willing to weep with those who weep, and rejoice with those who rejoice, even with those we shall never meet. And we can weep, and you can rejoice, because we have learned the language from those who have done it before; we are part of a continuum of faith.

The third level is participation in the very divine life itself, the triune life of God for the sake of the world. If you're doctrinal, you might want to say participation in the very triune dance of glory our ancestors, our mothers and fathers in the faith in the early church, talked about as *perichoresis*, union without loss of individual identity, the trinitarian God. Or, if you want another language, it's participating in the mystery of God. It has to do with singing, and listening, and praying, and speaking, and touching and being touched, and feeding and being fed, and healing and being healed. We do that as church in order to participate in the very life of God poured into this world.

Those are the three levels. I think, in our work, in our roll-up-the-sleeves hard work, when we're in despair at level one, we know that somewhere in our congregation someone has had and caught a glimpse of perhaps the third level, a kind of mystical moment in which they've said: "It came together for me this morning and God's life is here." And you, the preacher, are saying at the front door: "What? That was my worst sermon in six months." Never underestimate or doubt the grace of God and the work of the Holy Spirit to speak, touch, open people's eyes and ears. Maybe at the level of aesthetics it wasn't quite right. Maybe it was too simple, but it is said, "Sing God a simple song." Lenny Bernstein taught us that. Leontyne Price, coming to Atlanta many years ago to accept an honorary degree, was persuaded to sing. And everyone thought, ah, something from the sextet from *Lucia di Lammermoor*, because she could sing six voices at once. What did she sing? "This Little Light of Mine," a cappella. It was ravishing. Sometimes the simplest offering is right. After a service we did incorporating Fauré's *Requiem* into a liturgy for All Saints' Day, we followed—for the first time in that particular parish's experience—with the naming of all those who had died. One woman came up to me afterward and said, "I could finally let him go because I knew where he really was— with the company of saints. I no longer have to carry the burden of keeping him alive because he is already alive. And this service did that for me." That woman heard the *Requiem*, she sang, she listened, she prayed, but she was there as church. And clearly, by her testimony, she was there participating in the mystery of God to whom her beloved had gone. All three levels of participation. She was not alone any more.

There it is. When we sing, when we pray, when we participate, we can hear ancestor voices. We hear and share the memory of those gone before, but also we hear and see and occasionally taste what God has faithfully promised. Worship can be eschatological, even in "ordinary time." These moments when language is made active by the singing and the gesturing and the praying and the movement, the reading and the listening, can release the flow of grace over our living and our dying, our hoping. We have a mystery of death, of life, of forgetting, of loving, and losing, and gaining again. These are the things offered us in authentic worship. These are the things we are called to tend to. This is why we must pay attention to the quality of text we ask people to sing, and to the music, but also to the way a congregation hears, and the way a congregation may or may not be able to enter into levels two and three. We cannot simply throw out the old, but certainly we cannot deny that for generations unborn there are songs yet to be composed, there are forms yet to open unto them.

To conclude: we do, as human beings, need beauty. Check yourself. You need those times when you are fully taken up by something not yourself: By seeing a single rose in a jar on a pew where someone now deceased once sat and worshiped. By seeing the child who breaks free of his parents when his little sister is to be baptized and runs all the way down the center aisle to leap in slow-motion video into the arms of the pastor, breaking open the notion of what this baptismal rite signals. Or perhaps it is just that moment when all of your life is interpreted in a single sound, the sound of a bell, the sound of a drumbeat. Ah, the sound of the voices, the sound of the voice of the congregation. Those are hints and guesses. We have so much to offer one another and the people who are seeking, in their own idioms, what human beauty points toward, namely, the glory of God; the beauty of God; the terrible beauty of God; the creating, redeeming beauty of God that is part of the intrinsic life of the Trinity.

Let's end with a story, because so much is contained in narrative. A few years ago at Saint John's Abbey, the large Benedictine abbey in Minnesota where I've been associated for now thirty years, there was a service of healing. As we gathered we noticed an open space in the center of that great Breuer choir, a marvelous circle of grace around the altar. And slowly the monks from the infirmary came in wheelchairs, on walkers, some helped in walking. I had met some before; a few I recognized from an earlier time. They sat in the center. After the singing of a simple psalm, opening prayer, and the blessing of the oils, the two deacons and the abbot began to circle among them. And then a strange and moving thing happened. We were invited down to come lay hands on the sick. And so we did, with some fear and trembling, I may say. As we moved around, I came to touch Father Alfred, with whom I had been on a retreat many, many years ago. And as I reached out to touch his shoulder with a blessing, with his one good palsied hand he reached out and touched my face. I ask you, who were the healers, and who were the healed? Who were the pray-ers and who the prayed for? The gift of worship contains that for which the world yearns so deeply, where blessing and healing and joy and sorrow co-mingle, and where our names are known, and where we know the names of all whom God cares for and will bring to the consuming vision of grace at the end of all things. Would that we had, now and then, a foretaste, a forehearing, a little touch, a little teasing taste of what's to come. And is that not the goal of our liturgical life?

3

Musical Mystagogy
Catechizing Through the Sacred Arts

Michael S. Driscoll

Music has been my lifelong companion. From as early as I can remember, I have always had music in my ears. I can never remember a time I was not singing in a choir or learning to play an instrument. What is it about singing that comes so naturally to us? Why do we spontaneously break into song when we're happy? Or when we are sad? As Berthold Brecht said: "In the dark times will there also be singing. Yes, there will also be singing about the dark times."[1] What is it about music that conveys persistent memories with profound feelings and associations?

The human voice is the one instrument with which we come into the world. Even instrumentalists depend upon their voices in shaping the musical line. For example, when the late Isaac Stern visited Beijing after the Chinese cultural revolution, he spoke with young musicians who had learned their instruments by rote and in a mechanical fashion. Stern discovered that technically they played flawlessly. But something was lacking—musicality! After the students would play their instruments, Stern would ask these young violinists first to sing the line. Then he would instruct them to play their instruments following the same sense of line. This informed them how to phrase the music and where to add the breath.

What is it that prompts the song? Myles Connolly in his book *Mr. Blue* makes the claim that love is what prompts singing: "If one loves anything, truth, beauty, woman, life, one will speak out. Genuine love cannot endure silence. Genuine love breaks into speech. And when it is great love, it breaks out into song."[2] The human imperative to sing begins with and in our bodies. We begin with the beating of the heart and the sound of our breathing—inhaling and exhaling. In and with our bodies, we make sounds. From the very moment of the birth our first cry marks our tonal advent into the world. The world of sound constitutes the very elemental rhythms of human life itself. We move from hearts beating and lungs breathing to making music without the aid of musical instruments. We stamp our feet and clap our hands, further demonstrating the origins of music and song as an embodied experience. Music, therefore, is not merely the language of the soul, but also of the *soma* (body). Music is the embodiment of the language of life. The Quaker community understood this phenomenon very well. Music springs from within the body and the soul and it simply cannot be stifled. Consider the text of this Quaker song:[3]

> 1. My life flows on in endless song
>   Above earth's lamentation.
> I hear the real though far off hymn
>   That hails a new creation.
>
> *Refrain*
> No storm can shake my inmost calm,
>   While to that rock I'm clinging.
> Since love is Lord of heaven and earth
>   How can I keep from singing?
>
> 2. Through all the tumult and the strife,
>   I hear that music ringing;
> It sounds and echoes in my soul;
>   How can I keep from singing?
>
> 3. When tyrants tremble, sick with fear,
>   And hear their death knells ringing;
> When friends rejoice both far and near,
>   How can I keep from singing?

This song explains why "I" cannot keep from singing. What about "us"? What is it about song that brings solitary people together in community? Why is it that when someone lights a campfire, before long, everyone is seated around it and singing songs together? The fact that we sing by putting words on the breath implies that to sing with others is to mix or blend our breath with others. Singing in a group is a kind of conspiracy, if we take the root of the term *"cum-spirare"* (to breathe together) seriously. It is little wonder why singing lent itself to the very understanding of the Trinity itself, the Persons of the Father and Son mixing and blending their breath in the Holy Spirit to form a perfect unity.

But song as a communal experience does not stop there. We find all kinds of songs which accompany groups of people as they work and play together. Don Saliers notes:

> Planting the crops, harvesting, working on the chain gang—these, too, have generated song. Armies sounding brave drum and pipe, or with ambiguous valor singing of blood and earth and "fatherland" or march-ing off to war, singing in every language some equivalent of "When Johnnie Comes Marching Home Again," stirs the patriot's heart. The dirges of women crying out of loss when Johnnie or Dietrich or Maria does not return are also heard in every culture.[4]

These are all songs of the body and the soul. What we are talking about here is the act of singing together. This is deeply and indelibly human. When we sing, words are given greater range and power than when we speak.

But as Gabe Huck warns us: "Every place we give to inferior and un-worthy words is a place not given to strong words."[5] Yet something is shared in singing that goes beyond the words alone. Among religious people, this something has taken shape over many centuries in a prac-tice that expresses our deepest yearning and dearest joy: in what Don Saliers calls "the practice of singing our lives." Saliers goes on to say:

> There is something about human beings that needs to make music, something that insists on song. Every culture sings about the world it ex-periences, in its own distinctive sound. In fact, we come to know about a people by listening to what they sing and bring to expression in their music. *What* we sing and *how* we sing reveals much of who we are, and entering into another's song and music making provides a gateway into their world, which might be much different from our own. Sharing our song with others who do not know us is sharing a gift, akin to the shar-ing of food at a common table.[6]

Did not the musical metaphor serve Ignatius of Antioch well as he struggled with questions of diversity and unity at the beginning of the second century? "Therefore," he writes:

> it is fitting for you to run your race together with the bishop's purpose— as you do. For your presbytery—worthy of fame, worthy of God—is at-tuned to the bishop like strings to a lyre. Therefore by your unity and harmonious love Jesus Christ is sung. Each of you must be part of this chorus so that, being harmonious in unity, receiving God's pitch in unison,

you may sing with one voice through Jesus Christ to the Father, so that he may both hear you and recognize you, through what you do well, as members of his Son. Therefore it is profitable for you to be in blameless unison, so that you may always participate in God.[7]

Nowadays, we find we have similar concerns. The act of singing together at the liturgy is more than simply decorating the ritual action. Singing actually constitutes us as a worshiping community. Song gathers us from our individuality and isolation and brings us together into an assembly. Isn't it interesting that Dolores Dufner, O.S.B., uses the same musical metaphor in her "Sing a New Church"[8] when she writes:

Let us bring the gifts that differ,
And, in splendid, varied ways,
Sing a new church into being,
One in faith and love and praise.

In a similar way, Clement of Alexandria employed the musical metaphor of *symphonia* in opposing duality and disharmony in the early Church. The greatest possible harmony was pursued as the musical expression of the union of soul and of the community, as it prevailed in the early Christian liturgy. It is in this sense that the entire community of Christians, according to Clement, becomes a single *symphonia*:

We want to strive so that we, the many, may be brought together into one love, according to the union of the essential unity. As we do good may we similarly pursue unity. . . . The union of many, which the divine harmony has called forth out of a medley of sounds and division, becomes one symphony, following the one leader of the choir and teacher, the Word, resting in that same truth and crying out: "Abba, Father."[9]

Here Clement uses singing "in one voice" as an image of the unity and harmony of all Christians. He finds no more beautiful comparison of the universe than that of the primitive Christian singing the Psalms of David. If the expression *una voce dicentes* applied to the early church to speak about fundamental unity despite significant diversity, might we not apply it to music in liturgy today?

Finding Our Voice

A theme found in literary criticism but also strongly suggested by music is "Finding Our Voice."[10] The expression "finding one's voice" is most often associated with the literary world. In this context it means a kind of breakthrough that poets and writers achieve when they abandon past styles. When writers or poets move away from mere imitation of their teachers they are said to have found their voice, reaching an important moment of maturity. As a musical metaphor I am struck by the truth and the clarity enunciated by the Fourth Council of Carthage in the fourth century, whence comes this expression: *"Vide ut quod ore cantas, corde credas, et quod corde credis, operibus comprobes.* Take heed that what you sing with your mouths, you believe in your hearts, and what you believe with your hearts you show forth in your works."[11] Finding our voice in this context is singing reality into being. Music is akin to the creative Word of God that called creation into being by simple utterance.

The arts, particularly music, are a potent means for coming into contact with the transcendent. Many people confess to deeper religious experiences in the concert hall or the art museum than in church. This affirmation should not be regarded as an affront to liturgical worship but a positive evaluation of the arts. The arts have a profound power to access the transcendent, and there is a growing interest in aesthetics and theology.[12] Rather than pitting the concert hall or the art museum against the chapel, it is more desirable to affirm all these places as *loci theologici*. Instead of opposing the liturgy to the arts, I am inclined to agree with Bishop Albert Rouet of Poitiers, France, who writes: "The liturgy is an art that uses other arts. Art and liturgy, when they join forces, express transcendence."[13] A person easily recalls a liturgical service where a certain piece of music or a poem moved them to tears, or where the liturgy itself has been tended to with great care so it touches the person particularly due to the aesthetic dimension.

Mystagogy of the Arts

My principal purpose in this essay is to explore how the liturgical arts shape the worship and theology of those who enter into prayer. I would like to extend the idea of mystagogy, which has its roots in the initiatory practices of the early Church, to the realm of music. Just as Kathleen Hughes explored the use of mystagogy in sacramental rites beyond Christian initiation, so too I, by way of extension, would suggest that mystagogy also include the sacred arts, especially music. Hughes writes:

> How do we make the world of sacraments accessible to the head and heart? How do we talk about the liturgy and, in the process, impart not just a knowledge of facts and their history, nor even the relationship of

one part to another, but that deep-felt knowledge of head and heart and faith, the knowledge that nurtures whole human persons and inspires a knowing from the inside out?[14]

She proposes a method almost as ancient as the Church, namely, mystagogical catechesis. Historical research on the initiatory practices, particularly of the fourth and fifth centuries, has rekindled in us a desire to teach and preach in creative ways—ways that take seriously the liturgical rites. Rather than placing our sacramental catechesis before the reception of the sacraments, mystagogical catechesis teaches us to take seriously the power of the rites to convey deep meaning and truth. By means of an experiential pedagogy we come to know the truth about God and faith from within, not simply from looking at it from outside. The mystagogical pedagogy has also been extended to preaching. For example, Craig Satterlee, a Lutheran pastor and professor of liturgy, explored in his doctoral research how preaching might be rejuvenated by the mystagogical method.[15] Since 1972 the church at large has come to a renewed understanding of this method when the revised *Rite of Christian Initiation of Adults* was promulgated, and we are still discovering its extended possibilities not only for initiation but also for the other sacraments. Furthermore, mystagogy can become a way of doing pastoral ministry in general that values the experiential rather than the dogmatic and discursive, particularly in catechetical matters.

Mystagogy—the "interpretation of the mysteries" or "teaching of mystery"—was the postbaptismal interpretation of mystery offered to those who had just joined the community. They first had to experience the water bath, the anointing, and the meal in the course of the Easter Vigil. They then were able to talk about it, but not before. It is like love poetry. Unless you have fallen in love, you cannot have full access to the poetry. But once you are in love yourself, you feel compelled to add to the growing collection of love poems. Mystagogy was a form of instruction that attempted to plumb the depths of the rites that had been experienced for their spiritual import. First, the experience, then the teaching.

Craig Satterlee describes mystagogy as a sustained reflection on the mystery. So we are looking for a means to sustain our reflection, a way to savor the mystery. What better way to lead us to a heightened experience than the sacred arts? The arts by their very nature are experiential. And what better way to savor the mystery? In a poetic text, for example, something which we know from everyday life can be said in such a way that we see new possibilities. The arts have the power to transform us and lead us deeply into the mystery of God. The arts give us a unique access to the mystery of God which otherwise would remain totally ineffable.

Seen in this perspective, the sacred arts provide us with a lifelong way of knowing. Technically speaking, we know mystagogy is for neophytes and that it corresponds to the fifty days of Easter, but in the broader sense mystagogy is a commitment to learning, deepening, knowing, understanding, and loving. All the baptized are on a lifelong mystagogical journey. But as Kathleen Hughes notes: "The language of mystagogy is more like poetry than prose."[16] It is the language of poetry, in particular, and the sacred arts, in general, which permits us to talk about what is most precious to us. How could one speak about love until one actually falls in love? And how can one speak about a loved love without lapsing into poetry or song? When we fall in love, we cannot find adequate words to communicate the reality of our experience. We speak of profoundly moving experiences as "too deep for words," at least too deep for ordinary words.

But the language of the arts helps us give expression to these highly exalted sentiments. No wonder St. John of the Cross composed his best theology in the form of a poem. No wonder Johann Sebastian Bach used music as the medium for expressing his relationship with God. It is no secret that Bach signed all his scores with the epithet *Soli Deo Gloria*—to God alone be the glory. When ordinary language fails us, we look to the heightened language poetry and music provide. It is not that we exhaust the mystery before us, but we come closer in approximating it in a language accessible to us. A challenge still faces us about finding adequate artistic forms to support the mystery. Julia Upton on many occasions has signaled the clarion call that the rites and artistic forms we use must be up to the task of supporting the mystery. Trite artistic forms tend to banalize the experience of God. Liturgy that is trivial can actually impede one's access to the transcendent mysteries.

Discovering God and enacting our relationship with God and one another through liturgical worship means the words must be more like poetry than prose. In the presence of the ineffable God our language may well come across as half-sentences, images, metaphors, all of it part of the interpretation of the mysteries, which is what mystagogy is at heart.

Of course, the most critical element for successful mystagogy is well-celebrated rites. The American bishops said it well in the document *Music in Catholic Worship*: "Faith grows when it is well expressed in celebration. Good celebrations foster and nourish faith. Poor celebrations may weaken and destroy it."[17] What prophetic words—particularly from a church only a few decades earlier concerned with sacraments working *ex opere operato*—if you merely said the correct words using the proper elements. And this experience of celebrating the rites well has not been lost on our people. The number of Catholics who travel around in search of good liturgy is but one sign liturgy has been working in transforming the lives of believers. People innately come to know what constitutes good liturgy, particularly as good ritual experiences have transformed their lives.

What does it mean to celebrate the rites well? What are the criteria we use to judge? Again in *Music in Catholic Worship* we read these words:

> To celebrate the liturgy means to do the action or perform the sign in such a way that its full meaning and impact shine forth in clear and compelling fashion. Since liturgical signs are vehicles of communication and instruments of faith, they must be simple and comprehensible. Since they are directed to fellow human beings, they must be humanly attractive. They must be meaningful and appealing to the body of worshippers or they will fail to stir up faith.[18]

In a word, if the rites are to be fully effective, we must tend to the aesthetics of worship.[19] Excellent, careful, well-planned, and well-executed liturgy is first-level mystagogy. Good liturgy is requisite to rich symbolic participation and contemplation. But if liturgy is to be mystagogical it presumes an ability to experience the liturgy deeply, and then to reflect upon the experience. For mystagogy to be successful, we need to be able to identify and talk about our experience. That demands we know what our experience is, that we are in touch with our own inner world and attentive to what we are doing when we gather for prayer.

Four decades of liturgical renewal have led toward a retrieval of those forms of expression most appropriate for liturgy. The forms of expression best suited to bring about an experience of the mystery of Christ and the church are images, symbols, and ritual actions. These languages of liturgy are meant to engage the imagination rather than the discursive thought. As the liturgical languages engage the human imagination the liturgy moves us to active participation and opens us to experience presence, the mystery of God-with-us.

Because images and symbols are the proper forms of ritual expression, worship as an expressive form must include an aesthetic dimension. Images, symbols, and rituals are properly aesthetic modes of expression. The languages involved in ritual should excite and open the imagination to an experience of the presence of mystery. This is accomplished through engaging the imagination. Ritual, like liturgy, is an art. These languages are not just rubrics to be followed or texts to be read. Rituals, in their best sense, are a kind of drama, and as such, must be embodied and enacted.

Herein lies a fundamental problem with postconciliar liturgical renewal. We might say that the reform of the books and the rituals has been achieved. But the work of the deeper renewal is just beginning. This is a problem liturgical scholars and worship practitioners have only begun to face. Liturgy has not been approached sufficiently as an art. It has not been sufficiently understood as aesthetic in its human expressive core.

Ritual as a dramatic art is performative. Patrick Collins compares ritual to drama, dance, music, and poetry. He writes:

> Like drama, ritual enacts a story. It plays out the continuing saga of God's dealing with people, which includes past, present and future dimensions. Like music, ritual has innate rhythms. Each moment prepares for the next and each element flows out of what precedes. Again, like music, ritual involves the building of tensions and resolutions through the use of sounds and silence that create an aural experience of passage. Like dance, ritual involves movement becoming gesture, movement with symbolic meaning, such as processions, upraised hands, the laying on of hands, and eating and drinking. Like poetry, ritual uses words, not for explanation and communicating knowledge, but for exploration and creating insight into truth with feeling.[20]

It is important to understand that ritual's proper mode of celebration is aesthetic. It is equally important to stress that ritual is not merely a hybrid of these four performing arts. One should not speak of liturgy *and* the arts.[21] The liturgy does not *use* the arts in order to become aesthetic. Let me emphatically reiterate the words of Bishop Albert Rouet, "The liturgy is an art which uses other arts." Liturgy is an integral aesthetic form, and although it resembles other arts, liturgy must become its own integral art form. Liturgy takes other art forms into itself much the way an opera takes a story, dance, and music to draw them into a creative unity. Or, in the same way a poem when set to music becomes a song. The words of a song are no longer merely a poem when they have been transformed into music. Music becomes the commanding aesthetic form binding words and melody together.

In the example of the song, the art of music subsumes the art of poetry. The similar transformation of art forms takes place when any art is integrated into ritual. Like opera, liturgy uses dramatic action, musical sound and silence, and poetic expression. All elements meld in aesthetic ritual. When the constitutive parts are not smoothly integrated, the ritual action stalls.

But an aesthetic approach to liturgy contains at least one potential danger. In addressing the performative aspect of liturgy, there is again a tendency to make ritual merely a performance by the ministers whereby the assembly is rendered passive. If this were to happen, it would be pre-Vatican II worship revisited—although isolated individuals may attempt to act like a community. To avoid making the assembly inactive, ritual must be conceived, created, composed, and choreographed as an art of a performing assembly. The artists of ritual are not the folks up front, the multiple ministers. The artists of ritual are none other than all of the members of the assembly, including ministers. Ritual as art must not be done *for* but rather *with* the assembly, which is, in a very real sense, a community of believers, not merely isolated individuals.

Call to Artists

I have spoken about the role and responsibility of the assembly in conjunction with the liturgical ministers. I have also focused on liturgy as an art as well as the role of the sacred arts in bringing us to a deeper understanding of the mystery we are encountering. Now let me turn my attention to another important factor, namely, what role artists play in our mystagogical experience. There are two benchmarks I would like to examine with you—one at the end of Vatican II and another more recently. Both are papal elocutions addressed to artists.

At the end of the Second Vatican Council, the essential role of artists in helping with the liturgical reform was strongly underlined. In the "Closing Messages of the Second Vatican Council to the Artists" (Dec. 8, 1965), Paul VI engaged the subject of the role the arts and the artists play. Listen to his words, now forty years old:

> We now address you, artists, who are taken up with beauty and work for it: poets and literary men (and women), painters, sculptors, architects, musicians, people devoted to the theater and the cinema. To all of you, the Church of the Council declares to you through our voice: if you are friends of genuine art, you are our friends.

The church has long since joined in alliance with you. You have built and adorned her temples, celebrated her dogmas, enriched her liturgy. You have aided her in translating her divine message in the language of forms and figures, making the invisible world palpable. Today, as yesterday, the Church needs you and turns to you. She tells you through our voice: Do not allow an alliance as fruitful as this to be broken. Do not refuse to put your talents at the service of divine truth. Do not close your mind to the breath of the Holy Spirit.

The world in which we live needs beauty in order not to sink into despair. It is beauty, like truth, which brings joy to the heart of [people] and is that precious fruit, which resists the wear and tear of time, which unites generations and makes them share things in admiration. And all of this is through your hands. May these hands be pure and disinterested. Remember that you are the guardians of beauty in the world. May that suffice to free you from tastes which are passing and have no genuine value, to free you from the search of your ideals, and you will be worthy of the Church which, by our voice, addresses to you today her message of friendship, salvation, grace, and benediction.[22]

These words are as true today as in 1965. You might say they are even more resonant as we have struggled (and struggle) with what constitutes good liturgy. Since the council there has been much criticism from some quarters claiming that our postconciliar worship lacks beauty, that *Sacrosanctum Concilium* unwittingly fostered a rite marked by the worst aspects of a discredited Enlightenment aesthetic that exalts rationality and utility over mystery and complexity. But in fact the Constitution on the Liturgy, par. 8, sees the church's liturgy as a pilgrim's journey, driven by desire toward "the holy city of Jerusalem" where Christ sits at God's right. As the International Committee for English in the Liturgy works to get the words right, we ask ourselves if this is the only measure of what constitutes good liturgy. Good liturgy has to be more than faithfully translated texts. The liturgical arts contribute vitally to the quality of the liturgy.

The second benchmark is from Pope John Paul II. In many respects, we can look to him not only as pontiff or bridge builder, but also as poet and playwright, as someone who understands the arts with an insider's understanding. In his 1999 letter *To Artists*, an elaborate text of fourteen pages, he summed up the church's teaching on art. There is a shift away from the 1965 language addressed to artists who are "taken up with beauty and work for it." He writes to "all who are passionately dedicated to the search for new 'epiphanies' of beauty so that through their creative work as artists they may offer these as gifts to the world." Perhaps John Paul's high-flown formulation represents a deeper reflection on the sacramental character attributed to art by the Constitution on the Liturgy. The first section of the Pope's letter ("The Artist, Image of God and Creator") reflects on the difference between Creator and artist; the Creator makes "something out of nothing," while artists use something that already exists, giving it form and meaning. Since the divine Artist passes on to the human artist a spark of God's own surpassing wisdom, God calls the artist to share in the divine creative power. John Paul writes: "Artists, the more conscious they are of their 'gift,' are led all the more to see themselves and the whole of creation with eyes able to contemplate and give thanks."

The next section ("The Special Vocation of the Artist") treats the distinction between the task of crafting one's own life, which is of moral character, and that of making art "by giving aesthetic form to ideas conceived in the mind." Although there is a distinction between morality and art, the two can be connected. Artists reveal their personalities by means of their works, and through these works they communicate and speak to others. The Pope writes: "In producing a work, artists express themselves to the point where their work becomes a unique disclosure of their own being, of what they are and of how they are what they are."

In the third section ("The Artistic Vocation in the Service of Beauty") the Pope focuses on the Greek concept of *kalokagathía* (the Greek concept for that which is beautiful, good, and true). "The artist has a special relationship to beauty. In a very true sense it can be said that beauty is the vocation bestowed on the artist by the Creator in the gift of artistic talent." If beauty is defined as artistic talent, the artist who follows his or her inner voice and vocation should be on the right track. This is verified in what the Pope goes on to say: "Those who perceive in themselves this kind of divine spark which is the artistic vocation . . . feel at the same time an obligation not to waste this talent but to develop it, in order to put it at the service of their neighbor and of humanity as a whole." From this follows logically the fourth section ("The Artist and the Common Good") dealing with an ethic, even a spirituality, of artistic service, which contributes in its way to the life and renewal of a people. Here, John Paul expects dedication; the artists "must labor without allowing themselves to be driven by the search for empty glory or the craving for cheap popularity, still less by the calculation of some possible profit for themselves." These are the ideals a great many artists follow in their work.

The question of epiphany is treated in section five ("Art and the Mystery of the Word Made Flesh"). The Pope quotes from Exodus: "God is the transcendent 'I am who I am'" (Exod 3:14). In the epiphany of becoming human, the Son of God "unveiled a new dimension of beauty." Sacred Scripture is thus an "immense vocabulary" for artists to draw on. The Old Testament, read in the light of the New Testament, provides an endless stream of inspiration. In effect: "On countless occasions the biblical word has become image, music, poetry, evoking the mystery of 'the Word made flesh' in the language of art." So that "works of art inspired by Scripture remain a reflection of the unfathomable mystery which inhabits and engulfs the earth." Here John Paul, by describing what has been the case indirectly, recommends a text-related approach for making new ecclesiastical art.

Section six ("A Fruitful Alliance between the Gospel and Art") takes the notion of genuineness[23] as a point of departure, and thereby continues the explanation of *"epiphanies* of beauty." The Pope writes: "Every genuine artistic intuition goes beyond what the senses perceive and, reaching beneath reality's surface, strives to interpret its hidden mystery. The intuition itself springs from the depths of the human soul." Therefore, "true artists above all are ready to acknowledge their limits." And finally, "every genuine art form in its own way is a path to the inmost reality of man and of the world. It is a wholly valid approach to the realm of faith." Genuineness denotes that which draws near to the transcendent reality and "true artists" are those who seek it. This means the church regards "every genuine art form" as a "valid approach to the realm of faith." In John Paul's understanding, this realm of the "inmost reality" is part of the Christian mystery, what reveals itself as beauty. Therefore, artists "by their very nature are alert to every 'epiphany' of the inner beauty of things." It seems as though the term *epiphany* may correspond to the certainty that artists experience when they succeed in making something; the feelings of satisfaction and joy accompanying a solution of formal problems. If so, it is the very righteousness of form that has transcendence and beauty.

The letter continues with a survey of art in a Christian context through history. Section ten ("Towards a Renewed Dialogue") deals with the "modern era" and openly admits "the separation of the world of art and the world of faith." However, "the true art has a close affinity with the world of faith, so that art remains a kind of bridge to religious experience. Insofar as it seeks the beautiful . . . art is by its nature a kind of appeal to the mystery." The Pope addresses not only those who are involved in the sacred arts but all artists and all arts in general. He writes: "Even when they [the artists] explore the darkest depths of the soul or the most unsettling aspects of evil, artists give voice in a way to the universal desire for redemption." Even the act of producing art may be regarded as an act of hope, since it is an effort to communicate with others. This statement expresses precisely the situation of many contemporary artists who have desperately sought to express something that eventually might reveal a structure and meaning in their lives.

Section eleven ("In the Spirit of the Second Vatican Council") refers directly to the documents of the council and offers friendship and dialogue with contemporary artists. The importance and value of art for theology is made clear; art is "not only aesthetic representation but genuine 'source' of theology." Here is an invitation and challenge to artists to present contemporary, visual, and aural theology. Section twelve ("The Church Needs Art") proclaims the church's dependence on artists, because art is needed "in order to communicate the message entrusted to her by Christ." The church needs art to translate into meaningful terms what are ineffable in themselves; to nourish intuition of the faithful; and "to make perceptible, and as far as possible, attractive, the world of the spirit, of the invisible, of God." Here the persistent demand for beauty is subordinated to a request for art "as far as possible attractive," a formulation radically inclusive of and open to works of art when compared to the initial "epiphanies" of beauty.

The question "Does Art Need the Church?" (the heading of section thirteen) is answered by pointing to the fact that "Christianity offers artists a horizon especially rich in inspiration." And in the subsequent section fourteen ("An Appeal to Artists") artists are invited to "enter into the heart of mystery." At this stage, there can be little doubt that John Paul is addressing artists in general. He writes, "I appeal especially to you Christian artists" and he invites them to rediscover the depth of the spiritual and religious dimension typical of art in its noblest forms in every age. Here we see the terms spiritual and religious linked to what is regarded noble. And the noble is expressed in the title of the final section ("Beauty That Saves"). Like Paul VI's message to the artists, this takes the form resembling a prayer. Artists are encouraged to work for the church—to work for beauty. "Beauty," John Paul states, "is a key to the mystery and a call to transcendence. It is an invitation to savor life and dream of the future."

In sum, Pope John Paul II's *To Artists* invites contemporary artists in general, and Christian artists in particular, to be inspired by Christianity and work for the church. The Pope asks for an art based on genuine artistic intuition that strives to interpret this hidden mystery characterized by beauty and make perceptible the world of the spirit, especially on the literary, musical, dramatic, and figurative levels. He concludes his letter with an appeal to artists: "May your art help to affirm that true beauty which, as a glimmer of the spirit of God, will transfigure matter, opening the human soul to the senses of the eternal." Clearly these are words from the poet and playwright Pope, an artist in his own right addressing other artists.

Liturgical Arts Society, 1928–72

Finally, in this last section, let me discuss how we regard the sacred arts and where I would hope to see us go. To do this we need to look at the liturgical movement in the United States during the twentieth century and the role the sacred arts played. "The Liturgical Arts Society established in 1928 was a national effort to devise ways and means for improving the standards of taste, craftsmanship, and liturgical correctness in the practice of Catholic art in the United States" (Masthead, *Liturgical Arts*, vol. 1:1 to 40:3). Founded and led by laypeople, the Liturgical Arts Society's membership included men and women from all levels in the church who felt that objects of art used in public worship should be in keeping with the spirit of the liturgy and thereby aid in the revitalization of Christianity and society as a whole.

In 1931 the Society began publication of a quarterly magazine. For four decades, *Liturgical Arts* exerted one of the strongest influences on American artists and architects designing and furnishing Roman Catholic churches. It provided a forum for the views of the leaders of the liturgical movement, American and European, on the place of the arts in liturgical renewal. A key player in the Society was New Yorker Maurice Lavanoux, who kept the Society and its journal going even in difficult times. Unfortunately, toward the end of his life he had financial difficulties, and the last issue never saw its way to print. When Lavanoux died in 1974, so too did the Society and the journal. His papers were subsequently sent to the University of Notre Dame where they can be found today in the archives. Anyone who remembers this journal recognizes the contribution it made to the artistic and liturgical life of the church and regrets its passing.

I think that in many respects the day of *Liturgical Arts* had come and gone by the mid-1970s. *National Pastoral Musician* was in the offing. Other journals of art or architecture were already on the horizon. But there has yet to come on the scene a more multidisciplinary journal than *Liturgical Arts*. While all of the current journals have made wonderful contributions, both scholarly and pastorally, I think it is time to resurrect *Liturgical Arts* journal since nothing exists currently of the same quality or addresses *all* the sacred arts per se. A journal like a revived *Liturgical Arts* would allow and encourage the sacred arts to speak to one another in constructive ways and provide a scholarly outlet for those working in liturgy and the sacred arts.

Recently I was reminded of the need for the interplay of the sacred arts when I visited the restored Central Synagogue in New York. This major landmark suffered a catastrophic fire several years ago and has been in the process of restoration for some time. A conflict arose about whether the room is for the spoken word or music. The same types of arguments arise when new churches and synagogues are being built. In the case of Central Synagogue, it occurred to those working on the restoration that this dichotomy was false. They needed to work for a resolution favoring both the spoken and the sung word. The decision to install two sound systems is a good example of how technology helps us design spaces that do not oppose the sacred arts. A similar example arose at the University of Notre Dame when the new Performing Arts Center was still in the planning stages. The architects had provided for a new organ recital hall, but no serious organ builders would entertain a contract because the room was inadequate. To resolve the apparent impasse, acousticians were brought in to mediate the dispute between organ builder and architect. In the end, everything was resolved favorably, and the new firm building is now adorned with its new pipe organ by the Paul Fritts & Co. firm of Tacoma, Washington.

Notre Dame is working on an interdisciplinary program called Liturgy and Sacred Arts, to be housed in the Theology Department but reaching out to interested faculty in other departments, like music, visual arts, art history, architecture, dramatic arts, and homiletics. Initially, the project will target sacred music, but the ultimate goal will include all the sacred arts in order to foster dialogue and cooperation among the liturgical arts. The conversations that have led to this program have made us very aware of the growing need to further develop the liturgical arts. Our initiative capitalizes on existing structures at a university like Notre Dame, as well as the vibrant intellectual history of Catholicism and liturgical studies that we find there. It represents a new and coherent way of training students for the service in the church.

A core group of faculty in music and theology is leading the move to this cross-disciplinary approach, one that serves the church through the study and practice of music within the liturgy. We are interested in scholarly study and pastoral applications of how the arts interact one with the other and how theological and artistic principles come together in the arena of sacred arts. This is a sorely needed interdisciplinary venture. The emphasis focuses on the sacred arts in service to the liturgy as an art, in the context of ecclesial ministry. The sacred arts are a means to the end, not the end itself.

In conclusion, let me reference a statement issued in 2003 by John Paul II to commemorate the one-hundredth anniversary of the document *Tra le sollecitudini*, dealing with sacred music and promulgated by Saint Pius X in 1903. The Pope's new document is dated November 22, the feast of St. Cecilia, the patron of music, and in it he warns that not all music, even if sacred in nature, is suitable for liturgical use. He goes on to urge the Congregation for Divine Worship to "pay closer attention" to the issue of liturgical music. He repeats that exhortation in a plea for episcopal conferences to "pay closer attention" to the music used in the liturgy in their respective countries. One interpretation of these warnings could result in a paranoid fear that Big Brother is watching. I prefer to take the more benign reading and think the Pope recognizes the real power of music (as well as the other sacred arts) to transform us, to shape our life of prayer and our ways of thinking about God. The more benign reading suggests the sacred arts, particularly music, are not merely something we use to decorate the liturgy but an essential part of worship. As such they need as much care and attention as all the other details mentioned in the *General Instruction of the Roman Missal*.

Today liturgists face major challenges. The euphoria of Vatican II has ended. As the Constitution on the Liturgy fades in time, is it also fading in influence? Do we see a retrenchment from liturgical principles, a lessening of collaboration? Is there a liturgical backsliding that causes us to be disillusioned, dejected, disheartened? Those who work for liturgical renewal in the church should remember the words of St. Paul in his Second Letter to the Corinthians: "Because we possess the ministry through God's mercy, we do not give in to discouragement."

Notes

1. Alan J. Hommerding and Diana Kodner, eds., *A Sourcebook about Music* (Chicago: Liturgical Training Publications [LTP], 1997) 94.

2. Myles Connolly, *Mr. Blue* (New York: Macmillan Company, 1928).

3. "How Can I Keep from Singing?" Text: Robert Lowrey; tune: traditional Quaker Hymn.

4. Don Saliers, "Singing Our Lives," in *Practicing Our Faith*, ed. Dorothy C. Bass (San Francisco: Jossey-Bass Publishers, 1997) 182. I am deeply indebted to Don Saliers for the idea of finding our voice with regard to the phenomenon of singing in this essay.

5. *How Can I Keep From Singing? Thoughts about Liturgy for Musicians* (Chicago: LTP, 1989).

6. Saliers, 180–1.

7. "Ignatius of Antioch," *The Apostolic Fathers*, ed. Jack N. Sparks (Nashville: Thomas Nelson, Inc., 1978).

8. Delores Dufner, O.S.B. (Portland, OR: OCP Publications, 1991).

9. Clement of Alexandria, *Protrepticos* 9 (GCS Clem. I 65 Stählin).

10. I am greatly indebted to Nathan Mitchell and J. Michael Joncas for their insights.

11. Fourth Council of Carthage (fourth century).

12. Richard Viladesau, *Theological Aesthetics: God in Imagination, Beauty, and Art* (New York: Oxford University Press, 1999); Viladesau, *Theology and the Arts: Encountering God through Music, Art and Rhetoric* (New York: Paulist Press, 2000); and Frank Burch Brown, *Religious Aesthetics: A Theological Study of Making and Meaning* (Princeton, NJ: Princeton University Press, 1989); Brown, *Good Taste, Bad Taste, & Christian Taste: Aesthetics in Religious Life* (Oxford/New York: Oxford University Press, 2000).

13. Albert Rouet, *Liturgy and the Arts* (Collegeville: Liturgical Press, 1997).

14. Kathleen Hughes, *Saying Amen: A Mystagogy of Sacrament* (Chicago: Liturgy Training Publications, 1999) 2.

15. Satterlee, Craig, *Ambrose of Milan's Method of Mystagogical Preaching* (Collegeville: Liturgical Press, 2001).

16. Hughes, *Saying Amen*, 15.

17. Bishops' Committee on the Liturgy, *Music in Catholic Worship* (first edition 1972; rev. ed. NCCB, 1983) par. 6.

18. Ibid., par. 7.

19. For an in-depth treatment of the aesthetic dimension, see Patrick Collins, *Bodying Forth: Aesthetic Liturgy* (Mahwah, NJ: Paulist Press, 1992).

20. Ibid., 32.

21. Rouet, *Liturgy and the Arts*, 1.

22. W. M. Abbott, ed., *The Documents of Vatican II* (London & Dublin: Geoffrey Chapman, 1966) 732.

23. See Grete Refsum, "Genuine Christian Modern Art: Present Roman Catholic Directives on Visual Art Seen from an Artist's Perspective" (doctoral dissertation, Oslo School of Architecture and Design, 2000).

Part II

Historical Perspectives

4

An Anniversary Song
Pope John Paul II's 2003 Chirograph for the Centenary of *Tra le Sollecitudini*

Fr. Jan Michael Joncas

A handwritten document ("chirograph")[1] [hereafter Ch2003] produced by Pope John Paul II to celebrate the centenary of Pius X's 1903 Apostolic Letter on Church Music *Tra le Sollecitudini* is easier to describe by negatives. It is not: a decretal letter (e.g., reaffirming beatifications and canonizations), an encyclical epistle or encyclical letter (e.g., pastoral texts addressed to the universal Church clarifying doctrinal issues), an apostolic epistle or exhortation (e.g., less solemn texts addressed to single persons or limited groups within the church), an apostolic constitution (e.g., a doctrinal and disciplinary legislative text dealing with matters of import to the universal or a particular church), or an apostolic letter *motu proprio* (e.g., a legislative text issued on the pope's initiative). Nor does it appear to fit other typical categories of papal pronouncements, such as declarations, allocutions, homilies, radio addresses, or televised messages.[2]

Rather, Ch2003 is a creative "rereading" of earlier ecclesiastical documents in the light of contemporary developments:

> [I]n the light of the Magisterium of St. Pius X and my other Predecessors and taking into account in particular the pronouncements of the Second Vatican Council, I would like to re-propose several fundamental principles for this important sector of the life of the Church, with the intention of ensuring that liturgical music corresponds ever more closely to its specific function. [#3]

Thus Ch2003 parallels other documents produced by John Paul II, such as *Centesimus Annus* in which he "rereads" Leo XIII's great social encyclical *Rerum Novarum*, indicating both what is of permanent value in the earlier document and proposing new teaching in the light of a century's experience and changed social conditions.

To understand the significance of Ch2003, I wish to pose to it the same five questions I asked of nine seminal church documents in my book, *From Sacred Song to Ritual Music*:[3] (1) How does it define Roman Catholic worship music? (2) What is its purpose? (3) What are its qualities? (4) Who sings it? (5) Who plays it?

How Does Ch2003 Define Roman Catholic Worship Music?

As might be expected in a "re-reading" of earlier ecclesiastical documents, Ch2003 adopts the terminology employed in those documents. Thus, in contrast to "religious music," "church music," "liturgical music," or "Christian ritual music," Ch2003 prefers the term "sacred music." Most interestingly, however, Ch2003 also notes a difficulty in using this term: "Today, the meaning of the category 'sacred music' has been broadened to include repertoires that cannot be part of the [liturgical] celebration without violating the spirit and norms of the Liturgy itself." [#4]

Although reflecting on this range of terminology might seem esoteric and arcane, it actually has implications for pastoral practice. "Religious music" properly refers to any repertoire explicitly generated by a particular religious tradition (e.g., Jewish cantillation of biblical texts; Tibetan chanting). This stands in contrast to "sacred music" which may explicitly or implicitly (e.g., Wagner's *Parsifal*; Mahler's "Resurrection" symphony) deal with religious issues from any or no denominational perspective. "Church music" refers specifically to Christian music, but is not limited to Christian music employed in worship; church music may also be used in witness (e.g., singing "We Shall Overcome" during a civil rights march) or catechetics (e.g., singing "Jesus Loves Me" during a Sunday School class). "Liturgical music" refers to music employed in communal worship. Note that, depending on one's understanding of "liturgy" this may include Jewish worship music and/or the worship music of so-called "nonliturgical" churches. Finally, "Christian ritual music" designates music wedded to particular texts and/or actions contextualized by ritual behavior; thus an *Agnus Dei* actually sung during the breaking of the consecrated bread at Mass would exemplify "Christian ritual music" while the same piece extracted from its ritual context and sung as a concert piece would not. In the light of this varying terminology, I have opted for "Roman Catholic worship music" to designate music employed by Roman Catholics in liturgical (i.e., during celebration of the sacraments, sacramentals, and the Liturgy of the Hours) and devotional (e.g., music employed at paraliturgical services such as novenas, Stations of the Cross, etc.) settings. (See editor's comments in Introduction, p. x.)

Thus not all "religious" music is appropriate for [Catholic] Christian liturgy. We have appropriated psalms and canticles from the Jewish Bible (admittedly with interesting modifications—titles, antiphons, trinitarian doxologies, patristic referents, and psalm prayers—in order to "make them Christian"), but have not done so with, e.g., texts from the Qur'an or Upanishads, both of which have distinctive musical elements. The pastoral musician may be confronted with situations in which the religious or liturgical music of other Christian denominations is proposed for Catholic liturgy. While many Lutheran chorales, Episcopal and Methodist hymns, and nondenominational "praise and worship" music may be appropriate for use in worship by Catholics, occasionally their texts may bespeak a theology incompatible with Catholic beliefs or their music may carry anti-Catholic connotations.

Not all "sacred" music is appropriate for [Catholic] Christian liturgy: the late Beethoven C# minor string quartet evokes powerful religious sentiments in many listeners and critics, but would not appropriately accompany the opening procession at Eucharist. Singing the Schubert *Ave Maria* at Catholic weddings raises a host of questions: one could not use the original German text based on a passage from Sir Walter Scott's "Lady of the Lake" and, even with the Latin devotional text substituted, what element of the liturgy would it appropriately enhance (since the practice of carrying flowers to the Virgin's altar is a devotional custom appearing nowhere in the official liturgy)?

Not all "church" music is appropriate for liturgical use, as when music created for catechetical settings to inculcate lessons for particular age groups invades multigenerational communal worship. While parents and grandparents may be edified by hearing their blood kin singing "special music" at some points during the liturgy, do these practices tend to turn the children into performers entertaining adult listeners rather than involving children and adults in common acts of worship?

From Sacred Song to Ritual Music asserted that the documents studied offered varied taxonomies of what constituted Roman Catholic worship music. Thus, *Tra le sollecitudini* limited genuine Roman Catholic worship music to three categories: Gregorian chant, Roman school polyphony, and "more modern music" (understood as liturgical texts in the officially approved languages of Latin, Greek, and Hebrew set to music organized in key structures rather than modes and possibly accompanied by instruments). The 1958 Instruction nuanced and expanded these categories: Gregorian chant for the Roman Rite (with other chant repertoires for their proper rites); polyphonic compositions (in addition to those of the "Roman school"); "more modern music"; popular religious singing (employing the vernacular); and sacred organ music. Chapter six of *Sacrosanctum Concilium* reduced the categories to two: Gregorian chant as proper to the Roman Rite and "other kinds of sacred music, especially polyphony." Ch2003 continues to define Roman Catholic worship music in stylistic categories, but with some surprising emphases.

Gregorian chant maintains pride of place: "Among the musical expressions that correspond best with the qualities demanded by the notion of sacred music, especially liturgical music, Gregorian chant has a special place." [#7] But John Paul II clarifies Pius X's teaching that other forms of Roman Catholic worship music should aspire to Gregorian chant:

> With regard to compositions of liturgical music, I make my own the "general rule" that St. Pius X formulated in these words: "The more closely a composition for church approaches in its movement, inspiration and savour the Gregorian melodic form, the more sacred and liturgical it becomes; and the more out of harmony it is with that supreme model, the less worthy it is of the temple." It is not, of course, a question of imitating Gregorian chant but rather of ensuring that new compositions are imbued with the same spirit that inspired and little by little came to shape it. Only an artist who is profoundly steeped in the *sensus Ecclesiae* can attempt to perceive and express in melody the truth of the Mystery that is celebrated in the Liturgy. [#12]

Ch2003 likewise values what earlier documents referred to as "sacred polyphony," primarily noting the importance of "preserving . . . the centuries-old patrimony of the Church" [#8] in such choral music. Very surprising, however, is what appears to be a critique of how this repertoire is sometimes employed in the renewed liturgy: "[T]hose elitist forms of 'inculturation' which introduce into the Liturgy ancient . . . compositions of possible artistic value but that indulge in a language that is incomprehensible to the majority, should be avoided." [#6] It is unclear if this critique refers to singing texts that the majority of worshipers cannot understand (e.g., nonvernacular texts), to using styles of music that the majority of worshipers cannot appreciate without training (e.g., Notre Dame organa or Ars Nova polyphony), or both.

John Paul II devotes the most attention to the category of "more modern music," both positively and negatively. On the one hand, he offers encouragement to contemporary composers putting their gifts at the service of sung liturgical prayer:

> Since the Church has always recognized and fostered progress in the arts, it should not come as a surprise that in addition to Gregorian chant and polyphony she admits into celebrations even the most modern music as long as it respects both the liturgical spirit and the true values of this art form. . . . I have . . . intended in the Encyclical *Ecclesia de Eucharistia* to make room for new musical contributions, mentioning in addition to the inspired Gregorian melodies, "the many, often great composers who sought to do justice to the liturgical texts of the Mass." [#10] . . .
>
> I know well that also today there are numerous composers who are capable of making their indispensable contribution in this spirit, increasing with their competent collaboration the patrimony of music at the service of a Liturgy lived ever more intensely. To them I express my confidence, together with the most cordial exhortation to put their every effort into increasing the repertoire of compositions worthy of the exalted nature of the mysteries celebrated and, at the same time, suited to contemporary sensibilities. [#12]

Yet this optimism and confidence with regard to "more modern music" is tempered by a recognition that "not all forms of music can be considered suitable for liturgical celebrations" [#4]:

> I have . . . stressed the need to "purify worship from ugliness of style, from distasteful forms of expression, from uninspired musical texts which are not worthy of the great act that is being celebrated," to guarantee dignity and excellence to liturgical compositions. [#3] . . .
>
> [T]he sacred context of the celebration must never become a laboratory for experimentation or permit forms of composition and performance to be introduced without careful review. [#6] . . .
>
> It is . . . necessary to pay special attention to the new musical expressions to ascertain whether they too can express the inexhaustible riches of the Mystery proposed in the Liturgy and thereby encourage the active participation of the faithful in celebrations. [#7]

It should be clear that Ch2003 does not offer concrete solutions on how to determine which styles of music are inappropriate for Roman

Catholic worship. Perhaps recognizing that consensus on "ugliness of style," "distasteful forms of expression," "uninspired musical texts," etc., is difficult to reach, freed from individual bias and cultural insensitivity, John Paul II notes:

> Renewed and deeper thought about the principles that music be the basis of the formation and dissemination of a high-quality repertoire is therefore required. Only in this way will musical expression be granted to serve appropriately its ultimate aim, which is "the glory of God and the sanctification of the faithful." [#12]

In addition to employing the three stylistic categories employed by *Tra le sollecitudini* to define Roman Catholic worship music, Ch2003 also addresses the category of popular religious singing:

> The last century, with the renewal introduced by the Second Vatican Council, witnessed a special development in popular religious song. . . . This singing is particularly suited to the participation of the faithful, not only for devotional practices . . . but also with the Liturgy itself. Popular singing, in fact, constitutes "a bond of unity and a joyful expression of the community at prayer, fosters the proclamation of the one faith and imparts to large liturgical assemblies an incomparable and recollected solemnity." [#11]

Since the Liturgy may now be celebrated in the vernacular, the earlier distinction between "more modern music" in Latin, Greek, and Hebrew suited for the Liturgy and "popular religious singing" in the vernacular suited for devotions no longer holds. However, with the development of vernacular singing at the Liturgy, other issues have arisen: "In compositions written for divine worship . . . the particular Churches in the various nations are permitted to make the most of 'those special forms which may be said to constitute the special character of [their] native music.'" [#10]

How and to what extent the "substantial unity of the Roman Rite" will be maintained musically poses a profound challenge to contemporary pastoral musicians.

Clearly Ch2003 reiterates the desire of other twentieth-century official documents that Gregorian chant not be relegated to the status of a historical curiosity but be cherished as a vehicle for living liturgical prayer. Three problems immediately arise: textual, musical, and ritual. Textually, Gregorian chant employs Latin, Greek, and Hebrew, none of which are vernacular for the vast majority of contemporary Roman

Rite worshipers. Does one provide vernacular translations for singing (at the risk of distorting the quantity and accentual patterns of the original) or vernacular translations to be read while the text is sung in the original language? Musically, the Gregorian repertoire for Mass includes both "Proper" and "Ordinary" elements, with the musical glories of the tradition appearing in the neumatic and melismatic Introits, Graduals, Tracts, Alleluias, Offertories, and Communions found in the Proper. It is unlikely that these Proper chants could ever be assembly song (outside of religious communities) both because the texts vary from celebration to celebration and because the musical settings are quite elaborate (not to mention training the congregation to sing square-note, four-line notation and providing them with scores). Since the *Kyrie, Gloria, Credo, Sanctus-Benedictus,* and *Agnus Dei* texts of the Ordinary do not vary from celebration to celebration, they would be easier for a congregation to learn. The *Kyrie* and *Agnus Dei* would be easiest of all since their short texts repeat as litanies. Syllabic (*Kyrie* from Mass XVI; *Agnus Dei* from Mass XVIII), neumatic (*Kyrie* and *Agnus Dei* from Mass IX ["Cum jubilo"]) and melismatic (*Kyrie* from Mass VIII ["De Angelis"]; *Agnus Dei* from Mass XVII [neumatic, but wide range]) versions of these texts could be relatively easily memorized by the assembly. Congregational singing of the *Sanctus-Benedictus* would be slightly more difficult than that of the *Kyrie* and *Agnus Dei* since the text is not litanic, but syllabic (Mass XVIII), neumatic (Mass IV), and melismatic (Mass IX) versions could also be introduced and memorized by the assembly. Hardest of all for congregational singing would be the *Gloria* and *Credo* because of the amount of non-repeating text. However, the so-called Ambrosian *Gloria* (Chants "ad libitum" Gloria IV) and Credo III could be sung by the assembly, especially in alteration with a choir so that the assembly doesn't have to master the entire composition. One could also mention hymns and antiphons associated with particular feasts or seasons, usually syllabic or neumatic, that could likewise become part of an assembly's chant repertoire (e.g., *Pange lingua gloriosi, Veni Creator Spiritus, Salve Regina*). Ritually, the concern would be to adapt these chants to the demands of the reformed Order of Mass. For example, singing the *Credo* or the *Sanctus* by the choir alone without any vocal participation by the assembly would seem to violate their ritual function as the Profession of Faith of all the baptized worshiping and the Preface Acclamation sung by all with the priest. Similarly, the *Agnus Dei* appears as a "closed form" in the Gregorian repertoire; the number of repetitions of the text would have to be adjusted to cover the time it takes to break the consecrated bread and prepare vessels for Holy Communion.

Ch2003 also acknowledges sacred polyphonic compositions as part of the treasury of sacred music and appropriate to inclusion in the Roman Rite. Since these compositions never intended to include congregational singing, their placement within the reformed Order of Mass can be problematic. Certainly none of the Mass Ordinary movements would be appropriate since all call for the vocal participation of the assembly, with the exception of the *Gloria* explicitly cited as a text that can be sung by the choir alone. More realistic might be individual motets (e.g., Palestrina's *Sicut cervus*) that might be sung as prelude/postlude music, during the time of reflection after the homily, during the Preparation of the Gifts, or after the Communion procession.

Ch2003's treatment "more modern music" and "popular religious singing" clearly raises the opportunities and problems associated with these categories of Roman Catholic worship music. I believe the criteria proposed by the United States Conference of Catholic Bishops in *Music and Catholic Worship* and *Liturgical Music Today* can be very helpful in determining pieces from this repertoire appropriate to contemporary Roman Rite worship. These documents call for a judgment to be made musically (Is the composition well crafted, memorable, repeatable, able to bear the weight of mystery?), liturgically (Is the composition respectful of the text it enshrines, the personnel expected to execute it, the ritual activity for which it is intended?) and pastorally (Is the composition able to express and shape the faith of the concrete assembly who will be engaging it?).

According to Ch2003, What Is the Purpose of Roman Catholic Worship Music?

In delineating the purpose of Roman Catholic worship music, Ch2003 quotes the formula enunciated by Pius X in *Tra le sollecitudini*, a formula that has become venerable through repetition in ecclesiastical documents treating liturgical music in the past century:

> The holy Pontiff [Pius X] recalls that the special attention which sacred music rightly deserves stems from the fact that, "being an integral part of the solemn Liturgy, [it] participates in the general purpose of the Liturgy, which is the glory of God and the sanctification and edification of the faithful."

Thus for Roman Catholics worship is not simply a God-to-humanity movement (as in some forms of prophetic or charismatic religion) nor is it only a humanity-to-God movement (as in some forms of devotional or sacrificial religion). Rather, Roman Catholic worship involves both the divine equipping of human beings to offer proper devotion and the communal acts of devotion offered by living human beings in union with those who have already entered into God's eternity (the angels and saints). Properly speaking, God the Father (by appropriation) blesses the church through the Son in the Holy Spirit and the church offers its worship to God the Father (by appropriation) through the Son in the Holy Spirit. Liturgical music is one of the vehicles by which such worship takes place.

There is a slight problem, however, insofar as Ch2003 also quotes Vatican II's modification of this formula without adverting to a possible change in Pius X's teaching on the twofold purpose of liturgical music. The quotation appears toward the end of the final article:

> I hope that the centenary commemoration of the Motu Proprio *Tra le Sollecitudini*, through the intercession of their holy Author together with that of St. Cecilia, patroness of sacred music, may be an encouragement and incentive to those who are involved in this important aspect of liturgical celebrations. Sacred music lovers, by dedicating themselves with renewed impetus to a sector of such vital importance, will contribute to the spiritual growth of the People of God. The faithful, for their part, in expressing their faith harmoniously and solemnly in song, will experience its richness ever more fully and will abide by the commitment to express its impulses in their daily life. In this way, through the unanimous agreement of pastors of souls, musicians and faithful, it will be possible to achieve what the Constitution *Sacrosanctum Concilium* describes as the true "purpose of sacred music", that is, "the glory of God and the sanctification of the faithful." [#15]

Note that Pius X spoke not only of the "sanctification" but also of the "edification" of the faithful as part of the purpose of sacred music. The Vatican II version of the formula drops "edification," probably to avoid any hint of the "elitist forms of inculturation" mentioned in Ch2003 #6.

I think it is regrettable that Ch2003 does not allude to the functional categories that *Musicam Sacram*[4] proposed for determining the purpose of Roman Catholic worship music. This document acknowledges: (1) a decorative or alluring function by which the sacred texts are illuminated and made more memorable and spiritually effective; (2) a differentiating function by which the various roles of the worshiping assembly are embodied and clarified; (3) a unifying function by which the individual worshipers are formed into a community; (4) a transcendental function by which worshipers are led to the contemplation of spiritual realities; and (5) an eschatological function by which worshipers are given a foretaste of the worship of the heavenly Jerusalem. The challenge for the pastoral musician is to find, prepare, and critique a repertoire that not only glorifies God and sanctifies worshipers, but activates each of these functions.

According to Ch2003, What Are the Qualities Roman Catholic Worship Music Exhibits?

It is in Ch2003's treatment of the qualities Roman Catholic worship music should exhibit where it breaks new ground. This may be somewhat surprising since John Paul II uses *Tra le sollecitudini*'s three categories of holiness, true art, and universality as a framework for his own distinctive insights.

Unlike Pius X, who presented holiness as a quality inhering in music per se, John Paul II makes his own the more functional understanding taught by Vatican II that "sacred music increases in holiness to the degree that it is intimately linked with liturgical action." [#4] Rather than declaring particular languages, styles of composition, instruments, or methods of performance inherently holy, he cautions readers (quoting Paul VI) that "not all without distinction that is outside the temple [*profanum*] is fit to cross its threshold" [#4], i.e., it is easier to perceive elements of liturgical music lacking in holiness than to identify the contrary. And quoting his own teaching in *Ecclesia de Eucharistia*, he calls for deeper reflection on the relationship of holiness to the liturgical arts:

> St. Pius X's reform aimed specifically at purifying Church music from the contamination of profane theatrical music that in many countries had polluted the repertoire and musical praxis of the Liturgy. In our day, too, careful thought . . . should be given to the fact that not all the expressions of figurative art or of music are able "to express adequately the mystery grasped in the fullness of the Church's faith." Consequently, not all forms of music can be considered suitable for liturgical celebrations.

Perhaps surprisingly no mention is made of cultural codes influencing judgments about the holiness communicated by liturgical music.

The second quality Pius X identified for sacred music—sound form—inspires John Paul II to offer new criteria for determining appropriate music at liturgy:

> There can be no music composed for the celebration of sacred rites which is not first of all "true art" or which does not have that efficacy "which the Church aims at obtaining in admitting into her Liturgy the art of musical sounds." Yet this quality alone does not suffice. Indeed, liturgical music must meet the specific prerequisites of the Liturgy: full adherence to the text it presents, synchronization with the time and moment in the Liturgy for which it is intended, appropriately reflecting the gestures proposed by the rite. [#5]

Note that, while not denying that purely instrumental music may be a part of Roman Catholic worship music, John Paul II, in conformity with preceding church documents, emphasizes the role of texted music. Determining how music gives "full adherence to the text it presents" raises many questions. While some musical texts in the liturgy remain prescribed (e.g., the *Glory to God*, the *Holy, Holy, Holy*), others have become optional, either in the liturgical books themselves (e.g., the various tropes proposed for the *Lord, Have Mercy*) or by decision of episcopal conferences (e.g., the substitution of other texts for the antiphons proposed at the Entrance, Offertory, and Communion). Ch2003 teaches that whatever text is approved for liturgical use, the musical setting must not distort its intended communication (e.g., by omitting, disjointing, or unduly repeating words or phrases; by trivializing or treating the text with irony by pairing it with an inappropriate musical style; or by crafting a setting in which the text is assigned to inappropriate singers [such as an Institution Narrative sung by the choir alone]).

Synchronizing liturgical music "with the time and moment in the Liturgy for which it is intended" would seem to be a matter of performance, but in fact it raises questions about appropriate musical forms employed in the liturgy. For example, is a strophic hymn an appropriate accompaniment to the entrance procession? If the text is to be sung in its integrity, as the previous discussion suggests, then it should not be truncated simply because the ministers have arrived at their places; on the other hand, if the purpose of the entrance music is to accompany the procession of the ministers, its raison d'être to a certain extent disappears once the action of processing has ceased.

"Appropriately reflecting the gestures of the rite" also raises questions about the musical forms to be employed during the liturgy. For example, if the purpose of the *Lamb of God* chant is to cover the time it takes the ministers to break the consecrated bread and place it in ciboria, then musical settings of this text should be "open" (able to be modified as circumstances dictate) rather than "closed" (to be played note-for-note without compression or extension).

In the light of the foregoing, Ch2003 asserts that musical settings, rather than exhibiting a "holy homogeneity," should strive to differentiate the diverse acts of the liturgy:

> The various musical moments in the Liturgy require a musical expression of their own. From time to time this must fittingly bring out the nature proper to a specific rite, now proclaiming God's marvels, now expressing praise, supplication or even sorrow for the experience of human suffering which, however, faith opens to the prospect of Christian hope. [#5]

This presumes that one can determine the "nature proper to a specific rite," assisted by historical study and the guidance of the *praenotanda* of the various liturgical books. Thus, for example, when the General Instruction of the Roman Missal identifies the *Kyrie eleison* as a series of acclamations to Christ, a lugubrious setting in which the text is treated as petitionary or intercessory would be inappropriate.

Perhaps the strongest sign of how much Roman Catholic worship music praxis has changed in the past century appears in Ch2003's treatment of "universality." For Pius X, universality means that all human beings, believers or unbelievers, must receive a good impression when hearing Roman Catholic worship music sung or played. Later ecclesiastical documents shift the meaning of universality to music that believers would recognize as "their own" no matter what their ethnic background or wherever on earth they celebrated the liturgy. In contrast John Paul II associates the idea of universality in Roman Catholic worship music with his treatment of musical adaptation and inculturation:

> The music and song requested by the liturgical reform—it is right to stress this point—must comply with the legitimate demands of adaptation and inculturation. It is clear, however, that any innovation in this sensitive matter must respect specific criteria such as the search for musical expressions which respond to the necessary involvement of the entire assembly in the celebration and which, at the same time avoid any concessions to frivolity or superficiality. [#6]

Thus, Ch2003 treats "universality" not as something inhering in music per se, nor something immediately recognizable by those initiated, but as a necessary component of any encounter between the Gospel and particular cultures. *All* cultures, universally, must undertake the arduous tasks of identifying and rejecting what is irretrievably bound up with falsehood and superstition and of identifying and embracing what can express the Mystery in all of its cultural elements, music included.

At the pastoral level, this raises many issues. Should culturally homogeneous congregations sing not only texts in Latin, Greek, and Hebrew, from the Gregorian chant tradition as well as their own vernacular, but also songs in other vernaculars as a sign of solidarity with other members of the faithful throughout the world? Or is such a practice patronizing of other cultures and inauthentic in the culturally homogeneous congregation? In culturally diverse congregations, how does one achieve a balance of vernaculars: e.g., providing a "Spanish" Mass to which Anglo parishioners are invited, but at which no English is employed (or vice versa) but at which printed translations are provided (like the earlier Latin-vernacular hand missals); providing a "Taize"-styled Mass at which common refrains are sung in Latin, Greek, or Hebrew, while individual verses are sung in various vernaculars; providing a "mixed" Mass at which some elements are sung in one vernacular while others are in another vernacular (taking care not to mix vernaculars within a macro-unit, such as singing the *Sanctus-Benedictus* of the Eucharistic Prayer in Spanish but the Memorial Acclamation in English); providing a "bi- or multilingual" Mass at which multiple languages are used within a single musical element (e.g., *Santo, santo, santo / Lord, God of hosts*)? How can a community identified with one cultural tradition (e.g., Mexican American Spanish-speaking communities) embrace and welcome other cultural traditions using the same language (e.g., Cuban, Puerto Rican, or Central American Spanish-speaking communities)?

According to Ch2003, Who Sings Roman Catholic Worship Music?

More than any previous ecclesiastical document known to me, Ch2003 presents a unified and holistic picture of who sings the renewed Roman Rite liturgy as the fruit of differentiation by liturgical roles and unification by ritual coordination:

> From the smooth coordination of all—the priest celebrant and the deacon, the acolytes, the altar servers, the readers, the psalmist, the *schola cantorum*, the musicians, the cantor and the assembly—flows the proper spiritual atmosphere which makes the liturgical moment truly intense,

shared in and fruitful. The musical aspect of liturgical celebrations cannot, therefore, be left to improvisation or to the arbitration of individuals but must be well conducted and rehearsed in accordance with the norms and competences resulting from a satisfactory liturgical formation. [#8]

Note that this document distinguishes between the role of the psalmist (presumably the one who proclaims in song the Responsorial Psalm), located along with acolytes, altar servers, and readers, and the role of the cantor (presumably the one who serves as a choir substitute and/or leads the assembly), located closest to the assembly. Other documents note that frequently these two roles are combined in a single individual.

Of all the musical roles listed in article 8, John Paul II singles out the importance of the choir in maintaining the "centuries-old [musical] patrimony of the Church." Quoting the teaching of both *Sacrosanctum Concilium* and *Musicam Sacram* on the topic, he concludes: "The schola cantorum's task has not disappeared: indeed, it plays role of the guidance and support in the assembly and, at certain moments in the Liturgy, has a specific role of its own." [#8]

According to Ch2003, Who Plays Roman Catholic Worship Music?

The question of which instruments appropriately play Roman Catholic worship music is cursorily treated in Ch2003, especially in comparison to the lengthy taxonomy of "forbidden" instruments in the primary document on which it comments, *Tra le sollecitudini*. Here John Paul II first acknowledges the teaching of both Pius X and the Second Vatican Council that the pipe organ holds pride of place as an instrument to be played in the Roman Rite. He then notes that other instruments may also appropriately be used, but only if they exhibit the qualities that the Second Vatican Council already demanded:

> [I]t should be noted that contemporary compositions often use a diversity of musical forms that have a certain dignity of their own. To the extent that they are helpful to the prayer of the Church they can prove a precious enrichment. Care must be taken, however, to ensure that instruments are suitable for sacred use, that they are fitting for the dignity of the Church and can accompany the singing of the faithful and serve to edify them. [#14]

In summary, although Ch2003 is quite brief, it is far from being a lightweight document. Although it does not advance very far the discussion on the purpose of Roman Catholic worship music, who sings it, or who plays it, it does offer new insight into the role Gregorian chant might play in inspiring new compositions, new encouragement for continued liturgical composition, new criteria for determining the "sound form" of liturgical compositions, and new nuances in conceptualizing "universality" as a quality of Roman Catholic worship music. As such it is a welcome addition to continued reflection on sacred sound at the service of common prayer.

Notes

1. Chirograph of the Supreme Pontiff John Paul II for the centenary of the Motu Proprio 'Tra le sollecitudini' on Sacred Music" electronically stored at http://www.vatican.va/holy_father/john_paul_ii/letters/2003/documents/hf_jp-ii_let_20031203_musica-sacra_en.html. The numerals preceded by # refer to numbered subdivisions of the text.

2. See R. Kevin Seasoltz, *New Liturgy, New Laws* (Collegeville: Liturgical Press, 1980) 169–81, esp. 172–4.

3. Jan Michael Joncas, *From Sacred Song to Ritual Music: Twentieth-Century Understandings of Roman Catholic Worship Music* (Collegeville: Liturgical Press, 1997).

4. The Latin text appears in *Acta Apostolicae Sedis* 59 (1967) 300–20. An English translation appears in International Commission on English in the Liturgy, *Documents on the Liturgy 1963–1979: Conciliar, Papal, and Curial Texts* (Collegeville: Liturgical Press, 1979) nos. 4122–4190, pp. 1293–1306.

5

Forward Steps and Side Steps in a Walk-Through of Christian Hymnody

Bert F. Polman

In a relatively short time I would like to take a walk with you through the history of Christian hymnody. But in so doing, I'm going to start as a professing Christian with some biblical material that will become the glasses through which I will then read the history. This is the outline we're going to work through: I'll give you the biblical model first, and then five steps of the history. I'm using biblical material not only to read history but also as my source of normativity. I'll make judgment calls on what happens historically based on certain biblical criteria.

Biblical Criteria

We'll start then with the Old Testament material and particularly the book of Psalms. I hope all of you know the psalms well, a very rich source of textual material. One-third of them are laments in which you ask God to deal with illness, enemies, disasters, and you, in faith, ask God why and how long must my neighbor suffer with cancer and children die of starvation. The psalms give us words when we do not know what to say. If you look at an average modern hymnbook, that whole important phenomenon of lamenting before God in faith is largely missing. And it is the strength of people of faith to not only be able to say "Allelu Yahweh," praise the Lord for this, that, and a whole catalog of things, but also to say, "Lord, how long are you going to let me struggle?" or "Why are you silent, Lord, when my life is so difficult?" That takes a heart of faith, and that is what the laments help us do. Yes, there are also lots of praise psalms, there are great creation hymns like Psalms 8, 104, and 148. There are lovely, narrative psalms: 78, 105, 106, 135, and 136, and the wisdom teaching of didactic pieces like Psalm 1, 37, and 127. The book of Psalms is a rich repertoire to "feed the soul," to "nourish the Christian community."

The psalms didn't come out of David's mouth as one complete package, though sometimes we are led to think that way. The psalms developed over about 1500 years. The earliest psalm that we still have in the Psalter is the Psalm of Moses, Psalm 90. We have many ascribed to David or, if you read the Hebrew carefully, in the style of David. Obviously, something like Psalm 23 we think is definitely by David, but many others are at least in David's tradition and probably come from the early monarchy period. But there are later psalms, even postexilic psalms like 126. Scholars assume that under reform kings like Joash and Hezekiah, and later, Nehemiah and Ezra, various smaller psalm collections were produced. Thus we have a Yahweh Psalter, a Davidic Psalter, an Elohim edition, psalms of pilgrimage, and so on. These various "books" were then eventually edited and collated so that by the time we get to the Dead Sea Scrolls, approximately 100 years before Christ, we have the 150 psalms as we know them today. Sometimes the editors weren't completely on their toes, for there are duplicate passages in the book of Psalms. In any case, the process of editing is a process of discernment. Whoever these editors were, they chose to put in some of the psalms, and they also chose to ignore other pieces. We know the Israelites had victory psalms, but none of those got into the Psalter; they were a part of their life, but they didn't make it into the final book, so to speak. Evolving an anthology for God's people to sing is an ongoing process.

While it is true that some psalms are personal confessions or songs of praise sung by an individual, it is clear that the book of Psalms is a corporate expression of worship. It is a congregational effort, it is for the people to sing, whether they sing an old song like the Psalm of Moses or whether they sing a new song which they are always commanded to do in the book of Psalms. It is for the people to sing. Now they might have help. Certainly in the temple tradition, they had all kinds of professional people to help them sing. We're not sure what happened to corporate singing during the Exile, nor in the later synagogue tradition, but at least this much is clear: singing the psalms is a community experience for God's people.

When we get to the New Testament, we take this to a next step. You know the famous phrase of St. Paul in Colossians and Ephesians: "sing psalms, hymns, and spiritual songs." It doesn't really matter right now whether you take those as three separate genre or think that Paul meant two genre, "psalms and hymns," both of which are "Spirit-filled songs." We certainly do know that the early Christians, being Jewish Christians, continued to sing the psalms. They might eventually add a Christian doxology, a *Gloria Patri*, to the singing of the psalms, but psalmody stayed in their bloodstream. Then we get various New Testament hymns. You open the Gospel of Luke, chapters 1 and 2, and you get the famous four Lukan canticles: the Song of Mary, the Song of Zechariah, the Song of the Angels, and the Song of Simeon. Scholars assume these were early Christian songs that Luke incorporates into his Gospel. Similarly with Paul: his famous credo in Philippians 2:5-11 was presumably an early Christian creed that was sung, and he quotes this in his letter to the church of Philippi. The Johannine doxologies in the book of Revelation—all these marvelous, powerful texts about glory and strength and power and dominion (and so on) "to the Lamb forever and ever"—are also thought to be early Christian hymnic material John wove into his visions.

Not so much from the New Testament itself, but from very early Christian testimony in the second century, we certainly know the Christians sang. They were well known for their singing. Again, it was a congregational, participatory action. There are debates whether they used instruments at that point, but they certainly sang as a community of people.

Now let me summarize this rather quickly because, in a nutshell, we have what I call the biblical model or the basis, the basic principles, by which I'm now going to read the history that follows. First of all, there is a textual use of lament and praise in all of its various subgenres in the Jewish-Christian worship of God. Second, the biblical evidence suggests a concept of an ever-evolving songbook for which people make choices and discern what is helpful for singing in worship. They draw on the past history of song but also incorporate the "new song" each generation again. It's what I call this evolving, historically based anthology, but which is always fresh and open to singing to God a new song. Third, it's very clear this is to be a communal experience of singing, not essentially vocal solo material nor instrumental performance, even though solo voices and instruments may be involved. But the heart of this repertoire means that the family of God of all times and places sings together in song. The worship songs of God's people are no doubt addressed primarily to God; but, in so doing, they bridge the generations, different ethnic groups, males and females, class and economic structures, and so on.

Now, I haven't said anything about music style. And that is, as I usually tell my students, because the tape recordings David made got lost in the Maccabean War, and we don't know with any precision how the Old Testament Jews sang their psalms. And St. John made a video-tape on the Island of Patmos, but it was taken away by the Romans and hasn't been seen since. So what I'm sketching here are some essential things that mostly have to do, first of all, with text; second, with an editing process that respects history and is open to new songs; and third, with communal performance-practice. But those old songs and the new songs can mean any number of things in terms of musical style characteristics.

1. Walking Through the Medieval Era

Let's jump into our walk through the history of congregational singing, and we'll start with the medieval era, roughly 600–1400 C.E. What we get during this time period (I'm letting you see some highlights) are the great Greek language canons or preaching hymns in the Eastern Church. The best example is John of Damascus, whose Easter Canon has spawned some fine Easter hymns in English translations. They had a series of these canons, based on biblical canticles and the church year, that produced hymnic, sermonic-type poems. And though we're not totally sure, we assume these monks and bishops (and probably some church mothers in the group as well) would chant this material.

In the West we have the great development of the Office hymns in the monastic tradition by writers such as Bernard of Cluny, Bernard of Clairvaux, Abelard, or even Hildegard. All of these people who produced these Greek and Latin hymns took seriously God's command to sing a new song in that day and age. But they were still fed by psalmody, too. If you are Benedictine, you work your way through the Psalter quite rigorously so that memory becomes easy after doing that for ten years. In addition, some folk hymns developed, such as German *Leise* (e.g., "Christ ist erstanden"), or Italian *lauda*.

Though some of the medieval hymns in Greek and Latin may have been intended for congregations to sing, the great majority of this repertoire became professionalized material in later medieval performance practice. It was sung by clergy or clergy-dominated choirs and probably was sung very little, if at all, by lay worshipers in many Christian communities. Thus we made some marvelous steps forward in the medieval era, but were sidetracked by the loss of congregational performance.

2. Walking Through the Reformation Period

By the time we get to the Reformation in the early sixteenth century, we see a development that occurs frequently in history: when the Spirit of God broods upon the face of the deep, things begin to happen in creation; when the Spirit of God re-creates a people and sets them on a new journey, they break out into songs. God called Martin Luther, Menno Simons, Jean Calvin, and John Knox (to name a few) to lead his people, and one of the results is a great outburst of new hymns, new psalm translations, new Spirit-filled songs in the Protestant community. Let me mention some important Lutheran collections. Michael Praetorius compiled *Musae Sioniae,* a multivolume work (edited around 1605 to 1610) that includes some 1,200 hymns set for unison singing or single voice all the way to polychoral 12-, 15-, to 18-part writing of hymn motets. Johann Crüger's *Praxis Pietatis Melica* (the first extant edition is 1645) expanded from some three hundred songs to become, over its next numerous editions, an important anthology of those early Lutheran *chorales* (hymns) in vibrant rhythmic settings. That rhythmic vibrancy is lost by the time we reach Johann Freylinghausen's *Geistreiches Gesangbuch* (1704), the hymnal Johann Sebastian Bach used for his own harmonically satisfying (but rhythmically static) settings of many Lutheran *chorales.*

That brings us to Calvin and his emphasis on psalmody. Some of you might see red at my doing this, but I'm a Calvinist and I'm here to say that though I understand very well Calvin's rationale for singing only the psalms, I submit that this is one of probably a few areas where Calvin is simply wrong. I love the tunes from the *Genevan Psalter* (1562), for I grew up with them: my mother breastfed me on them; I know most of the 124 tunes from the *Genevan Psalter* from memory—even those almost inaccessible to many congregations. It is a marvelous collection. But when Calvin insisted that only psalms may be sung, and no longer the old or new hymns the Spirit of God also inspires among his people, then we encounter a regressive step in our walk through history.

Whether you're a Calvinist, a Lutheran, an Anabaptist, or whatever your mainstream or more radical Protestant heritage might be, the bottom line really very crucial in the Protestant Reformation is that congregational singing comes back to the foreground. It is now again congregations that sing the hymns and psalms of the church. Whether they have limited repertoires or wide-open repertoires, at least a large group of Christians is now engaged in corporate singing. That's a very important recovery.

3. Walking Through the Eighteenth Century

In the eighteenth century, in England first of all, we get the work of Isaac Watts who freshly paraphrased most of the psalms (*Psalms of David Imitated*, 1719), though not all of them, for he didn't think Christians should sing the imprecatory psalms, the ones with curses in them. In his psalm versions, Watts adopted a decidedly christological hermeneutic, so that Psalm 72 now becomes "Jesus shall reign where'er the Sun doth his successive journeys run." But Watts is also known as the "father" of English hymnody, for he wrote some much-used and highly respected hymn texts. I submit that his greatest hymn, "When I Survey the Wondrous Cross on Which the Prince of Glory Died," is sufficient evidence to indicate that Calvin's insistence on singing only psalms was wrong. That hymn, in its four stanzas, is the most powerful sermon on the atonement that I ever heard. And frankly, it's the only one I've memorized, excellent preaching notwithstanding.

Back on the continent in Germany, we have the development of the Moravian Brethren that has long roots back to the pre-Reformer John Hus and the *Unitas Fratrum*. Herrnhut, the estate of Nicholaus von Zinzendorf, gets to be a great missionary community for the Moravians. It's from there that missionaries get sent all over the world, including the United States. Under Zinzendorf's leadership, they developed *Singstunden*, that is, prayer meetings and hymnsings. People would start singing a hymn, and after a stanza somebody else would pick up another hymn. In their daily communal devotions they sang what we would call hymn medleys. The *Brüder Gesangbuch* that Zinzendorf edited in London (1753–4) is a two-volume book because it contains some three thousand German hymns in chronological order! This wonderful collection takes in the great richness of Germanic hymnody from Anabaptist and Lutheran sources and adds a lot of new Moravian material, including a good number of new hymns by Zinzendorf himself.

From the Moravians, we get to the Wesleys who encountered some Moravian missionaries on the boat on the way to North America. Many of you probably know those stories. That kind of Moravian pietism was very influential in bringing both Charles and John Wesley to renewed faith and contributed to the start of the Methodist societies that eventually became the Methodist Church. Charles Wesley wrote some seven thousand hymn texts. Many of the great hymn texts of the church year that you and I know from memory were penned by Charles Wesley: "Come, Thou Long-Expected Jesus"; "Hark, the Herald Angels Sing"; "Christ the Lord Is Risen Today" and "Rejoice, the Lord is King." John and Charles published numerous hymnals; the best known is probably their *Collection of Hymns for the People Called Methodists* (1780). There were other important evangelical hymnals, too: for example, the *Olney Hymns* published by John Newton and William Cowper. Obviously, congregational singing continued and flourished. However, many of the tunes initially associated with these evangelical hymn texts haven't survived well. They were often melismatic tunes in which you sing several notes to each syllable of text. That is not a very congregational-friendly approach, shall we say, for a congregation (the one performance body I know of that has the gall to perform regularly without the benefit of rehearsal), which, with its mix of musically literate and illiterate, requires tunes with reasonable accessibility.

The rise and popularity of new hymnody in many Christian communities meant that the singing of psalms went into decline. Psalms may still be spoken, no doubt, but were sung less and less frequently in corporate worship. I think that's a serious problem because most of the hymns we have in our repertoire focus on praise to God and do not pick up sufficiently the lament side of what I think Christians also need to sing—captured so well in many psalm texts. At least if your congregation is like mine, we have enough divorce, unemployment, abuse, and cancer to keep us busy with prayers of lament and petition for a long time. And if by God's grace your congregation is spared some of those ills, at least in empathy with the seemingly endless troubles of the world all around us, we need to sing lament psalms and compose new hymns of petition.

4. Walking Through the Nineteenth Century

In the nineteenth century, we have some very fascinating things that begin to happen. First of all, because of the Oxford Movement in England and the sort of Romanticism that is part of the nineteenth century, we get English translations, in a large-scale way, of the old Greek hymns from the Eastern church, the Latin hymns from the Western medieval church, and of a large group of Lutheran and other German hymns. John Mason Neale and Catherine Winkworth are important representatives of such translators, and Christian hymnody became greatly enriched by their translations, many of which we still sing today.

English Victorian hymnody of the second half of the nineteenth century is found in a very important hymnbook, *Hymns Ancient and Modern* (1860–1, edited by Henry Baker and William Monk). Many of the unions of specific hymn texts with specific hymn tunes we think are customary were made in the various editions of this hymnal. At the tail end of this era is the *English Hymnal* (1906, edited by Percy Dearmer and Ralph Vaughan Williams), best known for its inclusion of folk tunes as hymn tunes.

In the U.S.A., we have the American nineteenth-century Gospel hymn tradition of Crosby, Hasting, Bradbury, and Bliss, that crystallizes in Sankey's *Gospel Hymns No. 1–6* (1894), and leads in the twentieth century to the more modern Gospel hymns published by Rodeheaver and Singspiration. We also have the important folk hymnals such as *Southern Harmony* (1835) and *The Sacred Harp* (1844). The texts are often from Watts or Wesley, but the music style draws much more on the generic, British Isles folksong tradition as read through the Appalachian experience (before the *Hee Haw* program). We also get the development of black spirituals in which we find not only some great narrative hymns but also some very powerful laments. When you think of the slavery and later segregation experience of Afro-Americans, they certainly had reason to lament. (My impression is that many white Christians had their reasons to lament too, but they tended to do it beyond the church walls in country-western repertoire.) Eventually, in the 1870s and thereafter, these black spirituals began to become known in white communities, in part, due to black choirs who, for economic reasons, begin to do choir tours into white communities to raise money for their schools—the Fisk Jubilee Singers probably being the best-known case of that.

In the nineteenth century, congregational singing certainly continues. There's lots of new hymnic repertoire to sing by congregations; but certainly in North America, and to some extent in Britain with its high Anglican revival, church choirs become more important again.

Church choirs may be able to make important contributions to Christian worship, no doubt, but they do have a tendency to usurp some of the congregational songs. And that's not a happy, progressive development, I tell my students, "in my humble but sometimes inerrant judgment." The nineteenth century also saw some terrible conflicts in church music and denominations. If you think there are wars right now sometimes in the music department of the church, you should have been around in the nineteenth century when people almost assassinated each other because you were in the camp that wanted to sing only Gospel songs; and you, over there, were in the camp that insisted we should sing classic hymns; and another group over here wants to sing only the psalms. And churches split and new denominations formed: see, for example, the history of Presbyterians and Baptists, to name but a few. It sounds familiar to the turmoil in church music many of us experience today.

5. Walking Through the Twentieth Century

In the twentieth century there is a recovery of psalmody, particularly in the second half of this century. If you look at recent hymn-books, you'll usually find a sizable psalter section. Modern psalmody incorporates chant music, neo-chants such as those by Joseph Gelineau, metrical settings, and sung antiphons for spoken psalms. So modern Christians are expected (again!) not only to say the psalms responsorially but also to really mean it and sing them, for I submit we mean the psalms more when we sing them, or (even better yet) dance them.

We have hymns in different sizes in the twentieth century. Some are short—what some of us call mini-hymns: these are short Scripture choruses such as "Seek Ye First the Kingdom of God," and the Taizé repertoire of simple ostinatos like "Eat This Bread," or "O Lord, Hear My Prayer," with their varying instrumental parts on repetition. In the last twenty years, global hymnody is becoming part of our bloodstream; it is a marvelous infusion of great ethnic diversity and richness in our Christian anthology of hymn singing, ably promoted by church musicians like John Bell (Iona) and Michael Hawn. Others in the twentieth century are long hymns: a great outburst, particularly in the second half of the twentieth century, of what I would call classic, modern hymnody. This includes the textual work of Fred Pratt Green, Jane Parker Huber, Timothy Dudley Smith, Tom Troeger, Carl Daw Jr., and Margaret Clarkson, and a much more varied group of tune composers.

In Roman Catholic communities, following the important worship changes implemented by the Second Vatican Council, congregational singing again gains prominence, and we notice a recovery of both classic Christian hymns (from medieval and Protestant sources) and a flourishing of new hymns as well.

In our modern era, there are worship communities in which performance-oriented praise teams have replaced performance-oriented choirs, with the result that such "special" music continues to place congregational singing in some jeopardy. There are also some Christian communities that have chosen to abandon the historically based anthology concept I've suggested is a biblical norm for me. These are communities of different stripes. Some sing only Gospel hymns—hymns of invitation, hymns of commitment, initial commitment to Christ, hymns that are more suited to the young in faith. They sing the milk of the Gospel. That is essential, but if that's all one sings, one needs to ask, how do you nurture that young faith? There are some who sing only solid, classic, hymns, hymnody that takes four or eight stanzas of solid theological, systematically well-argued, deep stuff by which, definitely, if you take that material seriously, you can grow. In other communities, simple hymns are sung only by children in Sunday school, and global hymns only by teen choirs, but not by the entire worship community. Then there are some who think you should sing only the new song God has given you in the shower last week. They sing only the most recent Christian hit parade of hymns. I have students who come to my college who, unfortunately, know only one classic hymn, "Amazing Grace." They do not know "A Mighty Fortress Is Our God." They do not know the doxology and cannot sing the psalms! But they do know a number of contemporary praise songs from CDs and from their experience of corporate worship in their home churches. I sometimes hold back a tear when I tell these students they are eligible for a UNICEF grant because they come from underdeveloped churches that have given them a "new song" to sing to God but have withheld important parts of the Christian anthology of "psalms, hymns, and spiritual songs."

Many modern praise and worship hymns focus on praise almost exclusively, and many of them might be charitably classed as simple "milk" songs of Christian faith. The virtual absence of laments in modern hymnody is a serious issue today: the churches I know that do a lot or almost exclusively praise and worship singing have had to find other ways to pray laments and petitions. And so these churches develop prayer circles where people can come up and can say to God in spoken words, "what do I do with my cancer or AIDS," or "what must we do about starving children." The history of Christian singing, at its best, has always held that the most profound way of praying those prayers is to sing them. So, what I do, for example, in my own practice is to take a lament psalm we might sing and surround it with a praise song. So we get something old and something new. We get praise and lament in much closer proximity together, as typically happens in the book of Psalms.

Conclusion

What I've tried to sketch for you is some of the ways I think there is a basis, a common foundation you and I could share. It's a biblical basis that emphasizes both praise and lament and values corporate congregational performance, and therefore leaves stylistic questions open. I've tried to show how such biblical criteria can be used to read the development of Christian singing of "psalms, hymns, and spiritual songs" as we walked through various periods in history. I've noted many forward steps and some digressions or even regressive steps. I think we live in a fascinating era in which the Spirit of God is inspiring a great outburst of new songs. But one of the history lessons we might have learned is to recognize that the church, at its best, has been able to integrate the best of the new songs with the best of the historic ones. So let's not get too upset by periodic side- or backward steps in the largely forward steps in the development of Christian congregational song. As a Christian, I believe in the resurrection of the dead accomplished in Christ, in new life processed by the Holy Spirit, and then it becomes relatively easy for me to trust that God will correct our human foibles, our squabbles over church music, and our current obsession with sometimes ephemeral repertoire.

Part III

Contemporary Cultural
Considerations in the Light
of Biblical Mandates

6

The Sorrow Songs
Laments from the Old Testament and African American Experience

Wilma Ann Bailey

This paper examines the laments of the ancient Israelites and the African American slaves.[1] These two communities, of disparate time and place, find a connection in a common experience of bondage, suffering, loss of a homeland, and exile. The connection goes beyond that of a shared experience to the manner of responding to that experience through laments set to music that functioned both as catharsis and mnemonic device. Of particular interest are those laments that evidence an absence of closure, ending not with resolution but a steady uncertainty.

Connecting these two diverse communities, James Weldon Johnson wrote in 1925,

> It is not possible to estimate the sustaining influence that the story of the trials and tribulations of the Jews as related in the Old Testament exerted upon the Negro. This story at once caught and fired the imaginations of the Negro bards, and they sang, sang their hungry listeners into a firm faith that as God saved Daniel in the lion's den, so would He save them; as God preserved the Hebrew children in the fiery furnace, so would He preserve them; as God delivered Israel out of bondage in Egypt, so would He deliver them.[2]

The laments we read in the Hebrew Bible are the lyrics of songs sung in the cultic life of ancient Israel. We no longer have the melodies to the songs, but we do have ample references to musical instruments used in worship and, most likely, musical notations in the text. Biblical scholar Toni Craven indicates that laments are the largest single category of psalm in the Hebrew Bible.[3] The Psalms are notoriously difficult to date and connect with particular events. Psalm 137 is a notable exception. The setting is Babylon following the destruction of Jerusalem in 537 B.C.E. The psalmist reports that the disheartened Judahite expatriates cannot sing the Lord's songs in the land of exile. They pronounce a curse upon themselves if they forget Jerusalem and call for retribution. The psalm ends with the disquieting image of infants being smashed against rocks. Fortunately, most of the psalms of lament end on a more pleasant note.

According to Craven, the laments of the ancient Israelites are characterized by the following elements: an address to God, a statement of complaint, a confession of trust, a petition, words of assurance, and a vow of praise.[4] Shocking to modern ears are the frequent calls for vengeance upon the perpetrators of the violence inflicted upon the psalmist and the visioning of pain and suffering in their house.[5] One cries out, "The righteous will rejoice when they see vengeance done; they will bathe their feet in the blood of the wicked" (Ps 58:10).[6] And from time to time, in the laments of ancient Israel, God is directly accused of causing the suffering or standing silent in the face of it. One declares: "The Lord has destroyed without mercy all the dwellings of Jacob, in his wrath he has broken down the strongholds of daughter Judah" (Lam 2:2). Yet another demands: "Why do you sleep, O, Lord? . . . Why do you hide your face? Why do you forget our affliction and oppression?" (Ps 45:23, 24). But in the same psalm where the poet demands: "Let burning coals fall on them! Let them be flung into pits, no more to rise" (Ps 140:10), an assurance of faith is heard: "I know that the Lord maintains the cause of the needy, and executes justice for the poor. Surely the righteous shall give thanks to your name; the upright shall live in your presence" (Ps 140:12-13). Such psalms must be read within the historical context in which they were written. Here was an oppressed, disfranchised community that actualized its grief only in its words. The venting of anger and grief in this way functioned not only as a catharsis but as a recognition that there was a fundamental dichotomy between the life experience of the community at that particular time and their theology, a theology that paradoxically, affirmed the goodness of God and God's desire to bring blessing to all the people of the earth (Gen 12:3). Therefore with utmost confidence, they call upon God to act according to the divine mores.

The April 28, 1848, edition of *The North Star*, a weekly abolitionist newspaper published by Frederick Douglass in Rochester, New York, contained the following anecdote:

> I once passed a colored woman at work on a plantation, who was singing, apparently, with animation, and whose general manners would have led me to set her down as the happiest of the gang. I said to her, "Your work seems pleasant to you." She replied, "No massa." Supposing she referred to something particularly disagreeable in her immediate occupation, I said to her, "Tell me then what part of your work is most pleasant." She answered with much emphasis, "No part pleasant. We forced to do it."

The celebrated Dr. Rush of Philadelphia, in one of his published medical papers entitled "An account of the diseases peculiar to the negroes in the West Indies, and which are produced by their slavery," says:

> We are told by their masters that they are the happiest people in the world, because they are "merry." Mirth and a heavy heart, I believe, often meet together, and hence the propriety of Solomon's observation, "In the midst of laughter the heart is sad." Instead of considering the songs and dances as marks of their happiness, I have long considered them as physical symptoms of melancholy, and as certain proofs of their misery.[7]

As is well known, the laments of Africans in diaspora in America were brought to the attention of the world initially by a group of students from Fisk University. Eight of the nine students ranging in age from fifteen to twenty-five were former slaves or descendants of slaves. In 1871 they started out on concert tours to raise money for the university. Their popularity increased when they changed their repertoire from classical European music to the songs of the folk tradition of the American Negro. Other African American schools followed suit, and those teenagers and young adults are to be credited with saving a vast collection of traditional music that would have been lost. The Jubilee Singers sang primarily for white audiences because their purpose was to raise money for Fisk. The songs they chose to sing thus represented those spirituals that would please a white audience rather than those songs and the versions of those songs perhaps most significant in the African American community. In addition, the songs were sung in choral arrangements or as art songs to entertain. How were these songs originally sung? Frances Ann Kemble, a Philadelphian socialite who spent several months among the slaves on a Sea Island plantation in the winter of 1838–9, described the singing of the African slaves in a journal that she kept at the time. She writes:

> [T]hey all sing in unison. . . . Their voices seem oftener tenor than any other quality, and the tune and time they keep, something quite wonderful; such truth of intonation and accent would make almost any music agreeable.[8] The way in which the chorus strikes in with the burden, between each phrase of the melody chanted by a single voice, is very curious and effective.[9]

The Jubilee Singers were at first reluctant to sing the plantation songs in concerts because the songs were being used in minstrel shows to caricature African Americans. Therefore, George L. White, choir director of the first Jubilee Singers, was careful to create a way of singing that would distance the plantation songs from the minstrel representations. John W. Work, a successor of White at Fisk, writes:

> Mr. White decided on a style of singing the spiritual which eliminated every element that detracted from the pure emotion of the song. Harmony was diatonic and limited very largely to the primary triads and the dominant seventh. Dialect was not stressed but was used only where it was vital to the spirit of the song. Finish, precision, and sincerity were demanded by this leader. . . . Mr. White strove for an art presentation, not a caricature of atmosphere.[10]

The changing of the social context in which the songs were sung, the rearrangements of the tunes, the redirected purpose of the songs, and the new audience, all influenced which of the spirituals are remembered today and how they are remembered. In 1925 James Weldon Johnson and his brother Rosamund published a collection of popular spirituals. They included "Go Down Moses," "Swing Low, Sweet Chariot," "Deep River," "Roll Jordan Roll," "Joshua Fit the Battle of Jericho," "Little David, Play on Yo' Harp," and "Steal Away to Jesus." Except for "Steal Away," all use themes and imagery from ancient Israel. In fact, most of the biblical images used in the spirituals are taken from the Old Testament. The next year, the brothers published a collection that included some lesser-known spirituals. Among them were "I Want to Die Easy When I Die," "God's A-Gwineter Trouble De Water," "Mary Had A Baby," and "In That Great Gittin' Up Morning"—all spirituals that are well known today.

Particularly intriguing are those songs called spirituals with no religious content or where the religious content is vague and there is a lack of closure: for example, "Motherless Child," "Hush, Hush, Somebody's Callin' My Name," "Freedom Train A-Comin," and "I Didn't Hear Nobody Pray." Consider the last of these, "I didn't hear nobody pray. (2X) Way down yonder, by myself and I didn't hear nobody pray." There is no grace in the lyrics of that song. There is no denouement. There is no comfort. It is sung because it permits an expression of grief, not because it provides an answer.

Contrary to popular belief, the majority of Africans in America were not explicitly Christian until the Civil War era[11] when they began to enter the black churches, mostly Baptist and Methodist, in droves. The earliest of the spirituals of the African American community can only be traced back to the 1840s because that is when people starting collecting them. Is it possible then that this vast repertoire of spirituals with Christian or biblical themes had its origins in the slave period? Certainly many of them did. In addition to the songs themselves, there are collections of conversion stories, autobiographies, and poems that affirm Christianity's presence in the African American community. But some of the spirituals were certainly Christianized later on. In his 1901 autobiography *Up From Slavery*, Booker T. Washington writes:

> Most of the verses of the plantation songs had some reference to freedom. True, they had sung those same verses before, but they had been careful to explain that the "freedom" in these songs referred to the next world, and had no connection with life in this world. Now they gradually threw off the mask, and were not afraid to let it be known that the "freedom" in their songs meant freedom of the body in this world.[12]

Frances Kemble, citing lyrics of a song sung by Negro boatmen, relates that the slaves frequently sang "an extremely spirited war song, beginning 'The trumpets blow, the bugles sound—Oh, stand your ground!'"[13] The slaves referred to this as "Caesar's Song," and Kemble was intrigued by what she thought may be an allusion to Julius Caesar. She did not comment on the meaning or implications of the words.

Although it is widely known that the spirituals sometimes functioned as coded messages, for example, to send information about a planned escape, the implications of that are not widely recognized. These were not necessarily songs of piety. They *were* coded messages using the language of the Church in order to appear harmless. Arthur C. Jones writes that the use of Christian stories and symbols does not mean the slaves themselves were believers.[14]

Further, it is likely the oldest of the spirituals were not specifically Christian in their original form; religious, at times, but not necessarily

Christian. Fisher, for example, refers to a song the original title of which was "Run, Nigger, Run." It informed slaves of the presence of patrols in the area that were on the lookout for secret meetings. This song morphed into "Run, Mary, Run," recalling Mary at the tomb of Jesus who runs to tell the disciples he has risen.[15] "Steal Away" signaled an impending escape attempt. Because the Church preserved the spirituals, those explicitly Christian or that could be easily Christianized were kept; others were lost.

The origin of the slave songs is a matter of contention. Scholars of African American music have tried to determine how much of the content, tunes, and rhythms of spirituals are to be attributed to African roots and how much to the hymns and Gospel songs of the Church. James Weldon Johnson, weighing heavily on the former side, wrote, "by sheer spiritual forces . . . African chants were metamorphosed into the Spirituals. . . ."[16] Bessie Mayle notes similarities in style between African songs and those of Africans in America, particularly in what we call the "call and response."[17] To be sure, European-American Gospel songs did have an influence on some of the spirituals as George Pullen Jackson demonstrates in his book *White Spirituals in the Southern Uplands*,[18] originally published in 1933, and his second volume titled *White and Negro Spirituals*.[19] Jackson estimates that a third of the Negro spirituals, at least the tunes, had their origin in the white church.[20] Jackson pairs spirituals with what he believes to be precedents in the white church. For example, he pairs "O for a Thousand Tongues to Sing My Great Redeemer's Praise" sung to the tune Gaines rather than the more popular Azmon with "Swing Low, Sweet Chariot,"[21] and "Jesus, Thou Art the Sinner's Friend" with "Do Lord Remember Me."[22] While the former pairing is unconvincing, the latter has some merit. If these are two versions of the same song, the differences are striking. In the white version, the singer appeals to Jesus, placing himself or herself in the "bowels of [Jesus'] love," and refers to himself or herself as a sinner. In the black version, the more general term "Lord" rather than the specific "Jesus" is used. There is no reference to the singer being a sinner. No location is given for the singer. Even in the spirituals that derive from Gospel songs of the period, there is a notable difference in theology and worldview.

Miles Mark Fisher, in his 1948 dissertation entitled "The Evolution of the Slave Songs in the United States," asserts that:

> the so-called "Slave Songs" of the United States are best understood when they are considered as expressions of the experiences of individual Negroes, which can be dated and assigned to a geographical locale.

They are, in brief, historical documents. Further, the writer has come to agree with Frederick Law Olmsted, who, in 1863, concluded that the religion the Negroes sang about was not derived primarily from the American Christianity of the nineteenth century. This is to emphasize the African Background patterns.[23]

Fisher notes that Lucy McKim, a young woman who collected slave songs from the Sea Islands off the coast of South Carolina in 1862, also believed the spirituals to be historical in nature although "characterized as otherworldly."[24] He recalls that Talley believed Nat Turner, who led an unsuccessful slave revolt in 1831, wrote "Steal 'Wa,'" on the eve of his execution. Moreover, Earl Conrad attributed spirituals to Harriet Tubman.[25] Fisher cites a spiritual that sings about joining a band moving toward Jerusalem. Jerusalem is specifically identified with Courtland, Virginia, the destination of Nat Turner's slave revolt in 1831.[26] If Fisher is correct, then at least some of the pre-emancipation spirituals should be understood as describing historical events and situations, giving them something in common with the collection of laments in the biblical book of Lamentations. While it is unlikely most of the spirituals are historical in nature, it is likely some of them are, or to be more specific, were. Even those tied to a specific historical event[27] were sung in other contexts, changed and spiritualized to the point where the origin was lost.

In sharp contrast to the laments of ancient Israel, the Africans in America never understood God to be responsible for their suffering, nor did they blame themselves. They did envision God as the one who could remedy their situation in this world or the world to come. They believed that ultimately God was on their side. The religion of their oppressors would turn against them in the end. As a line in the spiritual, "I Got Shoes," proclaims, "Everybody talkin' 'bout heaven ain't agoin' there!"

The laments of ancient Israel were more fully developed than the African American spirituals likely because even those that did spring from the heart of the common people were appropriated for formal worship and made more complex, even as the simple two-line praise song of Exodus 15:21 expanded into the victory hymn of Exodus 15:1-18.

The Africans in America identified with the Israelites and adopted the same method of expressing their grief—laments set to music. The Africans in America also had in common with the ancient Israelites the use of song to record particular historical events or situations, though in many cases the historical contexts were forgotten as they were molded and shaped in the folk tradition. For both, the laments function as an aid to grief, to help people to grieve, to encourage them to grieve. In both these communities there are some laments that lack closure, so that the process is not cut short. The grieving could not come to an end until they were free to live as whole human beings.

Notes

1. A less concise form of this paper appears in *Yet with a Steady Beat: Contemporary U.S. Afrocentric Biblical Interpretation*, ed. Randall C. Bailey (Atlanta, Georgia: Society of Biblical Literature, 2003).

2. James Weldon Johnson, *The Book of American Negro Spirituals* (New York: De Capo Press, 1985, reprint of the 1925 and 1926 editions) 20–1.

3. Toni Craven, *The Book of Psalms* (Collegeville: Liturgical Press, 1992) 26.

4. Ibid., 27.

5. See Psalms 3:7, 5:10, 6:10, 10:15, 28:4, 63:9-10, 69:28, 79:6, 139:19, 140:10.

6. All biblical quotations are taken from the New Revised Standard Version unless otherwise noted.

7. *The North Star*, April 28, 1848. No page number and no author given.

8. Frances Ann Kemble, *Journal of a Residence on a Georgian Plantation in 1838–1839* (Athens: University of Georgia Press, 1984) 163.

9. Ibid., 259. Kemble does not describe tunes, singing styles, or lyrics of religious songs. She notes that the slaves were forbidden to attend Church services on the island. Some were permitted to go to a Church service once a month elsewhere. (See 261–2.)

10. John W. Work, *American Negro Songs and Spirituals* (New York: Crown, 1940) 15.

11. Mark Miller Fisher, "The Evolution of Slave Songs of the United States" (doctoral dissertation, University of Chicago, 1949) 34–5.

12. Booker T. Washington, *Up From Slavery* (Norwood, MA: Norwood Press, 1901) 19–20.

13. Kemble, 260.

14. Arthur C. Jones, *Wade in the Water: The Wisdom of the Spirituals* (Maryknoll, NY: Orbis, 1993) 8–9.

15. Fisher, 155 along with n. 38.

16. Johnson, 21.

17. Bessie Mayle, "The History and Interpretation of the Pre-Reformation Carol and the Negro Spiritual" (unpublished thesis, Boston University, 1932) 61–8.

18. George Pullen Jackson, *White Spirituals in the Southern Uplands* (Hatboro, PA: Folklore Associates, Inc., 1964).

19. George Pullen Jackson, *White and Negro Spirituals: Their Life Span and Kinship* (New York: Da Capo, 1975; reprint of the 1943 edition).

20. Ibid., 267.

21. Ibid., 182–3.

22. Ibid., 164–5.

23. Fisher, i.

24. Ibid., 37.

25. Ibid., 56.

26. Ibid., 163–5.

27. Sarah Thrower notes that, when asked, Sea Islanders indicated the songs they sang were connected to happenings in their lives. See Sarah Selina Thrower, "The Spiritual of the Gullah Negro in South Carolina" (unpublished thesis, College of Music of Cincinnati, 1953) 18.

7

The Virtue of Liturgical Discernment[1]

John D. Witvliet

Near the opening of the book of Philippians, Paul records his prayer for the Philippian Christians: "And this is my prayer, that your love may overflow more and more with knowledge and full insight to help you *to discern* what is best, so that in the day of Christ you may be pure and blameless, having produced the harvest of righteousness that comes through Jesus Christ for the glory and praise of God" (Phil 1:9-11). At the heart of this prayer is Paul's desire that his readers will exercise the virtue of discernment. He wants them to be able to make good choices, to "determine what is best."

I want to reflect not only about the *subject* at hand, but also about *the manner or rhetoric* of our conversation. Many of our discussions about worship and music feature what we might call the rhetoric of persuasion. That is, most often when people gather in churches, conferences, seminaries, and schools of music to discuss issues in contemporary church music, we gather with our minds already made up, eager to be affirmed in our viewpoint. We gather (a) to be affirmed in our own views; (b) to convince others of our well-founded positions; or (c) to amass ammunition to do that better in the future. The church today has no lack of opinions about church music, and no lack of willingness to share them.

So, in contrast to this rhetoric of persuasion, I want to call for a rhetoric of discernment. My goal is to isolate, define, and explore this virtue and then imagine what it might look like for conversations about church music today. My goal is to make an ethical appeal. I don't want to supply more ammunition for worship wars. I want to dare to pray that discernment would make us more virtuous leaders and better people, people who nurture and then hone a Christ-like mind.

I. Need of Discernment/Present Status

We need this virtue especially today because of a series of significant and at times bewildering changes in the practice of Christian worship. Consider seven (actually eight) currents in the contemporary sea of change.

First, the liturgical movement, symbolized by Vatican II, continues to influence our worship. The study of historical patterns of Christian liturgy and ecumenical encounters over the past thirty-five years has yielded an impressive harvest. Mainline denominations have worship books that look more like each other than has been the case at any generation since the Reformation. The liturgical movement has led Methodists and Presbyterians to sing their eucharistic prayers, evangelicals to light Advent candles, Roman Catholics and Episcopalians to nurture congregational participation in psalmody, and some Mennonites, Brethren, and Nazarenes to form Lectionary study groups. If you doubt God's existence, then consider this miracle: Catholics concerned about preaching, mainline Protestants concerned about sacraments, and evangelicals concerned about the early church. New ecumenical interest in the catechumenate (a period in the process of Christian initiation) is the most recent result of this movement. At the same time, a conservative trend in several Roman Catholic dioceses is evident, and there is a perceived reassertion of the authority of Rome.

Second, and in somewhat contrary fashion, the church growth movement has given us a new vocabulary for worship. This broad movement has encouraged congregations both to make worship services more accessible to those who are not yet Christians and to plan events specifically to address their needs and concerns. One result of this movement has been worship designed for specific groups of people, an approach that generated a whole new vocabulary for liturgical events: seeker-sensitive worship, seeker-driven worship, boomer worship, and so on. Church growth theorists of both mainline and evangelical stripes invite us to purchase subscriptions to *Net Results* and buy books entitled *Entertainment Evangelism*. The key thing to notice here, for good or ill, is the prominence of economic metaphors, including concern for a congregation's market niche, as well as the way that music can function as a tool to appeal to a wide spectrum of people.

Third, a concern for the active participation of the congregation has led to a renaissance in hymnody. Since the mid-1970s, nearly every denomination has published a new hymnal. In the late 1990s we have moved beyond new books to an era of hymnal supplements. More than ever before, these hymnals and supplements have been produced with cooperation among hymnal editors of various worship traditions. This ferment has led to a small industry of related efforts: the publication of dozens of single-author hymn collections, regular hymn-writing competitions, conferences on hymn writing and hymn accompaniment. There probably has never been as many single-author hymn collections in print as there are today. In the journal *The Hymn*, the Hymn Society's book service is printed in a smaller and smaller font with each issue in an attempt to cram all the new publications in those four pages.

Fourth, cultural diversity has enriched worship for Christians of all backgrounds and traditions. This diversity has led to the sharing of musical and textual resources among cultural traditions. Nearly every hymnal published in the past decade contains music from almost every continent and many North American cultures. Nearly every denomination is busy introducing or developing hymnals for ethnic minority congregations. And growth of global song has even Christian Reformed and Presbyterian churches buying conga drums. Significantly, this musical diversity is expressed not just within denominations, but within congregations. Many ethnically *homogenous* congregations are looking to become musically *multilingual*, singing songs and hymns from a variety of cultures.

Fifth, worship in nearly every Christian tradition has been influenced by the charismatic movement. A series of revivals in the late 1960s, which resembled the earlier Pentecostal outpourings at the beginning of the twentieth century, soon led to important changes in weekly congregational worship in many traditions. Closely related to (and perhaps a second generation of) the charismatic movement is the praise-and-worship movement. Emphases of "P & W" worship include exuberant praise as the basic act of worship; the use of several simple Scripture songs or praise choruses and the use of a sequence of actions that leads the congregation from exuberant praise to contemplative worship; and direction by a team of lay worship leaders often called a "worship team." This movement has resulted in the publication of Scripture choruses in many denominational hymnals or—more prominently—in the printed and projected replacements to traditional hymnals. This movement has generated an independent industry complete with published and recorded music, copyright licensing procedures, magazines, and conferences.

Sixth, the past several years have seen dramatically differing patterns for the role of children in worship. In many congregations, children have been segregated from public worship, with separate worship services or education sessions designed specifically for them. At the same time, a number of churches have looked for ways to integrate children into the regular pattern of Sunday worship—not just with "cutesy" anthems, but in leading the most significant parts of the liturgy, reading the Scripture lessons, singing the invitation to the Eucharist, or providing cover art for a printed worship order. Both changes have implications for children's music programs in the church—segregation generally leading to the demise of children and youth choirs, and integration leading to the view that children's choirs, like their adult counterparts, are best thought of not as a musical ornament on the service, but rather as a form of liturgical ministry.

Seventh, technology continues to shape innovation in worship. Video projection and sound amplification have forever changed how thousands of congregations worship. Hundreds of congregations have already left the overhead projector in the dust, and now plan worship services on PowerPoint, projecting not just song texts, but sermon notes, Scripture readings, video clips. As for sound amplification, we could travel to almost any city and find churches of widely divergent denominations arguing about the origin of musical sound for worship.

Certainly none of these developments is isolated from the others. Worship in a particular congregation will likely reflect the influence of several of them. In fact, when historians look at us some day, they may identify "eclecticism" as the central feature of much public worship at the beginning of the new millennium among North American Christians. Churches today either build diversity by offering a menu of services or packing it all into a single, eclectic, blended, fusion, stir-fry service.

The remarkable thing about all this change is how diverse and often contradictory it seems. Some say that worship has become irrelevant; others say that it has become irreverent. No single vantage point allows any of us to really understand how profound and far-reaching these changes are. We might say that rarely, if ever before, has the church been revising its worship in so many directions at once.

Part of the complexity of all this is that we have so many different issues. Some of us talk about the dozens of American Guild of Organist colleagues who have lost jobs in churches that are locking up the organ and buying a new Yamaha keyboard, about churches where the alternative service has become the main attraction. Some of us face parishioners who are sympathetic to our hopes and dreams, but where the senior pastor is deeply skeptical. Some of us have church music students who want training in music we deem unworthy of college study. Some of us are masters of Victorian hymnody, but don't know what to make of global song, or how to make it happen. All of us find ourselves in conversations about the complexity of contemporary culture.

Now in this world of change, it is easy to lose our bearings. Consider some of these real-life examples from North American congregations:

1. In one nearby town, a pastor issued an edict on worship styles, fired the long time AGO member church musician, locked up the organ, and purchased a new video projection system. He has proceeded to recommend and enforce whole-scale liturgical change on the basis of attending one conference on worship and evangelism, without so much as one month's discussion and prayer with the congregation.
2. Conversely, in another, three well-intentioned members of a high school youth group approached an organist/music director asking for help in forming a praise team. The organist, rather than seizing the nice teaching moment, responded quickly, "read my lips: 'that will happen over my dead body.'" A year later, two music staff people, an organist and a guitarist, coexisted in this congregation without ever talking to each other.
3. Members of the congregation are not immune to this, either. In one congregation, a group of choir members protested the use of Scripture choruses because they simply repeated the same line ten times over, and then went on to ask their music director if more Taizé services could be scheduled.
4. Conversely, in another congregation, a worship leader protested the use of any written prayers, because they were so predictable. When the worship committee reviewed tapes of earlier services, they discovered that this worship leader had, however, "spontaneously" come up with the same prayer in four consecutive services. The same worship leader, who had previously protested the overuse of a dozen traditional hymns, now lapsed into overuse of about a dozen choruses.
5. In another, a church council refused to adopt a proposal to celebrate Communion more frequently because "it would cease to be special," an argument that is rarely applied to preaching.
6. In another, cathedral-like church, the rector and parish musicians planned a brilliant service on the feast of the Annunciation that

included three settings of the *Magnificat* (an anthem, a metrical hymn, and a Scripture reading). Yet the fifteen people around me were entirely oblivious to the connections in that planning, so great was their biblical illiteracy. Here was a liturgical feast, which none of those around me had the enzymes to digest.

What we have here are situations in which committed Christians somehow lost their theological and pastoral equilibrium. Some of them may have been advocating important and helpful positions, but they lacked with the love, knowledge, or insight to help their congregations approach them in discerning ways.

II. The Anatomy of Liturgical Discernment

So what exactly is discernment? Discernment is a classical virtue, a common theme in Hebrew Scriptures, New Testament, and classical philosophy. And it merits our attention beyond simply giving a dictionary definition.

- Discernment is what Solomon asked for when he asked for "an understanding mind . . . to discern good from evil" (1 Kings 3:9).
- It is what Paul discusses in Romans 8 when he says that the "renewing of our minds" will help us "discern what is the will of God."
- Discernment or prudence, says Augustine, is "love distinguishing with sagacity between what hinders it and what helps it . . . prudence is love making a right distinction between what helps it towards God and what might hinder it."[2]
- Joseph Pieper identified it as "a studied seriousness . . . . a filter of deliberation," and "the perfected ability to make decisions in accordance with reality . . . the quintessence of ethical maturity."[3] Lewis Smedes, more colloquially, says that it is "having a nose for what's going on under the surface."[4]

Discernment, then, is nearly synonym for a slightly larger category— wisdom. More specifically, consider six ingredients in the recipe of discernment.

1. Openness

First, discernment can't occur without an openness to examine innovation. We can't make discerning choices without knowing the options. Discerning people are always willing to give a person, a movement, or a worship style a fair hearing. So, a discerning hymnal committee casts a wide net to gather lots of possibilities in its search for the gem that will distinguish their final publication. So does a discerning organist or choir director who is programming for an upcoming year.

For us to exercise discernment on the church's behalf means that we need to give a host of approaches a fair hearing. We don't need to like them. We don't need to adopt them. But we do need to examine them— to see what might be surprisingly lovely, honest, authentic, and beautiful about them. Their very existence in the Body of Christ demands that we attend to them.

So while it is fine to criticize Prince of Peace or Church of Joy or Ginghamsburg Church or your bishop or your youth director or whoever your favorite punching bag is, it's not fine to do that without giving them a fair hearing, without traveling there, without talking to them, without seriously reading what they have to say, without searching for the gem of truth to which they bear witness. And, conversely, it is fine for any of them to critique the work of AGO members, but only after talking with us.

2. Becoming Self-Conscious about the Choice between "Yes" and "No"

Second, discernment finally requires making choices, saying "yes" to some things, "no" to others. A discerning person doesn't give everything a blanket endorsement, nor does one stonewall every innovation.

Notice that we inevitably make choices for and against things all the time. Every time we choose hymns for next Sunday morning, we say "yes" to a few possibilities, and "no" to most. Over time, these choices add up. They gain significance. We end up ruling out hundreds of good hymns from our congregation's repertoire, and keeping some. The challenge is becoming *self-conscious* about that choice, being aware of what we are saying "yes" or "no" to, and the implications.

This also requires consistency. If we don't like contemporary prayers of confession because they sound too positive or upbeat, then we can't turn around and program the most upbeat, convivial *Kyrie* from the traditional Western musical repertoire. Our criteria must apply across the board.

If we don't like sentimental Christmas songs and anthems that show up in pop music, then we can't program sentimental anthems from the traditional Western church music—even if these sentimental anthems are written for English choirboys. (Let me also add that if we don't distaste sentimental Christmas texts, then we should.)

Let us admit at least this: Some of us suffer from not being open to any innovation. Others suffer from never meeting an innovation they don't like. The same prayer of confession won't work for both people. Some of us need to confess being obstinate, while others need to confess being indiscriminating.

3. Requires Knowledge

Third, discernment, according to St. Paul in Philippians 1, requires "knowledge and full insight." We can't make good choices unless we have a measuring stick or plumb line by which to judge a given innovation or practice. To make good choices, we need to be learners, readers, questioners. We need knowledge and insight, and it needs to be in search of truth.

Now it's true that a lot in music happens by instinct. But instinct is not enough. Not when we have churches where instincts seem to be headed for direct collision. In periods of competing tastes and competing instincts, we need to have articulated criteria (subject to intense scrutiny and criticism) which can serve as a rudder to our instincts.

The search for knowledge also demands humility. I recall the comments of a seasoned church musician who said that early in his career he attended American Guild of Organists meetings to tout his accomplishments and late in his career he attended them to learn from his colleagues, "to take my colleagues as my mentors." He had become, in his words, "a forever learner." What a difference this would make in hundreds of parishes.

This is also why congregational education is so absolutely crucial. In our parishes, we need to teach our people what worship and worship music are, and why we do what we do. In our professional conferences, we need not only to hone our musical skills, but also to nurture our pastoral sensibilities. In our seminaries, we need to teach liturgical literacy, not just to our musicians, but also to every single future pastor and church leader. And imagine what our church music conversations would be like if every typical organist and every typical praise team member would read two or three books in liturgical theology each year—or if every pastor would seek to learn our Christian musical heritage.

4. Love—Pastoral Judgment

Fourth, as St. Paul reminds us, discernment requires love.

This is especially true in matters of worship. John Calvin agreed. When discussing whether Christians should kneel in worship, for example, Calvin observed that some worship practices will inevitably change to accommodate to the culture of the age, but warned against rash, sudden, and poorly reasoned change, and then concluded: "But love will best judge what may hurt or edify; and if we let love be our guide, all will be safe."[5] In this passage, which is often misused to justify almost anything, Calvin portrays love in service of discernment.

This is not sentimental love that baptizes every fad. It is deep, pastoral love that seeks to promote worship practices that lead to the long-term health of the church. This is tender, empathic love that will take seriously the testimonies of fellow Christians about their own experiences of worship, and tough love that will allow us to challenge each other when we lose our way.

5. Community

Fifth, discernment happens best in community. Again back to Philippians 1, where Paul used the first-person plural to pray that "you (all) may determine what is best." He prayed for a *community* that would determine what is best. Indeed, Psalm 19:12 asks, "Who can discern his (their own) errors?" None of us by ourselves has the perspective to see the whole picture.

Yet think of how many people in the current state of church music face it in isolation. An isolated church consultant guru sits in a corporate office somewhere and writes a five-step program for revitalizing your congregation. A pastor, isolated in fear about the future of a congregation, reads this book in isolation and decides to impose significant liturgical change. A musician, isolated from any discussion on the topic, is informed of this decision, and complains (and rightfully so) to other musicians. An isolated bishop tries to keep Rome and home happy, but often without serious conversations on either end. Isolated church music professors might go for months without talking to a practicing church musician in many of the denominations that their students will serve. So often, we are ships in the night that pass each other by, without any genuine conversation about key topics.

In fact, think of how individual our models for church music are. Parish musicians choose music, study scores, attend conferences, and select music in splendid isolation. How much better when models of mentorship, team-building, and corporate decision making are central to our work.

6. Gift of Spirit

Finally, discernment, like all virtues in the Christian life, is less an accomplishment to achieve than a gift to receive. The chief ally and agent in any communal discernment process is none less than the Spirit of God. Discernment is a Pentecost virtue, and as such, it is something for which we pray. Discernment is the church's way of responding to complicated patterns of change. Wise leaders of Christian churches envision a process of communal discernment, an ongoing conversation. Now, of course, discerning conversation by itself is not enough. Having nice, hospitable conversation won't, by itself, change the world. We shouldn't be naïve about this. Instead, think of this process of discernment as setting the context of trust, honesty, and keen perception that will lead us to a deeper level of renewal. We are creating an environment with seeds of hope for the future.

Significantly, one of the places that we receive this gift is in worship itself. The psalmist declares "In your light, we see light" (Ps 36:9), and speaks of God's sanctuary as a place of true perception (Ps 73:17). Orthodox theologian Alexander Schmemann echoes this theme, calling true worship "the arrival at a vantage point from which we can see more deeply into the reality of the world."[6] Full, conscious, active participation in worship forms in us the kind of humility, courage, wonder, and sense of divine purpose that is necessary for discerning ministry.

III. Discernment at Work

This notion that discernment should be a sought-after gift in the area of liturgical music is, of course, not new.

- Augustine applied his definition of discernment almost verbatim to defend the singing of psalms and hymns, memorably challenging his inquirer to press forward "when there is greater hope of gain than fear of loss."[7]
- Likewise, Luther called for and modeled discernment in searching for texts and that preserved both accessibility and poetic excellence.
- Perhaps the best examples of discernment at work in our field come to us in the process of serving on a hymnal committee. Hymnal editorial committees have thousands of examples from which to choose, and need to find a way to sort out which examples are the most lovely, excellent, honest, and authentic.

What would a discerning mind look like today? Consider a dozen topics that are common in today's discussion, discrete topics that have been the subject of recent writing. In each case, consider the kinds of questions that might move us beyond easy and entrenched positions:

1. *Inculturation*: Will we distinguish cultural engagement from cultural capitulation and, conversely, will we distinguish cultural resistance from cultural retrenchment? Will we discern which aspects of worship are properly contextual, which are transcultural, which are candidates for cross-cultural sharing?

2. *Aesthetics*: Will we really ground our musical and aesthetic judgments in something other than taste? Might we ground musical judgments in terms of how music enables us to carry out the actions and purposes of Christian liturgy? That is, can we ground our musical judgments, in part, on distinctly liturgical criteria? If we allow church music to become simply a matter of taste, we might as well pack our bags, close up shop, and go home. We need musicians to challenge this assumption. Church music should critique my taste, challenge me to see something that is quite countercultural as quite good.

3. *Liturgical History*: Will we discern when history is being used as propaganda? For example, is John Wesley, who was deeply committed to the regular and profound celebration of the sacraments, legitimately invoked in defense of seeker worship? Is Luther's use of musical idioms with indigenous origins really a precedent for use of popular music today? Conversely, is J. S. Bach, who united doctrinal precision with pietistic warmth in his cantatas, invoked either to preclude or to include the use of more pietistic texts in current worship, and both apart from a concern with doctrinal precision? Using bad arguments in good causes eventually catches up with us. We must hold ourselves to historical honesty in the examples we invoke.

4. *Cultural Analysis*: Will we discern how given contemporary traits offer *both* challenges *and* opportunities to the Christian faith? That is, can we be prophets against the excesses of our culture without losing the ability to draw on strengths and opportunities of this cultural moment? Some church growth advocates describe every cultural phenomenon by sophisticated surveys and then remake the church in the image of our culture. Some traditionalists become masters at cultural jeremiads and fail to envision how the

Gospel might speak with clear and lucid tones to today's environment. May we honestly assess the bane and blessing of each trait of contemporary culture. That culture is not all bad, nor all good; that worship is inevitably shaped by culture, but need not baptize everything that comes along.

5. *Liturgical Theology*: Will we discern the difference between merely talking about worship and actually engaging in worship as primary theology? The danger in all of our discussions about worship style is that we will become so focused on talking about worship that we will fail to actually do it.

As Craig Dykstra asks in his book *Growing in the Life of Faith: Education and Christian Practices*, "We go to worship on Sundays, but when we worship, is each of us actually engaged in the practice of giving praise and thanks? Or are we just 'singing the hymns' or 'conducting the worship service'?"[8] Eugene Peterson, in *Working the Angles*, worries that pastors have become shopkeepers. Perhaps we must worry that church musicians have become background noise.

6. *Theology of Liturgy*: Will we have an operative understanding of Christian liturgy that is sufficiently specific, imaginative, and theological to provide a rudder or plumb line by which to assess liturgical innovation? Discerning people must ask tough questions: Why do churches with a high doctrine of Scripture often feature so little Scripture reading in Sunday worship? What about a church that confesses the power of the Word of God and then demands that its preacher use either high-gloss rhetoric or emotional manipulation to talk people into the kingdom of God? What about a church that holds to a Chalcedonian christology, but whose hymns praise only the human Jesus? What about the church that proclaims a gospel of grace and then implies that true worship demands that one conjure up certain emotions? What about the church that confesses that God is both transcendent and personal, but only sings songs that emphasize one of these attributes? What about churches with a high view of creation that nervously dismiss the contributions of visual artists?

7. *Pastoral Music*: Will we discern the difference between musical expressions that are accessible and those that are simply vacuous? Will we discern the difference between *simple* offerings that protest the noise and busyness of modern life and *simplistic* offerings that reduce the Gospel to therapy? In light of these questions, will we

find ways to minister with depth to people with almost no biblical literacy?

8. *Global Music*: Will we be able to tell the difference between inclusivity and "ethnotourism," that is, producing worship services that function as "a liturgical buffet"?

9. *The Tradition*: Will we discern the difference between defenses of the tradition that are pretentious forms of cultural elitism and those that speak to the genuine genius and spiritual insight of ancient liturgical patterns?

10. *Divisions over Worship Style*: Will we discern which descriptions of "opposing forces" in recent worship wars are merely caricatures and which are accurate and useful? Will we take the time to learn about those parts of the Body of Christ that we are inclined to ignore or ludicrously exaggerate?

11. *Congregational Discussions of Worship*: Will we be able to tell the difference between discussions of worship that focus on worship's content, purpose, and form, and discussions that focus on its style and mechanics? And will we have the guts to insist that a good deal of our conversation should focus on the former? Part of our problem is that we are so reticent to speak forthrightly about the spiritual and theological dimensions of worship. Some talk only about the art form of music. Some only about the realities of the market. How do our churches enable people to feed on the Bread of Life? How effectively do we proclaim to the world the Gospel of Jesus Christ?

12. *Economics*: Will we discern how much of our distaste of certain worship styles and our preference for others is really a form of socioeconomic classism? That is, will we discern how much of our preference is genuinely driven by spiritual concerns and how much is driven by attitudes about the company we keep? And how much of the move away from traditional music is really a reaction against old-money, upper-middle-class Protestantism?

Here are twelve areas where hastily formed simplistic judgments leave us without a rudder to negotiate this sea of change. Here are twelve areas in which there have appeared brilliant and insightful writings in the past decade to guide and challenge us. Here are twelve areas where initial work at discernment has begun.

The problem, as I see it, is not that a discerning position cannot be imagined, but that relatively few are willing to exert the energy to get there. Our discussions are long on turf-building rhetoric, and short on communal discernment.

But what does this elusive alloy of openness and rigorous evaluation look like in real life? I close with a series of examples of thoughtful, discerning people I have encountered from across the country. The best part of my job is to listen in on very different worship-related congregations across the country.

- One musician set up a worship training program for all lay worship leaders. The training program focused not on the mechanics or style of worship, but on its purpose and meaning. The result was a common understanding of what worship is. Agreement emerged on a host of criteria: that the congregation was the primary choir, that worship needed a balance of prayer that included praise and lament, that worship needed a balanced diet of scriptural themes, that nothing in worship should be haphazard or glib. There was common ground from which future growth could be charted.
- Another pair of discerning leaders, a professor of church music and a professor of worship at a leading church music graduate program, have set up a colloquium series for this current academic year in which the worship, music, and evangelism leaders from a half dozen very different congregations have presented congregational case studies for graduate students at this program to ponder. Imagine dozens of organ/church music graduate students encountering not only Vatican II-type Roman Catholic parishes, Episcopal cathedrals, and tall steeple Presbyterian churches but also Pentecostal and seeker-sensitive congregations. Not all these students may enjoy every presentation, but their awareness and powers of perception will be unmistakably challenged.
- One denomination set up a program to challenge pastors to reflect together on their role as worship leaders. The result, a program called PALT, Pastors as Liturgical Theologians, features small groups that meet regularly to read, pray, to engage in discernment.

Here, then, are several congregations blessed with wise, pastoral leaders who are cultivating the gift of discernment. Here are people pursuing the love, knowledge, and community that will create an environment for making good decisions about worship. Here are people who are refusing to allow the church to be governed only by power, politics, and personal taste.

Conclusion

At the end of the day, a lot of our problems about worship aren't as much about worship as they are about the shape of the Christian community. That is, we often don't have strong enough communities to sustain the kind of honest, open process of discernment that will serve us. But there are signs of hope as we attempt to model the rhetoric of discernment. Can we commit ourselves to doing specific things to foster a conversation of discernment in our own places of service? Could the result be nothing less than hundreds of communities each committed to deeper reflection, more intentional prayer, more honest dialogue about worship's deep meaning and purpose?

In the end, the activity of discernment is a tool, a means to a higher end, a way of helping us become, through the Spirit's power, "pure and blameless, having produced the harvest of righteousness that comes through Jesus Christ for the glory and praise of God." May we yearn for and cultivate this gift, and then see it bear fruit in worship that is God-honoring, Christ-centered, and Spirit-inspired.

Notes

1. Portions of this essay appeared in an earlier form in John D. Witvliet and Carl Stam, "Worship Transformed: A Time of Change for Choral Musicians in Christian Churches," *Choral Journal* 38, no. 8 (arch. 1998) 55–62; and John D. Witvliet, *Worship Seeking Understanding* (Grand Rapids, MI: Baker Academic, 2004).

2. Augustine, "On the Morals of the Catholic Church," in *St. Augustine: The Writings Against the Manichaens*, vol. 4 of A Select Library of the Nicene and Post-Nicene Fathers of the Christian Church, ed. Philip Schaff (Grand Rapids, MI: Eerdmans, 1956) 48.

3. Joseph Pieper, *Prudence* (London: Faber and Faber, 1960) 36.

4. Lewis B. Smedes, *Choices: Making Right Decisions in a Complex World* (San Francisco: Harper & Row, 1986) 97.

5. John Calvin, *Institutes of the Christian Religion [1559]*, Library of Christian Classics, vols. 20–21, ed. John T. McNeill, trans. Ford Lewis Battles (Philadelphia: The Westminster Press, 1960) IV.X.30.

6. *For the Life of the World* (Crestwood, NY: St. Vladimir's Seminary Press, 1988) 27.

7. Augustine, Letter 55, Chapter 18, Patrologia Latina Series Completa, ed. J. P. Migne, vol. 33 (Paris, 1880) 220–1.

8. Craig Dykstra, *Growing in the Life of Faith: Education and Christian Practices* (Louisville, KY: Geneva Press, 1999) 54.

8

Reverse Missions
Global Singing
for Local Congregations

C. Michael Hawn

If the liturgy of the church in the United States is to continue to have vitality, then we must listen to new voices and incorporate them in our worship experience. Among these voices are those from places that we considered in the past to be our "mission fields"—Latin America, Asia, and Africa. The songs, prayers and confessions from the global community can add depth and energy to worship that is too often complacent and culturally bound. What we need is a little reverse missions!

A ndrew Walls, career missionary to Sierra Leone and Professor Emeritus of Christianity in the Non-Western World at the University of Edinburgh, offers an enticing metaphor for the human situation in an episode entitled "The Human Auditorium."[1] It goes like this:

Let us begin with a visit to the theatre. It is a crowded theatre, with a huge stage, and a stream of actors passing across it. Everyone in the packed auditorium can see the stage, but no one sees the whole of it. People seated in one place cannot see the entrances left, though they can hear the actor's voice as he enters from the wings. Seated somewhere else, the view is obstructed by a pillar, or an overhanging balcony. Go up into the balcony, and the proscenium arch cuts off the top of the set. As a result, though everyone in the audience sees the same play and hears the same words, they have different views of the conjunction of word and action, according to their seat in the theatre. Those on one side get a sharply focused view of certain scenes which those placed elsewhere do not have to the same degree, and people in the balcony are puzzled to hear laughter in the stalls when they themselves have seen nothing to cause it. But the position is reversed when the scene changes, and the main action is on another part of the stage.

Of course, it is possible to get up and change one's seat; but while this may provide a different view of the stage, it will not enable a view of the whole stage at once; and the way a person who changes seats understands the performance as a whole will still be affected by where they were sitting for the first act.

Walls is speaking of our experience in culture at large. I would like to apply his metaphor to the liturgical arena. When we worship together we participate in the drama entitled "The Story of the Salvation of All Humanity." Each week another act unfolds as we praise and adore God, invoke the Holy Spirit, confess our sins, and hear and respond to the biblical witness. The largest part of this witness embraces the Incarnation—the presence of God in human form within our space and time. Jesus was born in a specific place for all places, at specific time for all times, of a specific culture for all cultures. As participants in the greatest drama of all time, most Christians view the action from one cultural perspective. Some of us have the opportunity to take a different seat in the human auditorium, and we learn to see the play of salvation from an entirely different perspective. Most of us will maintain a cultural bias for the place where we were first seated in the theater of human experience. A few will learn to enjoy the great drama so well from a new perspective that they have trouble coming back to their original seat in the theater.

I am proposing that worshipers in the United States need to experience the drama of salvation from a different cultural perspective—a different seat in the theater—in order to understand and more fully appreciate the sacrifice and salvation of the Incarnation. It is natural, of course, for us to view the biblical witness from only one seat in the theater. I imagine many of us recall a moment, however, when we realized we were not the center of the cultural universe—a kind of Copernican revolution in which we understood that human experience does not revolve around our cultural perspective, but all perspectives revolve around the Creator of all cultures. I recall a time when I became aware that my cultural view of the Incarnation was limited.

During the summer of 1996, I attended a conference of Asian Christians in Kuala Lumpur, Malaysia. Approximately fifty Asians gathered from over twenty countries to investigate the topic "Doing Theology with Asian Resources."[2] I was the only non-Asian observer at this event sponsored by the Programme for Theology and Culture in Asia, a theological forum growing out of the Christian Conference of Asia. As we listened to the diverse stories of those assembled, a recurring theme emerged: Can one be both truly Christian and truly Asian? Asian Christians often face a conundrum. While they are grateful to Euro-American Christian missionaries for a legacy of the Good News of Jesus Christ, they are frustrated for feeling like cultural aliens in their own land. Euro-North American influences remain stifling, especially in the area of worship ritual and congregational song.

At one point in the conference, a Malay woman stood and reframed the dilemma this way: "We need to remember that Jesus was born in far western Asia and sought refuge in northern Africa." Then she seemed to look at me and concluded: "He never visited the United States." Her statement implied a struggle: Who is at the center of Christian experience, and who is on the periphery? We all want to feel we are at the center of the Gospel. No one wants to be on the cultural margins.

The early church faced a similar situation. Paul encountered a struggle between two cultural groups at the church at Ephesus. Jewish Christians felt they were nearer the center of the Gospel story than Gentile Christians. He responded as follows:

> So [Christ] came and proclaimed peace to you who were far off and peace to those who were near; for through him both of us have access to the Father. So then you are no longer strangers and aliens, but you are citizens with the saints and also members of the household of God, built upon the foundation of the apostles and prophets, with Jesus Christ himself as the cornerstone (Eph 2:17-20 [NRSV]).

Musical anthropologist John Blacking spoke of living not only *"for culture"* but *"beyond culture."*[3] Blacking expressed the need for musicians to become a bridge between the particular and the universal. The liturgical ramifications of this perspective are pregnant with possibility. We do not worship only with an isolated local congregation, but with the saints of the church universal throughout time, past and present. How do we gain a sense of the universal body of Christ? Singing with the worldwide church opens up possibilities. The Ephesians passage just cited also suggests another perspective on this situation. Can we worship as fully when we are not aware of the ethnic aliens and strangers among us? Can we engage the diverse ministries of the Holy Spirit when worship reflects only a central cultural perspective and is not open to a wider spectrum of ways of singing and praying? Thinking about the strangers and the aliens among us may help us consider the rich possibilities of observing the drama of salvation from a different seat in the theater.

Stepping outside our culture of origin is impossible. Few people learn to function equally well in two cultural worlds. In most cases those who do are members of co-cultures within a normative societal context. These people are truly bicultural. While liturgy can be greatly enriched through bicultural leadership, this is not the goal of praying and singing globally. Those who live liturgically beyond culture become self-conscious about their bias. Through complex symbol systems, the cultural milieu provides the means for people to participate in society by preserving, transmitting, communicating, perpetuating, and developing knowledge out of all that comprises meaning.[4] A healthy bias is inclusive of other worldviews and presupposes there are also other cultural ways of making meaning equally valid. Bias becomes prejudice when it assumes an exclusive posture toward other cultural perspectives, that is, what Blacking calls "living for culture."[5]

It is easier to distinguish bias from prejudice when the latter is most blatant. Hilaire Belloc's famous assertion made in 1920, "The Faith is Europe's and Europe is the Faith,"[6] could not survive the two world wars that took place before that century's midpoint. The decline of Christianity's influence within Europe during the second half of the twentieth century and continued atrocities in Eastern Europe right up to the end of the century expose the fallacy inherent in this prejudiced assertion.

Musicians and musical theorists have also made bold claims about the superiority of the Western tonal system above all others. Deryck Cooke proposed that the Western tonal system was grounded in a natural harmonic structure. This "natural" system supplants less deserving musical styles: "Wherever Western European civilization has penetrated another culture, and set the people's thoughts along the road to material happiness, the tonal music of Western Europe has begun to oust the music of that culture from the people's affections."[7] While it is true that both classical and popular styles of Western music have gained prominence throughout much of the world, Cooke falls short on at least two fronts: First of all, popular Western styles have always been modified and enriched by local musical traditions. Furthermore, the reverse situation is recently becoming quite common. During the last decade of the twentieth century, popular global music, especially from Africa and Latin America, has begun to influence popular music in the West, usually under the guise of "world music."[8] Second, the "material happiness" that Western civilization was to bring to the world at the time of Cooke's assertion in 1959 has turned out to be a combination of neocolonial exploitation and economic ruin, the latter often perpetuated by the indigenous leaders of nascent post-colonial nations. Regardless of one's views on the superiority of Western music, contact with Western European civilization and its culture does not guarantee a journey on the "road to material happiness." Vibrant musical traditions are usually the result of cross-fertilization. Music, like the greater culture in which it participates, rarely stands in isolation, but adapts organically to nurture new forms.

An example may be found in the work of ethnomusicologist and Catholic priest David Dargie. Before the liturgical reforms of the Second Vatican Council in 1963, he found that Xhosa congregations were singing music that had no cultural significance to them, subject to the level of musical abilities of the priest. One of Dargie's most lamentable examples was the singing of the venerable Latin chant *Tantum ergo* to the tune "My Darling Clementine." The indigenous music of the Xhosa people is based on various forms of musical bows with overtones created through a variety of resonance chambers from larger gourds to the oral cavity itself. Drums such as those used by the neighboring Zulus are not a part of the traditional music. As much as Dargie appreciated the indigenous tradition of musical bows, it was obvious they could not support congregational singing. Looking north to the Shona people, primarily in present-day Zimbabwe, he discovered a vital marimba tradition. Dargie introduced marimba ensembles, tuned to Xhosa scales, and supporting Xhosa rhythms into the churches. He engaged traditional musicians in workshops to write music for various parts of the Mass.[9]

I suggest that the presence of a wider variety of musical styles from Christians around the world could enliven our worship, broaden our understanding of Christ's incarnation—that is how Christ is among us—and give us glimpses of a time when all Christians of every place and time will gather in one celestial feast. According to Harold Best, the North American church of the twenty-first century needs to look beyond its Western roots in order to "fill out [our] praise."[10] I want to suggest that we need to experience "reverse missions" to keep us mindful that Western (or northern) church is not the center of God's realm and the Incarnation was a gift for all humanity. Living out this assertion calls us to search for alternatives to two common approaches to music in worship: musical uniformity, especially as manifest in the Praise and Worship movement; and eclecticism, a blended approach that often gives little attention to the cultures a song comes from or the best placement of the song in liturgy.

Assumptions for Using Cross-Cultural Music in Worship

Six general assertions frame my understanding of cross-cultural worship rather than uniformity or eclecticism. The first three are stated negatively, while the remaining are positive assertions: (1) Cross-cultural worship is not "ethno-tourism." Madeleine Forell Marshall, commenting on what she calls "Third World/liberation" hymnody, cautions us against this danger. Congregations should not be allowed to think that showing solidarity with others by singing global song is the same as "having fun in the sun in Mexico."[11] (2) Using music from other cultures is not denying one's cultural heritage of faith in song, prayer, and ritual. It is a conscious effort to lay one's cultural heritage and perspective alongside another's, critique each, and learn from the experience. Margot Fassler and Peter Jeffery express well the importance of established musical forms within the contemporary context:

> Chant and polyphony will not go away, indeed they are more popular among some of the general public than they have been for centuries. Just as the church, while it must be open to new theological insights from every quarter, can never abandon its biblical and historical Greek and Latin heritage, so the church, while it must penetrate and redeem every culture on the modern world, can never forget its musical heritage.[12]

(3) Using music from other cultures does not necessarily imply a synthesis of styles into one "universal" form. To the contrary, it is an acknowledgment of and participation in a diversity of voices within a liturgical structure. Inevitably the juxtaposition of styles has an influence on each other.[13] Cross-cultural musical participation implies, however, that we attempt to appreciate *sui generis* the contribution of each perspective to our understanding of God. Rather than a melting pot that synthesizes, the image of a mosaic comes to mind. Each piece of a mosaic has its own shape and hue, yet it fits together to form a larger whole. Analogously, each cultural contribution has its own distinct cultural shape and hue, but all come together as they contribute to the overall shape of the liturgy.

Cross-cultural music-making has positive assertions as well. (4) Singing the songs from another culture is a *counter-cultural* expression of faith that calls into question the context of the normative culture in light of the *transcultural* message of the Gospel and the historical shape of Christian liturgy. As liturgical materials from others—persons beyond our cultural worldview also formed in God's image—are placed side by side with rites and rituals from our culture(s) of origin, unfamiliar prayers, creeds, actions, and songs may act as filters for our normative cultural assumptions, modifying or transforming our perspective and our local liturgical practices.[14] The juxtaposition and integration of cross-cultural rites and rituals in worship may guard against an inappropriate syncretism between culture and liturgy, avoiding those elements that undermine or contradict the Gospel. Liturgy, when under the intense influence of popular, media/market-driven forms of music and art, may be in danger of cultural captivity. Such captivity may lead to the idolatry of culture.[15] (5) Singing the songs of the world church celebrates the Incarnation as a *cross-cultural* manifestation of God among us—all of us. This does not deny the validity of our culture(s) of origin. Participating in the incarnational experience of others much different from us enables us to place in perspective our localized views of the Other who became one of us. Awareness of the universal deepens the experience of the particular. (6) Cross-cultural music making raises our consciousness of those who have been invisible to us—listening to, learning from, and sharing in their prayers, and joining with them in common intercessory prayer for the world.[16] The "voice of the voiceless"[17] becomes heard in our worship. In short, singing with Christians of every time and place offers us the potential of making room at Christ's table for all those who have been formed in God's image.[18]

Reactions to Multicultural Worship

At the same time we are becoming aware of the increasingly multicultural face of Christianity, more and more people feel isolated and alone. In the West, extended families are unknown for many people, and nuclear families are fragmented. Isolation and independence may combine to produce a sense of rootlessness. For many, the individualistic nature of society has changed the character of common worship from the gathered people of God called into community (*ekklesía*) to individuals searching for a comfortable community. These people may see themselves as consumers searching among an array of liturgical opportunities vying for their attention in the ecclesiastical marketplace. As consumers they are looking for a church that "feeds them" or "fits their needs." Such descriptions have become euphemisms for community defined as uniformity whether it is theological, political, racial, or social. The tendency to worship in homogeneous interest groups aligns the church as a sustainer of cultural fragmentation, allowing its members the sense of being with others without having to sacrifice their individuality. This practice leads to what Mark Searle calls "shared celebrations rather than common prayer."[19] M. Francis Mannion is on the same track when he speaks of the "intimization of society" or "the process by which social complexity is eschewed in favor of a model of human coexistence that puts ultimate value on bonds of intimacy, personal closeness, and radical familiarity."[20] Such an environment, Mannion concludes, fosters not so much a worshiping community, but a gathering of politically like-minded persons. Strangers, especially those noticeably different from normative society in terms of race, socioeconomic position, and disability, may be "regarded as threatening."[21]

Liturgy has responded to the paradox of increasing cultural diversity on the one hand and increasing need for intimacy on the other in several ways. In many cases congregations have clung to the security of the past, unwilling to admit any change into their rituals. The threat of a heterogeneous culture is too much to cope with. Worship then becomes an ethnocentric haven to preserve the stability of the dominant culture in the midst of what otherwise may seem to be culture anarchy. This response may be what Jaroslav Pelikan meant by "traditionalism," which he called "the dead faith of the living," a position he distinguishes from a healthy, vital tradition, "the living faith of the dead."[22]

Others float on the waves of current culture, searching for community, relevance, and intimacy. At its worst, this trend might be called "The Church of My Own Special Interests." Congregations taking this approach often shun most, if not all, of the practices and symbols of the Christian liturgical heritage. Charles Trueheart calls this the "Next Church."

> No spires. No crosses. No robes. No clerical collars. No hard pews. No kneelers. No biblical gobbledygook. No prayerly rote. No fire, no brimstone. No pipe organs. No dreary eighteenth-century hymns. No forced solemnity. No Sunday finery. No collection plates.[23]

These liturgical polarities have become manifest in the ongoing discussions between "traditional" versus "contemporary" worship pervading many local congregations and worship journals today. While the style of worship varies widely between these two poles, they may have more in common than is usually noted. I would suggest that Western culture's obsession with the individual and apprehension of an increasingly multicultural and religiously pluralistic society threaten both groups. Some respond by holding on to traditions apparently devoid of vitality. Others find excitement in the "shared celebrations" of like-minded individuals. In both cases there may be a loss of two elements vital to healthy liturgy: common prayer and service. Common prayer and service cajole us away from our individuality and pull us toward the needs of a broader world.

Music as Prayer as Theology

Prayers have been present in our singing all along, but the sheer number of words and the stanzas of ordered thought tend to obscure the recognition that while we are singing, we are also praying. In many ways the refrain form of the nineteenth-century Gospel song and its successors, the Scripture song or chorus, provide a clearer sense of sung prayer because they are easily memorized, make use of repetition, and use fewer words. For many people the Gospel song and its offspring became the folksongs of the faith.[24]

John Blacking offers insight from an anthropological perspective that may shed light on the actual mental processes that relate music and prayer. He draws from Susanne Langer who proposed in her aesthetic theory that music as a nonverbal medium is more precise than language in articulating the affective realm.[25] Sung prayer permeates the worship of many non-Western cultures. As songs from around the world find their way into our experience, along with newer forms from intentional communities such as Iona and Taizé, some congregations are discovering what Don Saliers has called "the integrity of sung prayer." He states that:

> At the heart of our vocation as church musicians and liturgical leaders is the question of how we enable the Church to "pray well"—to sing and dance faithfully and with integrity. . . . When we are engaged in sung prayer, we are not simply dressing out words in sound; rather, we are engaged in forming and expressing those emotions which constitute the very Christian life itself.[26]

I believe the future of vital congregational singing depends on reestablishing the link between prayer and song. Those of us in the Western world might learn the art of prayerful song from areas of the globe where the Christian faith is expanding vibrantly, from intentional communities of faith where prayer shapes the lives of those who live there as well as those who sojourn on pilgrimage, and liturgical traditions with deep roots in sung prayer.

There is also a long-standing tradition in the church suggesting that what we pray shapes our belief. To state this in the parlance of modern developmental psychology, experience or behavior should precede the explanation. Singing is a kinesthetic experience. The entire body is the instrument of the singer; in many faith traditions, prayer also implies a specific physical posture. Each of us has learned through our varied liturgical experiences to pray in a specific manner at once mental and physical. Such a practice can lead to a monotonous, though never boring, sense of "reverent waiting without expectation" in which one is nevertheless ready to hear the "still small voice" of the Creator. It is in such a manner that, over time, the content of our sung prayers merges with the patterns of our existence and shapes our belief. Albert van den Heuvel of the World Council of Churches supports this thesis clearly when he says:

> It is the hymns, repeated over and over again, which form the container of much of our faith. They are probably in our age the only confessional documents which we learn by heart. As such, they have taken the place of our catechisms. . . . There is ample literature about the great formative influence of the hymns of a tradition on its members. Tell me what you sing, and I'll tell you who you are![27]

That We May Be One

As stated earlier, the disparate forces of ethnic diversity and the tendency toward personal intimization appear to be threatening the formation of Christian community in the United States, especially the sense of *ekklesía* that binds together those called into the community of Christ. The unity of the Christian community has never been based on ethnic uniformity—"There is no longer Jew or Greek"—social position—"there is no longer slave or free"—or differences in gender—"there is no longer male or female" (Gal 3:28). Our worship should not exacerbate the differences that divide us, but facilitate the unity that binds us together in Christ. It is in this manner that sung prayer can function to bring unity out of diversity.

Sung prayer not only symbolizes the unity of the church gathered, it is per se an act of unity. In this manner it has transforming sacramental potential. Integral to music's nature to encourage unity is its ability to forge an "enhanced group identity . . . as [people] together sense similar types of affect."[28] John Blacking is more specific about the potential of music as a unifier of disparate groups within a society: "Music can bridge the gulf between the true state of human being and the predicament of particular human beings in a given society, and especially the alienation that springs from the class struggle and human exploitation."[29] Rather than singing only in the style of one culture, raising our voices in sung prayer with the songs of Christians around the world creates a parable of oneness in Christ. Musical anthropologist John Blacking speaks of living not *"for* culture" but *"beyond* culture."[30] Through a varied diet of sung prayer we may learn to pray *beyond* our cultural norm as we offer intercessions for the world. When a congregation engages in the ritual of intercessory prayer for the world, it is performing a priestly act of common prayer "for the sake of others."[31] This act may be strengthened by participating in sung prayers from other cultures, even the cultures for whom we are praying. Praying with forms beyond our normative culture broadens our experience of *common* prayer and deepens the sense of solidarity to some degree already a natural part of intercessory prayer.

The Pentecost paradigm hovers over the church. Acts 4:32 states that "the company of those who believed were of one heart, and one soul, and no one said that any of the things which he possessed was his own, but they had everything in common" (RSV). Though some might see an example of early Christian economic socialism in this passage, is it possible this verse refers also to the sharing of even more valuable resources—our ways of embodying our faith in rites, rituals, and songs, and expanding our common prayer across cultures?

We are not going to see the entire stage in the drama entitled "The Story of the Salvation of All Humanity" until we join Christ around the throne. But we have the opportunity for glimpses of this drama from many seats in the theater of liturgy by worshiping in ways that celebrate the songs of Christians of all places and times.

Notes

1. Andrew F. Walls, *The Missionary Movement in Christian History* (Maryknoll, NY: Orbis Books, 2002) 43.

2. This conference was part of an ongoing program on this topic. A summary of the work of the first ten years can be found in *Doing Theology with Asian Resources: Ten Years in the Formation of Living Theology in Asia*, John C. England and Archie C. C. Lee, eds. (Auckland, New Zealand: The Programme for Theology and Culture in Asia, 1993).

3. John Blacking, *How Musical Is Man?* 7. Italics in original. The theme of living beyond culture was very important to Blacking and reiterated later in *Music, Culture and Experience, Selected Papers of John Blacking*, ed. Reginald Byron (Chicago: University of Chicago Press, 1995), where he says: "If the artist who expresses personal experience may in the end reach universal experience, it is because he or she has been able to live beyond culture, and not for culture" (240).

4. From a classic definition of culture by Clifford Geertz, *The Interpretation of Cultures* (New York: Basic Books, 1975) 89.

5. The distinction between bias and prejudice is made in Alexander L. Ringer, "One World or None? Untimely Reflections on a Timely Musicological Question," *Comparative Musicology and Anthropology of Music*, Bruno Nettle and Philip V. Bohlman, eds. (Chicago: University of Chicago Press, 1991) 192–3.

6. Hilaire Belloc, *Europe and the Faith* (New York: Paulist Press, 1920) 261.

7. Deryck Cooke, *The Language of Music* (London: Oxford University Press, 1959) 55. For a more complete discussion of the assumption of superiority by Western musicians, see Anthony Storr, *Music and the Mind* (New York: Ballantine Books, 1992) 49–64.

8. Some examples of this trend in southern Africa are discussed in David B. Coplan, *In Township Tonight! South African's Black City Music and Theatre* (New York: Longman, 1985) and Fred Zindi, *Music Ye Zimbabwe: Zimbabwe Versus the World* (Gueru, Zimbabwe: Mambo Press, [1985], 1997).

9. For a discussion of David Dargie's work with Xhosa music and the Mass, see C. Michael Hawn, *Gather into One: Praying and Singing Globally* (Grand Rapids, MI: Wm. B. Eerdmans, 2003), chapter 4, "Singing Freedom: David Dargie and South African Liberation Song."

10. Harold M. Best, *Music Through the Eyes of Faith* (San Francisco: HarperCollins Publishers, 1993) 68.

11. Madeleine Forell Marshall, *Common Hymnsense* (Chicago: GIA Publications, 1995) 162.

12. "From the Bible to the Renaissance," *Sacred Sound and Social Change: Liturgical Music in Jewish and Christian Experience*, Lawrence A. Hoffman and Janet R. Walton, eds. (Notre Dame: University of Notre Dame Press, 1992) 115–6.

13. Such cross-stylistic influences are manifest in a variety of ways in music, including the combination of text, melody, accompaniment, instrumentation, and movement from two or more cultures in the performance of a single piece of music. Depending on the social dynamics of these combinations, they may be viewed as liberating or imperialistic. I-to Loh explores some of these dynamics in "Contemporary Issues in Inculturation, Arts and Liturgy: Music," *The Hymnology Annual: An International Forum on the Hymn and Worship*, vol. 3, Vernon Wicker, ed. (Berrien Springs, MI: Vande Vere Publishing Ltd., 1993) 49–56. At what point these combinations become a synthesis of styles is open to question. In "Toward Contextualization of Church Music in Asia," *The Hymnology Annual: An International Forum on the Hymn and Worship*, vol. 1, Vernon Wicker, ed. (Berrien Springs, MI: Vande Vere Publishing Ltd., 1991), I-to Loh prefers the term "syncretism" which he defines as "new compositions in the native style using traditional or contemporary Western harmonic idiom[s that are] skillfully integrated into a new composition. The melody may

be native, but the harmony remains Western, thereby elements of both are syncretized" (95). In other rites, a congregation using the Apostles' Creed might include an affirmation of faith or creed from another tradition. The existential reality is that the earlier creed, firmly in the memory banks of the people, is juxtaposed with the more recent creed simultaneously, opening up new meanings for both creeds.

14. The concepts of transcultural, contextual, countercultural and cross-cultural influences on liturgy are clearly stated in the "Nairobi Statement on Worship and Culture: Contemporary Challenges and Opportunities," *Christian Worship: Unity in Cultural Diversity*, S. Anita Stauffer, ed. (Geneva: Lutheran World Federation, 1996) 25–8. In this same volume, Gordon W. Lathrop develops the role of the transcultural core or *ordo* and the countercultural critique in the process of contextualization or localization of liturgy in "Worship: Local Yet Universal," 47–66. The value of cross-cultural critique, though supported generally in multicultural settings, is less explicit in the book.

15. The dangers of syncretism and cultural captivity are discussed by S. Anita Stauffer in "Worship: Ecumenical Core and Cultural Context," *Christian Worship: Unity in Cultural Diversity*, S. Anita Stauffer, ed. (Geneva: Lutheran World Federation, 1996), on pages 12 and 21 respectively. Stauffer's use of syncretism differs from I-to Loh's stylistic syncretism in note 13.

16. Melva Wilson Costen explores invisibility in liturgy in the context of the African American church in the United States in chapter 3, "Worship in the Invisible Institution," *African American Christian Worship* (Nashville: Abingdon Press, 1993) 36–49. Marjorie Procter-Smith raises this theme in the context of women as invisible throughout liturgical history in her book *In Her Own Rite: Constructing Feminist Liturgical Traditions* (Nashville: Abingdon Press, 1989) 14ff.

17. From Archbishop Oscar Romero's Fourth Pastoral Letter, "The Church's Mission amid the National Crisis" in *Voice of the Voiceless*, trans. Michael J. Walsh (Maryknoll, NY: Orbis, 1985), delivered August 6, 1979. Archbishop Romero uses this concept in his pastoral letter saying that the "church, then would betray its own love for God and its fidelity to the gospel if it stopped being 'the voice of the voiceless,' a defender of the rights of the poor, a promoter of every just aspiration for liberation, a guide, an empowerer, a humanizer of every legitimate struggle to achieve a more just society, a society that prepares the way for the true kingdom of God in history" (138).

18. This is the theme developed in *Making Room at the Table: An Invitation to Multicultural Worship*, Brian K. Blount and Leonora Tubbs Tisdale, eds. (Louisville, KY: Westminster John Knox, 2001).

19. Mark Searle, "Private Religion, Individualistic Society, Common Worship," *Liturgy and Spirituality in Context: Perspectives on Prayer and Culture*, Eleanor Bernstein, C.S.J., ed. (Collegeville: Liturgical Press, 1990) 37.

20. M. Francis Mannion, "Liturgy and the Present Crisis of Culture," *Liturgy and Spirituality in Context: Perspectives on Prayer and Culture*, Eleanor Bernstein, C.S.J., ed. (Collegeville: Liturgical Press, 1990) 9.

21. Ibid.

22. Jaroslav Pelikan, *The Vindication of Tradition* (New Haven, CT: Yale University Press, 1984) 65.

23. Charles Trueheart, "Welcome to the Next Church," *The Atlantic Monthly* 278:2 (August 1996) 37.

24. Carlton R. Young, *My Great Redeemer's Praise: An Introduction to Christian Hymns* (Akron, OH: OSL Publications, 1995) 80.

25. *Philosophy in a New Key: A Study in the Symbolism of Reason, Rite, and Art*, 3rd ed. (Cambridge, MA: Harvard University Press, 1942, 1971) 222. Though Langer introduces this theme in *Philosophy in a New Key*, she develops it further throughout several texts. See her chapter "On Significance in Music" in the work just mentioned. For further de-

velopment of the nature of music as a form that articulates feeling, see chs. 7 and 8, "The Image of Time" and "The Musical Matrix," *Feeling and Form: A Theory of Art* (New York: Charles Scribner's Sons, 1953) 104–32. It is here she introduces the concept of "virtual time" as "the primary illusion of music" (109). "Virtual time is . . . separate from the sequence of actual happenings . . . " (ibid.). Especially connected to the concept Blacking is proposing here is ch. 7, "On Living Form in Art and Nature," *Mind: An Essay in Human Feeling*, vol. 1 (Baltimore: The Johns Hopkins Press, 1967) 199–253. In this chapter Langer discusses the feeling of motion that emerges from melody and harmony (her assumptions at this point are Western music). Such a sense of motion "is a sound image of locomotion where nothing is transferred from one place to another" (236). It is, however, from this "direct and very pure abstraction of a feeling of pure temporal change" that we have a sensation or "'disembodiment' of an element emerging from organic structures" (ibid.).

26. Don Saliers, "The Integrity of Sung Prayer," *Worship* 55:4 (July 1981) 291–2, 293.

27. From Albert van del Heuvel, *Risk: New Hymns for a New Day* (Geneva: World Council of Churches, 1966), Preface. Quoted in James Rawlings Sydnor, *Introducing a New Hymnal: How to Improve Congregational Singing* (Chicago: GIA Publications, Inc., 1989) 114.

28. John E. Kaemmer, *Music in Human Life: Anthropological Perspectives on Music* (Austin: University of Texas Press, 1993) 148.

29. Reginald Byron, ed., *Music, Culture and Experience: Selected Papers of John Blacking* (Chicago: University of Chicago Press, 1995) 171.

30. John Blacking, *How Musical Is Man?* (Seattle: University of Washington Press, 1973) 7. See note 3.

31. Paul F. Bradshaw, *Two Ways of Praying* (Nashville: Abingdon Press, 1995) 64.

9

The Altar-Aesthetic
as "Work of the People"

Linda J. Clark and Joanne M. Swenson

Each of the essays in this book deals either directly or indirectly with worship planning. Using material from two extensive research projects[1] of various Episcopal and Methodist congregations in New England and one rural congregation in particular, we would like to describe and analyze an often forgotten aspect of this planning process—preserving, nurturing, and transforming the indigenous music traditions of local congregations through attention to and analysis of their style—what we call their altar-aesthetic. In these days of intrusive mass culture and instant, worldwide communication, the distinctive features of locality and of tradition need attention, not only for aesthetic reasons but also for religious ones.

In the first research project, *Music in Churches*,[2] we studied twenty-four Episcopal and Methodist congregations in New England. As I [Linda] traveled from one to another, I began to notice that, despite the fact these churches held a particular tradition and hymnbooks, prayer books, and other resources in common, each one of them was distinctly different as an aesthetic entity. That is, each had a distinctive style or "flavor." The second study, *Worship, Music and Religious Identity*, took the initial research a step further in an effort to explore this diversity of aesthetic cultures. What did it signal about the nature of these congregations? In choosing to study only three congregations in some depth, we were able to uncover and describe links between the aesthetic dimensions of worship and the faith of a community. Each of these communities exemplified Clifford Geertz's insight that an aesthetic object or event lays open a *world*—"a manifestation of a way of experiencing."[3] Communal worship creates such a world. Worship has an aesthetic cast—a style. In this stylized world, non-aesthetic materials from tradition, such as creeds and historical narratives, are appropriated and stylized, placed in new aesthetic contexts, to create a distinctive "habitation" for the people of God. Like tubes of paint through which a painter composes a picture, inviting us to grasp our world through the tonalities, textures, and emphases of that painting, everyday religious life provides a variety of materials that are composed into a world, distinctive in its style. A church makes decisions about how and when to recite the Apostles' Creed, about when the children should be present in worship, about the cadences and color of its singing, the use or not of ministerial robing. In this process, they establish levels of formality and friendliness appropriate for their worship. Each of these decisions is shaped by the congregation's implicit (and sometimes explicit) sense of its style. When one enters a new congregation, this style is suddenly and perhaps uncomfortably apparent. But with time, one is absorbed into the style of the community, and its distinctiveness may be less apparent.

What Is Style?

Style is an aspect of a congregation's culture. These cultures are "tool kits"[4] of stories, symbols, rituals, patterns of thought, worldviews with which people build a way of life. Regions of the country are known for these cultures—the frugal Puritan Yankee, the Norwegian bachelor farmers of Garrison Keillor's Lake Wobegon, the laid-back New-Ager of California. All of these cultures are influenced by their past, their region, their leaders, and their people. These cultures will have a style. Religious traditions come in various styles. Episcopalians are familiar with stylistic distinctions in their tradition: they label their churches "High Church," "Low Church," or "Broad Church." People might say, "I don't want to go to that church. It's too High (or Low) for me." Or among Baptists and Methodists in the South, you might hear people say, "That church is not 'down-home' enough (or too 'down-home') for me." In each of these instances, people are making value judgments based on the style of a congregation.

People also have styles. Their living spaces often reflect stylistic values. When people make choices about paint for the walls, where the TV set belongs, what to put on the bookshelves, or whether or not to convert the formal dining room into a room for Mom's souvenir teapot collection, they are making decisions based on their sense of style. Something "fits" in the way something else doesn't. Even ordinary room clutter or the lack of it has something to do with style.

Let's turn for a moment to conventional definitions of style. In general usage, style means the form or manner of a thing as opposed to its content or subject matter. One might say, "She gave that speech in a very concise style!" meaning that the form in which she delivered her ideas was clear and to the point. She didn't waste words. There weren't many flowery adjectives. When speaking ordinarily, we often make a distinction between substance and style—between the content of the speech and the way it is delivered. Yet in the discussion of style in the new *Grove's Dictionary of Music and Musicians* the distinctions between form or manner and content are not so neatly drawn. *Grove's* defines style as "manner, mode of expression, type of presentation . . ." and then says, "[T]o treat of the style of an epoch or culture, one is treating of import, a substantive communication from a society, which is a significant embodiment of the aspirations and inner life of its people." In other words, the manner in which an idea is presented communicates the "aspirations and inner life" of people.

In a six-page handbook on ushering written by a member of a large suburban church sometime during the 1950s, we found a wonderful illustration of a congregation's concern for style. According to the layman who authored the handbook, ushering for church services is a duty, but also an honor. "It is an honor because the usher stands before the community as one representing the highest attributes of the church membership as a group." What follows this statement is a description of the tasks—seating people in the sanctuary, taking the collection, greeting people at the door at the end of the service. It also describes the manner in which these actions are done. In seating the congregation: "With your friendliness, display dignity. Remember, in no way does our sanctuary resemble the scene of a twenty-fifth anniversary class reunion. People should, and most people do, guide their thoughts toward reverence for God and respect for His House of Worship as they approach the sanctuary." The usher is a *model of appropriate behavior* in the sanctuary, a representative of the church. "Carry out your duties with self-assurance. This is not demonstrated by slouching against walls or leaning on chairs. Stand erect. Walk erect. Your position is an honor to you—respect it as you would have others respect it."

The way things are done conveys a message about the style of this congregation. This church is distinctive because of the solemnity of its gatherings, the erect bearing of its seated parishioners, the careful attention given to any and all physical, public movement within the sanctuary. All of us would recognize our church's style when someone, perhaps a new pastor, departs from the way things are done. For example, the pastor of the rural church in the second research project changed the customary way Communion was practiced by adding a simple gesture of touch during the distribution of the bread and cup at the altar rail. However, the addition of touch remarkably altered the "feel" of the ritual. Even though everything was the same but this one small gesture, many were vocally upset by this change. Perhaps its style was too "touchy-feely" for this Yankee congregation.

As we can see in the handbook on ushering, style is not just a whim or fancy, like the latest type of tie or cut of the lapel on a man's suit. The style of a congregation is a disclosure of its inner, collective, spiritual world. It displays attributes of a people and their intimations of God; it also displays the appropriate relationship between the two. A church-shopper senses or intuits this world as he or she enters a church. When people church-shop, they are reading the stylistic clues given off, coming to grasp who these people are, and who God is for them.

The attention to the ways things are done—with respect and reverence—discloses the appropriate attitude toward God in worship. The kind of order brought to the act of ushering teaches a person how to approach God. It also indirectly teaches something about God—as One who commands respect and dignity. The worshiper does not greet God with a hearty "How are ya?" as one might an old friend at a class reunion. There is a respectful distance maintained between the worshiper and God.

To return to the twenty-four churches in the original research project, not only was I traveling from one *aesthetic* milieu (to use the vocabulary of Frank Burch Brown) to another, I was also traveling from one *religious* milieu to another. The piety-soaked aesthetica I encountered communicated images of God and of people and were not readily interchangeable from one congregation to the next. True, the Methodists were, by and large, using the same hymn book, but when they stood to sing those hymns, they did not sound alike. And their choice of which hymns to sing also differed. How they celebrated Holy Communion, how they prayed, how they gathered—all differed in style.

The Work of the People

Defining liturgy as the "work of the people" has become a favorite pastime of scholars. But what actually is this work? Of what does it consist? By and large, in worship people *use aesthetic objects* and *use objects aesthetically*. We wish to emphasize especially this latter action of appropriating explicitly non-aesthetic objects, occasions, and human actions, and aestheticizing them in liturgy and worship in general. We have observed that a great deal of religious life is given over to the appropriation of the non-aesthetic and aestheticizing it. For example, the practical, non-aesthetic act of walking into church is made religiously meaningful by patterning it, arranging the players in a certain order, marking and controlling their pace, accompanying it with music, banners, and symbols. By shaping and adorning an ordinary thing like walking, a procession is created. Likewise, complex doctrine (certainly not aesthetic but more properly grasped as metaphysical claims) are routinely aestheticized into banners, vestments, slogans (poetry), and praise choruses. The non-aesthetic becomes aesthetic, and thereby becomes "religious." We once saw an electric slow-cooker (a.k.a. "crock pot") used as a vase for flowers on the rural church's altar (not plugged in, of course). It was a perfect gesture for this community, sanctifying the ordinary and practical, mingling kitchen culture and religious adoration.

A congregation designs and adorns their sanctuary, creates rituals, and sings psalms, in order to create an exemplar, an objectification of their faith. This objectified style—the altar-aesthetic—is not an object in the traditional sense, for one cannot pick up the style of a congregation like one picks up the cross or a choir robe. But this aesthetic "objectifies" the faith of a community, and, we hope, is an "object" the congregation can come to recognize, think about critically, and intentionally develop.

This style is itself profoundly theological. Style subtly conveys images of God and of the people of God, not in creedal statements or doctrine, but in highly articulated events drenched in aesthetic qualities. Notwithstanding their implicit nature, these styles have the force of promulgated doctrine in many communities, as musicians and other leaders find out when they try to make significant changes in the worship practices of their local church.

The aesthetic provided by worship is itself a theological symbol. Therefore we call it an "altar-aesthetic." It is a style and a way of conceiving the world in terms of that style, taken by the individual or community as they move out of the confines of the church. It is not an objective state of the world, but the garmenting of the world in a distinctive style. In faith communities, the aesthetic materials include numerous and complex references to ultimacy—to the world's ultimate hope and destiny, to that which sustains life in the face of suffering and defilement, to God. It is important thus to recognize the theological dimensions of the aesthetic of faith communities.

And, in character with the implicit universalism of any theological symbol, this aesthetic seeks to reshape the larger world in terms of its vision. Therefore, while this theological symbol is aptly called an "*altar*-aesthetic," it can also be considered an "*alter*-aesthetic" by the way it alters one's sense of the world through the *use of the aesthetics of the faith community*.

The wedding of style and piety takes characteristic shape in every congregation, of making God seem especially alive. In these research sites we could identify certain acts of worship that exemplified the piety in a particularly vivid way. We designated them "signature symbols" because the congregation's own style was so well displayed in them. Someone witnessing the congregation enacting one of them will observe much that is characteristic of and significant for them. Typically, *signature symbols* are executed not only with familiarity but also with great competence, if not pride. The congregation "comes together" in a marked spirit of mutual understanding and expectation about the power (and the pleasure) derived from a familiar aestheticized activity or ritual. Signature symbols also carry significant memories for the congregation.

Signature symbols also have a history for the congregation, of making God seem especially alive. We've come to call these occasions "breakout" where people experience the presence of God "breaking into" their midst. A signature symbol, while made by humans and executed with a spirit of competence and pride, can yield to God's presence. This should not be surprising, for everyone brings implicit hope to any aesthetic event—religious or otherwise—that something revelatory will be experienced. Variously called artistic ecstacy, the sublime, or revelation, we have all experienced—and hope to experience again—the Truth that seems to surpass the merely human exertions of artist and audience, yet is mediated through their practiced efforts. So too in the local congregation: There comes to be an expectation that this familiar, well-performed and beloved moment in our religious life (for example, the gradual illumination of the sanctuary by candlelight during the Christmas Eve service) will bring with it a precious and powerful moment of awareness of God.

These signature symbols gain their meaning as others do—in a dynamic rather than a static fashion. Meaning is formed out of a congregation's present-day experience yet is also drawn from their particular past and the past of its religious tradition. Symbols are filled with past meanings that have formed and shaped the lives of parishioners; but, at the same time, they are subject to new meanings arising from their interplay with the congregation's present joys and sorrows. In this way, symbols become personalized, some even becoming "signatures." They take on the collective personality of the present-day congregation.

The philosopher Schopenhauer once said, "The style of a man is the physiognomy of the soul."[5] According to the dictionary, physiognomy means "the face; facial features and expression, especially as . . . indicative of character." The style of a congregation's life together envisages its soul, a vital expression of its character.

Working at Faith: "The King Is Coming"

We can illustrate what we have been discussing by reference to one of the signature symbols of the rural congregation—their favorite hymn. As we will show, it is replete with its altar-aesthetic. The culture of this church is heavily influenced by its origins in a rural community. "Familial" is the altar-aesthetic for the church, a style that shapes its understanding of human relationships and their breakdowns, God's nature, and the role of church and town. This altar-aesthetic was evident through the church's homey, "Come as you are!" intimate and inclusive conventions of worship and community life. On a more profound note, this familial altar-aesthetic conveyed a form of human dignity where, whatever the blows to one's dignity suffered in the workplace or small-town life, one's God-ordained worth was unconquerable.

The church's style conveyed an *alter*-aesthetic, an alternative way of responding to these difficulties. Over and over people expressed the feeling that, within the church, they were not being judged. They felt accepted despite job loss, illness, and family breakdowns. Everyone was welcomed in this family of God.

This signature symbol hymn is "The King Is Coming" by William and Gloria Gaither.[6] The text is filled with everyday images, painting a picture of an emptying world as people run to greet "the King" coming through the Gate of Heaven surrounded by the saints. The music is of the country-and-western gospel idiom, with a refrain repeating the line: "The King is coming!" It has a beat and energy that sweeps you up and carries you forward.

When we asked the people in the focus group to talk about this hymn, they began to talk about Richie, whose favorite it was. One Easter he was playing the guitar, and May was playing the organ before the service began:

> He'd be sitting there, playing the guitar and we came around . . . . He'd say, "Let's go, old girl." I loved that. Oh, gosh! And he wanted the music loud. His wife said he wants it loud, so I would blast. He didn't want anything soft. And boy, I'm telling you, there wasn't a dry eye in this place.

Richie plays an important part in the meaning of this song to the people in that focus group because he contracted cancer and died. In an interview, Jim Kelsey related the impact of Richie's dying on his own spiritual journey:

> I remember when I fractured my shoulder, our first youth group meeting, down at the hill here, and I ended up going down to the hospital, in the emergency room. At the time, Richie was in the hospital, you know, he was quite a bit towards the end of his life there. And I was feeling kind of down and, you know, pouting, "Oh God, look what I've done now!" and kind of whiney. . . . They finally got me into a room, waiting for the doctor to come in, and I started thinking about Richie upstairs, and all that he had been going through, and just how he handled it, and how he was an inspiration to everybody. I mean, he was going through so much pain. . . . But he was always in a good mood; he'd always tell you a joke, he'd raise your spirits when you were down, regardless of what he was going through, and I thought about that a lot. And before long, I was kind of laughing at what happened, and all of a sudden all the nurses just started coming in, saying, "What's wrong with that guy in there?" you know! So I had all the nurses coming in to see me, and I just had completely forgotten about what I was going through . . . because I was thinking a lot about Richie. That's the inspiration he was, and I know that God worked in my life, too, so that I would get to know Richie better.

The image of Richie sitting at the front of the sanctuary before the Easter service, yelling over his shoulder at the eighty-four-year-old woman at the organ behind him to play louder, and the experience of the music-making, evoke in the people the times they had with him in which their own lives were transformed. They associate the sound with spiritual transformation and God's love for them, made palpable through the beat and sound of "The King Is Coming." When they sing that hymn, they both create and enter their collective, spiritual, transformative world.

By analyzing this hymn, we can get a greater appreciation for the religious power of the aesthetic work going on in this congregation's worship. While we noted the historical reasons why this hymn became so central to the people in the congregation, we now want to address more specifically the aesthetic and religious questions raised by the prominence of this hymn in their lives. Here we have a congregation whose style is characterized by an informal intimacy. The image of the church as a family is central to their piety, as is the notion of the acceptance of everyone, warts and all. They frequently speak of being on a journey, a religious pilgrimage singly and together. How is this hymn an exemplification of these qualities?

> The market place is empty,
> No more traffic in the streets,
> All the builders' tools are silent, No more time to harvest wheat;
> Busy housewives cease their labors,
> In the courtroom no debate,
> Work on earth is all suspended, As
> the King comes thru the gate.
>
> *Refrain*
> O the King is coming, the King is coming!
> I just heard the trumpets sounding,
> And now His face I see;
> O the King is coming, the King is coming!
> Praise God, He's coming for me!
>
> Happy faces line the hallways,
> Those whose lives have been redeemed,
> Broken homes that He has mended,
> Those from prison He has freed;
> Little children and the aged Hand in hand sound all aglow,
> Who were crippled, broken, ruined,
> Clad in garments white as snow.
>
> *Refrain*
> I can hear the chariots rumble, I can see the marching throng,
> The flurry of God's trumpets
> Spells the end of sin and wrong;
> Regal robes are now unfolding, Heaven's grandstands all in place,
> Heaven's choir is now assembled,
> Start to sing "Amazing Grace!"

Taking a closer look at the text of this hymn, we notice how ordinary the images are, describing typical workers and their tasks. Builders, farmers, housewives, judges—all have suspended their daily round of work, leaving their ordinary lives behind as they prepare for the imminent appearance of the King. "The King is coming!" Since these are the ordinary activities of the people in a rural town, they easily place themselves in the shoes of the people awaiting the King. Here the Gaithers have exemplified the daily lives of the typical person in the pew who will need no long, metaphysical explanation to be able to say to themselves, "Yes, the King is coming for me! Let me join in the parade."

The text is not explicitly theological. It tells a story, building a dynamic image of movement toward an about-to-be-consummated event of the most extreme significance to the singers. The structure and images of the text creates this anticipatory state. The theology is implicit and very powerful. What actually *is* there? Not a dogmatic claim, but an image of the anticipated end of ordinary time, drawn in chords, cadences, images, and emotions near to the hearts of these parishioners. Is the song's image grasped metaphorically or literally? It doesn't matter: it effects or instantiates a *world*—"a manifestation of a way of experiencing."

Notice the use of the predicate nominative in that oft-repeated phrase, "The King is coming": the verb *is* links the subject *the King* and the gerund form of the verb *to come*. This usage gives the singer the sense of being right in the midst of something. An action has begun. There is movement. The King moves toward the people as they prepare for his coming. Indeed, all ordinary life has been suspended as the people await the act of the King—his approach. They are at a point immediately after the suspension of ordinary life and just before the King will come through the gate. It is quite a dramatic point in moving—one might say *marching*, given the music—time. This feeling-soaked time is instantiated through the sentence structure and dynamic images of the text.

In the second verse, the writers describe the healing of the people in the anticipation of his approach. Redeemed, healed, freed, and clothed in garments white as snow, they wait. The "end time" is envisioned; the longed-for horizon appears and helps to create the forward movement of the hymn. The reiteration of the refrain reinforces it, too. "The King is coming, the King is coming!"

In the third verse, the narrator appears and moves the action along, evoking this about-to-happen event through both sight and sound images. The anticipation is heightened; the climactic event of Christianity is just on the verge of happening, announced by the rumble of the chariots, the blaring of God's trumpets, the sound of the heavenly choir singing the most beloved of Christian hymns, "Amazing Grace," and, in the quintessential small-town Fourth of July activity—setting up the grandstands.

What a scene! But notice we are still on the brink of the event yet to happen. What the hymn provides is not the event itself but its anticipation. It exemplifies a particular interpretation of the world of the faithful—dynamic, expectant, exciting, anticipatory. It is not arrival but the journey.

The music works to enflesh the dynamism of the picture. The music is an "image of movement." It is Gospel music with its heavy, marching beat, its flashy piano accompaniment, and its verse and refrain structure. It is easily learned, easily sung, easily approached. There is no period of contemplative initiation into this music. When the people in the rural church said, "We don't do subtle!" they were referring to qualities they disdain in music. No. In this hymn, you are right there, immediately. That the group of singers and instrumentalists is in the act of creating this image makes it just that much more powerful.

As Roger Sessions once said: "[M]usic is controlled movement of sound in time. . . . It is made by humans who want it, enjoy it, and even love it."[7] It is "shaped time" with a beginning, middle, and end. In "The King Is Coming," melody, harmony, and particularly rhythm exemplify or pattern an important religious sensibility: yearning for Jesus' second coming, wanting, enjoying, loving its approach. In the singing, that yearning is enlivened, being made to live among us. Over a lifetime singing it, we learn about such yearning, and how to extend, apply this sensibility. Each time it is sung, present-day applications present themselves. The lost job, the marriage of a granddaughter, the answer to a prayer—these latch onto the "about-to-happen" sense of fulfillment of our longing for God.

The Discernment and Evaluation of This Work

In constructing aesthetica, artists' attentiveness to line, color, form, and so on, lead to the essential expressiveness of various media like sound and paint. Material that is not expressive cannot communicate the depth of religious meaning characteristic of the altar-aesthetic. One reason that walking in church is treated aesthetically is to give it expressive meaning. If one merely walks into church, the entrance is functional. If one patterns the entrance, one makes it meaningful. The act of entering takes on weighty import: "This isn't just an ordinary space—something significant is about to happen!"

In worship, people *use aesthetic objects* and *use objects aesthetically* to create this sense of significance. What particulars the altar-aesthetic consists in will vary from culture to culture, from tradition to tradition. The pastor in the rural church uses puppets to make points in his children's sermons. Those madcap characters belong in that congregation, but perhaps not in others. There they fit; they express the laughter and boisterousness of that community. As we saw in the case of Jim Kelsey in the hospital, laughter heals. It isn't just any laughter, but the sanctified laughter of the congregation's altar-aesthetic. It erupts in worship through the follies of the puppets, and the familiar joking between parishioners and pastor. Such laughter, however, may disrupt worship in other communities. What seems like "home" and "familial" in one congregation may be a barrier in another. Deeply idiosyncratic, a congregation's altar-aesthetic needs both careful discernment and evaluation. Given the limitations of any human construct that purports to symbolize God, the altar-aesthetic needs to be evaluated for its ongoing appropriateness to the evolving culture of a community, as well as for its theological integrity and expressive power.

A commonplace way of making judgments about the aesthetic has been to point to an object and say, "That's beautiful!" (or otherwise). However, this reduction of beauty to the realm of aesthetic objects is too narrow a vision. As the theologian Edward Farley writes in *Faith and Beauty:*[8]

> Whatever the importance of the arts in the history of the religious community, they are not the primary means by which beauty persists in the life of faith, for beauty is always already present in the *imago Dei* and its redemptive restoration, and it already shapes the world as being.

Thus we turn our attention to the tasks of *evaluating* the altar-aesthetic of a congregation and its manifestation in the various practices of worship. We will outline characteristics of this evaluative process and then add brief comments. Taken together, we hope that this discussion will provide the reader with a new understanding of the role of style in "the work of the people."

It is our belief that a congregation cannot radically change its foundational style without serious, negative consequences. Change takes place, but organically, over time. The altar-aesthetic evolves and *should*, as evidence of a congregation making contact with and being revitalized by what is going on in contemporary life. There is a necessary interaction between church and world that provides a creative dialogue between a tradition like Christianity and the secular realm.

We propose a method of working with and within the altar-aesthetic, becoming aware of this evolutionary process, acting to deepen and intensify its most enduring insights, and following the play of new paths and forms that spring from its depths. It is only through such reflective study that leaders and others can effectively deepen and develop this otherwise unexamined, implicit, yet pervasive faith-symbol.

We are indebted, in the following approach, to the late Mark Searle, a theologian and liturgical scholar who taught in the Theology Department of the University of Notre Dame, as well as other advocates of "pastoral liturgical studies." Their approach was described by Searle in a very influential speech given at a meeting of the North American Academy of Liturgy in January 1983. It was later published as "New Tasks, New Methods: The Emergence of Pastoral Liturgical Studies" in *Worship*.[9] There were several new questions Searle asked a room filled with scholars of worship who, until that time, had confined their scholarly interest to theological and historical statements and interpretations of liturgical texts. Acknowledging the immense value of that work, he then called for new directions for study. He shifted the focus to the gathered congregation and how worship is appropriated by people who enter the sanctuary to pray to and praise God. Thus how symbols are used by congregants, how they communicate meaning, and how they instantiate the cultural context of a community became objects of study.

Searle's emphasis on the congregation and its engagement in worship stems from his understanding of the nature of incarnation. In his remarks about the necessity to critique contemporary American culture, he says: "[the church] . . . takes the present moment seriously as being not only the context within which the church works, but the very flesh in which the grace of God is to be incarnated. . . ."[10] Our research stems from Searle's preoccupation with the "present moment" in a congregation at worship. Through study of various congregations, we uncovered the centrality of style and what we label the altar-aesthetic.

As was described at the opening of the article, the research that we at Boston University have undertaken in the last two decades stems from Searle's preoccupation with the "present moment" in a congregation at worship. Subsequently, through work among the people in various congregations, we uncovered the centrality of style and what we label the altar-aesthetic.

As we have asserted: Every theological symbol and practice a congregation receives from its forebears is clothed in an aesthetic that is a theological symbol in its own right. There can be no real understanding of the piety of a congregation without an understanding of its altar-aesthetic.

Discerning the altar-aesthetic and understanding its power demands practice, what Frank Burch Brown calls "disciplined attention."[11] It demands attentiveness to the aesthetic dimension, recognizing the transformation of materiality into expressive form; and it demands attentiveness to religious meaning, recognizing the faith embedded in expressive materiality.[12]

Briefly, we propose that . . .

(1) Congregations learn to describe their altar-aesthetic, paying attention to its manifestations and to its terms for characterizing it.

Perhaps the most straightforward way to teach congregations to "pay attention" to their altar-aesthetic is to have them reflect on "what works" in their worship, and to encourage them to unpack the meanings conveyed through these occasions of worship excellence.

Emphatically, when we think about "what works" in worship, this evaluation cannot be made on the merits of artistic excellence. No, attention to artistic truth comes later in the evaluative process. One morning, during worship at one of our research churches, an elderly woman stood up and began singing "her hymn." She knew the song by heart. In it the expression of meaning was hers but soon became everyone else's. Through her singing, everyone resided in meaning. Although her voice lacked the conventional qualities of good vocal sound, her singing possessed a power that many a professional singer would envy. To an audience in Symphony Hall, barely two blocks from the sanctuary, her song might not be considered beautiful. There the community's practices would have been effaced in order to pursue an aesthetic perfection beyond the capacity of most churches' resources. The milieu of a concert hall allows for focused attention on the aesthetic qualities of a beautiful object to the exclusion of its function within a practice like worship. Indeed, music that works to exclude its place in worship might be seen as detrimental to the community's practices.

Yet the woman in the sanctuary probably would not wish to sing her song on the stage. The symphony hall audience would not be an appreciative, prepared audience, an audience with a ready heart for worship. They would not be religiously trained to "read" the meanings performed by this spontaneously enraptured woman, moved by the Spirit to arise from her pew and sing for the pleasure of God. Amidst her congregation, she is freed to sing, because her "audience" is prepared, learned in the medium and meanings potential to her performance.

We wish especially to caution clergy and music leaders on this point about "artistic excellence." When you come to a church for the first time, you are entering something that has been in existence in a particular place and has carried the vitality of faith over time. In working with the altar-aesthetic of a congregation, one does not simply replace it, as one would substitute a newer computer disk drive for an older one. Contemporary American culture preaches the gospel of "the latest thing." Yet a vital altar-aesthetic could be centuries old! We advocate becoming good historians of a congregation, even if it is only twenty-five years old. Who are the people—and not necessarily leaders—who have shaped the congregation's style? What are its signature symbols? What do they mean? What do they show about the religious life of the congregation?

As congregations come to focus on "what works," they can think about the media that undergird these powerful moments or symbols. "Are we a pipe organ kind of congregation, or are we more deeply moved by vocal groups (or potluck suppers, or extemporaneous prayer)?" They may be prepared at this point to consider whether their congregation has signature symbols. This discussion, undertaken with a positive, affirming approach, will lead to insights about the congregation's particular altar-aesthetic (perhaps a list of adjectives), its historical lineage (a historical display of church photos and artifacts, showing the continuities and change in the congregation's style), and, inevitably, how the altar-aesthetic seems to be changing and developing (reflection on the aesthetic styles of their contemporary world and their religion's/denomination's culture: which ones attract them, which ones repel them?).

(2) Congregations learn to discern what their altar-aesthetic means and how these meanings get conveyed.

In this second moment of "paying attention," congregations take the big picture, assessing the meanings conveyed by their altar-aesthetic. Essentially, this is an anthropological moment, as the congregation attempts to describe what kind of "people" they are, as evidenced by their style.

This moment may open the way toward critical, evaluative thinking, if the congregation perceives a breakdown between how they understand themselves as a religious community, and what their altar-aesthetic conveys about them. Here it would be helpful to introduce the notion of aesthetic adequacy or even, so-called, "artistic truth." "Truth" in the realm of the aesthetic is not propositional truth. Rather, we are in the realm of assessing the experience generated by our symbols, as Susanne Langer points out:

> To understand the "idea" in a work of art is therefore more like *having a new experience* than like entertaining a new *proposition*; . . . There are no degrees of literal truth, but artistic truth, which, as all significance, expressiveness, articulateness has degrees; therefore works of art may be good or bad, and each must be judged on our experience of its revelations.[13]

What are the aesthetic qualities of an expressive object or event? How is meaning conveyed? If we return for a moment to "The King Is Coming," its authors were able, through their craft, to manifest "anticipation" in their song; they put us at that scene as Jesus is coming (note the verb form) through the gate. What do the Gaithers know about the materials of their craft? Through the various media, they "show" something, and we are caught up in this "showing," this appearance. It attracts us. We are drawn to it. Before we ask the functional question, "How do we use this hymn?" we need to ask, "What is this showing?" "How is it made?" "How does it mean?"

Showing is a form of creation, done by people attentive to the essence of materials that display themselves to the senses—in this case, sound. What is the logic of sound? A musician enters the realm of sound and thinks sound, not in the way one thinks words. With words, one moves into *their* logic, watching for nouns, pronouns, verbs, making sentences, changing topics, pausing, and so on. Sound has its own logic, its own intelligence. One is aware of movement, of highs and lows, of greater and lesser intensity shaped by the movement of harmonies. There are periods or sections one moves in and out of, ideas of sound that help shape the moving through time. In the Gaither hymn, there is a refrain that emphasizes and reinforces the meaning. Its melodic line is shaped through slight nuance of pace or emphasis. One approximates the expressiveness of the human voice in melodies. Tone has various qualities one appropriates for its sensuous appeal. The musical realm one enters is born of sound, but much more, since the shaping of sound in various ways leads to structure, and structure to architectonic constructs of meaning. It is shaped time, but not the time we associate with a clock and its insistent, unvarying, two-dimensional progress toward tomorrow. It is time as we experience it—the present or "presence" in all its sensuous grandeur. Susanne Langer calls music "the morphology of feeling," in that it consists of structures of vitality that ebb and flow, symbolizing the experience of being alive. Through these structures, hymns and other religious aesthetic objects become alive to us—a "presence."

Thus the broader question arises: is the symbol—in this case, a musical one, but it could also pertain to the pastoral prayer, the altar cross, the church wall hangings—adequate to the idea it embodies? The answer to this question leads us back to the process of attentive care that the Gaithers and others like them take in the creation of shaped sound. Aesthetic adequacy is an issue of "possession," according to Nelson Goodman.[14] An aesthetic symbol not only points to or refers to an idea (like "casual"), but it must also *possess* features conventionally grasped as "casual." A church may like to think its altar-aesthetic is "homey," "warm," "contemporary," but if its material objects are tattered and neglected and a hangover from the 1970s, it does not "possess" these features! Its symbols are not adequate to the ideas they seek to convey.

In an altar-aesthetic, aesthetic attributes include, among others, pace, tone, shape, color, and gesture. The way a congregation gathers differs if their style is formal or informal. Gestures may be contained or extravagant. One enters a silent room with a different attitude than one filled with jazzy organ music. These are features or possessions that contribute to the big picture, the altar-aesthetic. Taken together, they compose distinct "worlds," fashioned by the creativity of congregational symbol-makers.[15] They manifest a way of experiencing,[16] carrying enormous intimations of a people's identity and their God. To this last consideration—an altar-aesthetic's communications about God—we finally turn.

(3) *Congregations think theologically about how God is manifested in their altar-aesthetic and about the vitality and limitations of this "artistic version" of God.*

After thinking "anthropologically" about style, the third moment presents an opportunity to think theologically: what images, affects, and ideas about God are conveyed through our altar-aesthetic? Here the advanced theological training of pastors, musicians, and lay leaders is an advantage, as they possess a vocabulary to grasp, describe, and bring historical understanding to the representations of God inherent in an altar-aesthetic.

But the congregation is not voiceless or without wisdom in this consideration. For theology and theological symbols must find not only intelligible reception with the congregation. They must also prove their mettle by acting as mediators of human transformation. A pastor or musician may be excited about a new theological emphasis or a new musical idiom heralded by the academy or in heavy rotation on the local Christian Contemporary radio station. But it only gains its real authority when an actual congregation finds it life-giving.

In the church where I [Linda] am currently the choir director, and my husband is the priest, I made a stylistic shift in the music during Communion. People were very polite—I'm the minister's wife, after all—but emphatic about the music being too loud. "Isn't it supposed to be soft here?" "Not necessarily!" I responded, thinking there really wasn't any rule anywhere about the volume of music during Communion. But later, when I reflected on the consternation I had raised by making what I thought was a simple change, I backed off. There wasn't any rule in my book, but in theirs there was. I had inadvertently changed the nature of the piety of the Eucharist in the congregation. Other changes I made did not provoke any response. This one did, because Holy Communion was the center of their piety. By changing the music for Communion, I had struck at the center of the congregation's altar-aesthetic. The music not only didn't "fit"—it inhibited the full, life-giving experience of a signature symbol of their faith.

There are both anthropological and theological ideas imbedded in the style of taking Communion in this church. At some point in working with the altar-aesthetic, a critique of the limits of its theology should be undertaken. As Mark Searle's approach implies, leaders in the church are responsible not only for the "intended" meaning of worship, but for its "received" meaning. One's leadership task is only half over when one chooses hymns, poems, banners, and so on, for worship. The question, asked and answered over a prolonged period of time in a congregation, is about faith development. Are these symbols and forms working in this process? Do they engender the necessary self-transcendence in the life of faith?

In the instance of the Communion music, I am now working within the altar-aesthetic of the congregation to deepen it, making it more effective as a symbol of their faith. For example, one Sunday the organist realized the congregation was humming along while she was playing quietly during Communion. In order to make this participation by the congregation more effective, I am working with hymns and songs familiar to them. Occasionally I introduce something new through a choir piece, but repeat it frequently to draw the congregation into it.

Along with that process of making an existing altar-aesthetic more expressive, we are modifying it to make it more inclusive. Several years ago, we began supplementing the congregational music through the use of a new hymnal, *Lift Every Voice and Sing*. The "new" aesthetic, actually centuries old, broadens and changes the prevailing altar-aesthetic to encompass traditions underrepresented in the "regular" hymnal. There has been some resistance to these new hymns and songs, but by and large the response has been overwhelmingly enthusiastic. Had we replaced the standard hymnal by the other, we would have had mutiny on our hands.

Conclusion

These three moments of evaluating an altar-aesthetic open the door to a congregation's growth of faith in God. These steps are not only accomplished in an attitude of "spiritual inventory," but also of faith and openness to mystery. For here we must face the inherent limitations of our "artistic version" of God, and in so doing, give witness to the vast mystery of God, defying human symbolization.

A congregation can only create God-symbols out of its integral aesthetic—with its limiting materials, competencies, and imaginative horizons. This theological "taking stock" is also a moment of confession. Like any symbol, as Edward Farley points out, it is distorted by sin. No human construct can adequately capture the totality of God.[17]

But these can be moments of celebration and wonderment. For God uses our limited palette to present colors, if you will, new and hitherto unimagined, in moments of chastening and joyous breakout. Our limited religious cult, objectified in its altar-aesthetic, opens to a vaster communion beyond, both confirming the worth of our altar-aesthetic, but also chiding, "God is more, God is more . . ."

Notes

1. Some of this material has been previously published in Linda J. Clark, Joanne M. Swenson and Mark Stamm, *How We Seek God Together* (Herndon, VA: The Alban Institute, 2001).

2. The results of this project were published in *Music in Churches* (Herndon, VA: The Alban Institute, 1994).

3. Clifford Geertz, "Art as a Cultural System," *Modern Language Notes (MLN)* 91 (1976) 1478f.

4. This is a phrase borrowed from Anne Swidler's influential article "Culture in Action: Symbols and Strategies," *American Sociological Review* 51 (April 1986) 273ff.

5. Quoted in Arthur C. Danto, *The Transformation of the Commonplace* (Cambridge, MA: Harvard University Press, 1981) 131.

6. Words by William J. and Gloria Gaither and Charles Misull. Music by William J. Gaither. Copyright 1970 William J. Gaither, Inc. ASCAP. All rights controlled by Gaither Copyright Management. Used by permission. See *Hymns for the Family of God* (Nashville: Paragon Associates, 1976) 313f.

7. Quoted in Howard Gardner, *Frames of Mind* (Basic Books, 1983) 105.

8. Edward Farley, *Faith and Beauty, a Theological Aesthetic* (Burlington, VT: Ashgate, 2001) 110f.

9. *Worship* 57 (1983) 291–308.

10. Ibid., 303.

11. Brown, Frank Burch, *Good Taste, Bad Taste, and Christian Taste* (New York: Oxford University Press, 2000) 260f.

12. The Roman Catholic theologian Avery Dulles talks about the quality of religious symbols to merge both spirit and matter and thus to be like humans, spirit-filled bodies: "The structure of human life is . . . symbolic. The body with all its movements and gestures becomes the expression of the human spirit. The spirit comes to be what it is in and through the body." See his *Models of the Church* (Garden City, NY: Doubleday, 1978) 60f.

13. Susanne Langer, *Philosophy in a New Key* (Cambridge, MA: Harvard University Press, 1957) 262ff.

14. See Nelson Goodman, *Languages of Art* (Indianapolis: Hackett Publishing, 1976) 52ff.

15. "Countless worlds made from nothing [except] by use of symbols . . ." Nelson Goodman, *Ways of Worldmaking* (Indianapolis: Hackett Publishing, 1978) 1.

16. Geertz, 1478ff.

17. Farley, 84ff.

Part IV

Practical Considerations
in the Light of Biblical Mandates

10

Religious Meanings and Musical Styles[1]
A Matter of Taste?

Frank Burch Brown

The cover of the August 1996 *Atlantic Monthly* announced a Christian cultural revolution: "Giant 'full-service' churches are winning millions of 'customers' with [their] pop-culture packaging. They may also be building an important new form of community." Author Charles Trueheart described what he calls the "Next Church": No spires. No crosses. No robes. No clerical collars. No hard pews. No kneelers. No biblical gobbledygook. No prayer rote. No fire, no brimstone. No pipe organs. No dreary eighteenth-century hymns. No forced solemnity. No Sunday finery. No collection plates.

The list has asterisks and exceptions, but its meaning is plain. Centuries of European tradition and Christian habit are deliberately being abandoned to clear the way for new, contemporary forms of worship and belonging.[2] The Next Church and its many smaller, typically suburban relatives are held up as models of the options available to Christians who want to "catch the next wave."

Music provides the clearest indication of the revolutionary change. The musical idioms of the Next Church are contemporary (nothing dating from before 1990 in many cases). One twenty-four-year-old pastor characterized the predominantly rock music of his university-related church as "a cross between Pearl Jam and Hootie and the Blowfish"—in other words, somewhere between angst-ridden "grunge" and upbeat pop.[3]

Yet, as it happens in many of these churches, the spectrum of styles offered is actually quite narrow—as it has been in most churches throughout history. Country music is usually out of the question, as is religious jazz in the style either of Duke Ellington (in his "Sacred Concerts") or Wynton Marsalis (*In This House on This Morning*, 1994). Nor is there world music like that of Sister Marie Keyrouz, a Lebanese nun who has begun singing the chants of her tradition in an appealing, "secular" style that utilizes colorful instrumental accompaniments. The typical Next Music sound is club-style soft rock.

It would be unusual to hear anything in these churches so morally daring as certain songs of the Grammy-Award winning Indigo Girls, or anything so ironically and astutely probing as a song on ecological spirituality by James Taylor ("Gaia," from *Hourglass*), or music as alert to alternative spiritualities—African and South American—as Paul Simon's *Graceland* and *The Rhythm of the Saints*, or as achingly yearning in overall effect as k.d. lang's "Constant Craving" (*Ingénue*), or U2's "I Still Haven't Found What I'm Looking For" (*Joshua Tree*). Those are only a smattering of widely accessible, equally white, and mostly middle-class alternatives.

The more ritualized yet contemporary music from Taizé (composed by Jacques Berthier) and the newly composed yet folk-based songs of the Iona Community in Scotland apparently smack too much of traditional religion to find wide acceptance in the Next Church. And little of what is currently heard in the megachurch, or suburban church with contemporary worship, resembles contemporary classical "spiritual minimalism." Nothing in those settings sounds much like Arvo Pärt, Philip Glass, John Tavener, John Adams, Giya Kancheli, or (more Romantic in idiom) Einojuhani Rautavaara. Nor would such churches, which often make use of recordings, be tempted to venture into the recorded repertoire of more avant-garde classical composers such as Igor Stravinsky (by now virtually a classical icon), Olivier Messiaen, Krzysztof Penderecki, Sofia Gubaidulina, or James MacMillan—all more-or-less contemporary and almost shockingly spiritual, and frequently explicitly theological.

The current selectivity in church music, because it is more the rule than the exception, would be unremarkable except for the claim made by the Next Church and its more conservative Contemporary Christian relatives: that theirs is the truly contemporary alternative for Christian music today.

Exclusively Contemporary

In his book *Dancing with Dinosaurs: Ministry in a Hostile and Hurting World*, William Easum makes this very claim about worship and music. A former United Methodist pastor, William Easum works as a consultant with congregations and religious organizations. He describes major changes in worship as the "second stage" of the Reformation. Easum states: "The shift in the style of worship is the most obvious and divisive [of the changes]. This divisiveness is over the *style* of worship rather than doctrine or theology."[4]

Easum insists that the generations most vital to church growth—the midlife baby boomers and the baby busters (born after 1964)—do not want to be reverent or quiet during worship. Easum singles out music as the "major vehicle for celebration and communication." Few movies, he observes, make a profit without a solid sound track. And what sort of "sound track" should a church choose, given the variety of options? Easum claims that the right method for arriving at a suitable style is to determine which radio stations most of the "worship guests" listen to. "Soft rock," he declares, "is usually the answer" (4).

For Easum, classical music—and traditional church music in general—is a relic of a dying past. If you want life and growth, he says, make use of music, art, and media that are "culturally relevant." "Classical music was rooted in the native folk music of the time," he assures us. "That world is gone" (84). He quotes John Bisagno, pastor of the First Baptist Church in Houston, Texas, who "minces no words when he describes the debilitating effects that classical music has on worship in most settings":

> Long-haired music, funeral-dirge anthems, and stiff-collared song leaders will kill the church faster than anything in the world. . . . There are no great, vibrant, soul-winning churches reaching great numbers of people, baptizing hundreds of converts, reaching masses that have stiff music, seven-fold amens, and a steady diet of classical anthems. None. That's not a few. That's none, none, none (85).

If you want life and growth, Easum suggests, make use of music, art, and media that are "culturally relevant." He repeatedly emphasizes the importance of "quality music." But today, he insists, quality music is less likely to be produced by choirs and organs than by praise teams, soloists, a variety of instrumentalists, and small ensembles that use synthesizers, drums, electric guitars, and so forth. Quality music, especially in the context of youth evangelism, needs to be entertaining

(89). As for cultivating some sort of developed and mature taste for quality in worship music, he states curtly: "Worship is not the place to teach music appreciation" (86). In fact, according to Easum, it turns out there is only one question worship communities in the new paradigm need to ask about music: "Does it bring people closer to God?" Music is never "the message itself." Indeed, "No form is inherently better than another. Music is good if it conveys the gospel; it is bad if it does not" (86).

Easum is willing to cite historical precedents if he thinks they serve his purpose:

> Spiritual giants such as Martin Luther and Charles Wesley showed us the importance of culturally relevant music [by] taking the tunes out of bars, putting words to them, and using the songs in worship. They accommodated the needs of people in order to reach them with the message that would eventually change their lives. They did not conform the message, just the package (86).

Easum does make one concession to the music of the past. In cases where a congregation is aging and possibly declining, he says, it may be best to create two kinds of service, one of them using a style that is still able to validate the cultural needs of the older generation. But, according to Easum, that will not be the service that is "culturally relevant" (89).

Christians should be able to sympathize with many of Easum's pastoral and musical concerns. They are consistent with the need for what in Catholic circles has been known as the indigenous "inculturation" of the Gospel—something missionaries to foreign cultures have for some time now encouraged and attempted. Importing Vivaldi or Brahms or William Mathias into a church community whose native musical languages are closer to those of Madonna, Jimmy Buffett, or John Tesh might be compared with earlier missionary efforts to impose European or North American religious styles on drastically different cultures out of an imperialist or colonialist mentality. (Not that converts do not sometimes need and welcome a sharp alternative to their native cultural vocabulary. Chinese Christians have treasured the Gospel hymns brought to them by nineteenth-century missionaries, choosing them over songs using Chinese folk tunes or composed later by Chinese Christians and in a Chinese idiom.)

Easum makes a valid point, moreover, in claiming that music that was originally secular has repeatedly found its way into church. The boundary between sacred and secular has repeatedly been blurred or transgressed. No one style is unalterably sacred, nor another unalterably secular. And Easum is probably correct in saying that much of the soft rock or pop music that he advocates for worship has become a kind of generic musical product with no set of specifically worldly associations that would prevent its use in worship. One could make a similar observation regarding the baroque and early classical musical styles of the seventeenth and early eighteenth centuries (roughly from Handel to Haydn) that crossed rather freely from the operatic stage and concert hall to the church and back again.

Again, matching religious words with neutral or nonspecific popular music can bring out a suitable range of meanings the music might not have on its own. Amy Grant, Petra, Jars of Clay, and countless others can now adopt and adapt rock as a Christian musical style that their listeners find entirely consonant with their sense of Christian life and proclamation.

Finally, we can agree with Easum's implicit claim that church music has sometimes been unduly limited by traditional suspicions of pulsing or lively rhythms, "irreverent" instruments, and entertainment. (Religious music would be in trouble in much of the world, if it could never be rhythmic or animated.) Nevertheless, Easum makes several highly questionable assumptions. And his mode of argument exemplifies something very different from what I like to term Ecumenical Taste, which I regard as not only more justifiable but also more Christian and charitable at heart.

In Time but Out of Tune

William Easum claims nothing for himself if not that he is attuned to the times and to the needs of contemporary Christians. Yet, in reading Easum's argument as he sets it forth, many readers will find his assertions regarding church music not only uncompromising but also discordant and at points uninformed and misleading.

Easum advances his argument in terms evidently meant to rally support on the part of people who, whether or not they have realized it, are tired of the status quo in the church music of their own traditions. He does not couch what he says in terms meant to invite or encourage change on the part of people whose faith has been fed, and continues to be fed, by much of the more traditional music—except insofar as Easum can persuade them to see themselves as "dinosaurs"

standing in the way of vital change. People who love Jesus, he insinu-
ates, would not want to be guilty of standing in the way of using pop
and rock music in church.

Although one would think that the primary target of Easum's assault
on traditional church music would be professional church musicians (to
whom we are coming momentarily), it seems likely that Easum is operating out of an intuitive sense that an attack on classical music will accomplish two things at once. If he can depict the advocates of classical
church music as both elitist in taste and disloyal to the Gospel, he will
not only discredit them in the eyes of popular music lovers; he will also
gain the sympathy of those many Christians who, while populist in taste
and sentiment, have tended to accept "classical" styles because they associate rock 'n' roll with worldly activities and feelings.

Be that as it may, for the many professional musicians whose liveli-
hood is based in large part on their training and competence in more
traditional church music, no way of raising the issues could be more
threatening or alienating than this. Easum insists that churches that
want to survive and grow have no choice but to change the music they
use in worship. And, as we have seen, he argues the new music should
be the same music the "worship guests" most enjoy on the radio,
which he assumes will normally be "soft rock." The number of musicians in the American Guild of Organists who are both proficient in
playing soft rock and eager to use it as the basic musical style for worship is miniscule. That is to be expected, in view of the fact that it takes
great amounts of time, skill, and dedicated training to become even
moderately competent as a traditional organist. Easum is providing a
recipe for getting such people fired or retired.

Then there is the matter of how Easum states his own aesthetic
claims regarding church music. One might have thought that a person
who began his discussion of style and worship by remarking on the divisiveness of the issue would take considerable care with how he
phrased his own judgments. Unfortunately, Easum exemplifies just
how prone we all are to take our own judgments of taste, or the judgments of our own group, as universally valid. Kant was right, at a psy-
chological level: Most of us tend to think that our judgments in matters
of taste ought to be shared universally, even if we know they won't be.
In this case, Easum is unhesitating in his sweeping rejection of certain
music (classical) and completely confident in his endorsement of certain other music (particularly soft rock). Yet, aside from alluding to
radio listening habits and referring to the importance of popular music

in film soundtracks, Easum offers minimal evidence that classical music is virtually fossilized as a worship medium or that pop music is ideal. The primary proof he offers is that no big, soul-winning churches use classical or related music. While he recognizes many professional church musicians resist the changeover, he contends they are letting their own private taste stand in the way of the Gospel: "The source of . . . conflict comes primarily from trained musicians who often find these concepts repugnant and resist any change in the style of the music. . . . Many are more interested in music appreciation than in helping people find new life." In short, such musicians supposedly think "making disciples is not as important as making good music. It is time we recognize this problem and deal with it accordingly" (88).

Needless to say, professional traditional church musicians are not always pluralistic themselves and are seldom the best judges of the worship potential of popular music. But Easum, instead of encouraging dialogue, simply turns elitism on its head. A musical elitist assumes that any popular music must be bad. A musical populist, on the contrary, assumes that only popular music is good and that the most popular music is necessarily the best music—and indeed, the best music for worship. Operating on the basis of that populist principle, Easum argues the best music for church is nothing other than the music the greatest number of people like; and since we cannot formulate precise rules and concepts that will fully describe or guarantee high quality in music (on this point we can all agree), Easum asks us to look only at the results. The music that wins his contest is bound to be the music of those churches that grow the fastest.

It may be worth noting that a theologian such as Kierkegaard would have no sympathy with Easum's claims, since Kierkegaard was highly suspicious of any form of Christianity that might be thought compromising or popular. But we do not need to resort to Kierkegaard to suggest alternatives. With a little further reflection, we can see that Easum operates with a whole cluster of highly questionable assumptions:

- that religious quality and musical quality are both reliably indicated by numerical success;
- that liking a certain kind of music for light entertainment is necessarily the same as liking that very music for all the purposes of worship;
- that the key to musical quality, religiously and aesthetically, is immediate accessibility;

- that religious music is never, therefore, a medium one might expect to grow into and grow through as a part of Christian formation and development;
- that worship music today must always be upbeat and animated if it is to be "culturally relevant";
- that classical music in general is stodgy and fossilized;
- that religious words guarantee genuinely religious music, as long as the music is likeable;
- that music can be treated simply as a "package" that contains the Gospel message instead of being treated as an art that embodies and interprets the Gospel message by its structure and the way it sounds.

Finally, Easum assumes he is competent to make judgments about the viability of particular kinds of music without engaging in genuine dialogue with musicians trained in those traditions. Thus, far from exhibiting ecumenical taste, he takes a quite selective and dogmatic position disguised as welcoming obedience to a Gospel imperative to spread the Word.

In fairness, it must be said that the musicians Easum has generally dealt with might not have been open to much dialogue on these points. Traditional and classical musicians in the employment of churches have all too often waved off pastoral and worship concerns as irrelevant to their music-making. Not long ago a prominent New England composer of church music declared before a society devoted to religion and contemporary arts that he had a profound *un*interest in anything having to do with religious doctrine. "Music is my religion," he avowed—not proudly, but truthfully, without supposing for a moment that, when composing for churches, even an agnostic composer might want or need to find musical ways of enlivening doctrine itself. (One thinks of the contrast with Ralph Vaughan Williams, whose private agnosticism transcended itself in the very act of imagining faith in musical terms.) Still more recently, in a prominent classical music magazine, a young classically trained organist recounted how he had always been accused in English churches of playing too fast and too loud. With pleasure he recalled how he responded when he was told by the Dean of Worcester Cathedral that, as guest organist, he should tailor his voluntaries to the more subdued tastes of people in Elgar country. His answer was to let forth a "torrent of Widor." Asked by the bemused interviewer about his religious convictions, the organist replied: "Well, I spend a lot of time in church, but . . . let's put it this way: I would never go to church to hear a said Mass. No, music is my religion."[5]

Faced with the narrowly musical mindset and unchristian arrogance of certain professional "classical" church musicians, Easum and numerous others have evidently taken matters into their own hands. They have discerned and reacted to a level of congregational restlessness and dissatisfaction—which is something the more traditional musicians have been slow to notice and understandably reluctant to treat as relevant to their work.

That still does not mean, however, that Easum and others taking his approach exhibit the sort of taste and informed judgment that would make them reliable guides to Christian growth (or even church growth) in the sphere of music and the arts. Let us return to two points in particular: (1) the current status of classical music—and of certain other "minority" styles—in church and out; and (2) the use of "secular" musical styles in church, and hence the relationship between medium and message in worship.

A Closer Listen

Dinosaur or Phoenix?

The argument that traditional church music, particularly classical, is either extinct or well on the way toward extinction may seem to be a historical and cultural question of relatively minor theological consequence. Yet it is highly charged from the perspective of those Christians whose faith is significantly shaped through such music; it has a direct bearing on the whole question of assessing "cultural relevance"; and the way the argument is usually deployed (whether true or not) reflects a dubious understanding of the range of art needed for the whole of the Christian life.

Without pretending to have William Easum's clairvoyance regarding the future—he predicts, for example, the quick death of all symphony orchestras that do not soon begin to feature a significant amount of pop and rock music (84–5)—we can make a number of observations that run counter to his suppositions. They constitute the very sort of evidence regarding "cultural relevance" that he, as a consultant, treats as pertinent.

First, while it is true that classical music has lost some of its prestige and audience of late, it is worth pointing out that opera has recently experienced a tremendous revival, and not only among the senior generations. At present, opera houses in many parts of the world (including Easum's own United States) are filled to capacity and are adding series rather than trimming back.

Second, the number of people in North America who say they very much like classical music stands at a comparatively substantial 14 to 20 percent across the generations, which constitutes a more consistently favorable cross-generational response than most other styles elicit. Although the sale of classical recordings is a relatively small percentage of total audio sales, that can partly be explained by the fact that classical music is much less oriented toward the currently fashionable and the new, which is of course also quickly unfashionable and must therefore be replaced. As Mark C. Taylor remarks, in the course of rejoicing in the "profoundly superficial" surfaces of postmodern life, fashion—being "forever committed to the new"—speaks only in the "present tense."[6] That hardly argues against incorporating classic and classical styles in many church settings where riding each successive wave of fashion seems neither desirable nor even possible.

Third, it is well known that, for the past quarter century, "early music" (roughly European "classical" music before the eighteenth-century classical period itself) has attracted a significant and ardent audience, young and old. That audience augments the already considerable following of baroque music in particular, whose popularity is indicated by the enthusiastic reception accorded to Pachelbel's "Canon in D," Bach's *Brandenburg Concerti*, and Handel's *Messiah*. A concert by the women's medieval quartet Anonymous 4, by the Monteverdi Consort (directed by John Eliot Gardiner), or by the Tallis Scholars (directed by Peter Phillips) is normally "packed" almost anywhere these and comparable groups sing, be that in Rome, London, or Indianapolis.

Fourth, recent years have seen a surge in the popularity of chant and chant-like music among people of all ages. The widespread introduction of religious services using music from the religious community at Taizé, France, fits with this trend, since much of it tends to be rather contemplative and in harmony with the moods if not modes of chant. The attraction of such "boring" ritual music certainly challenges Easum's notion that "culturally relevant" music must be lively and entertaining.

Fifth, such trends have themselves been accompanied by rising interest in "spiritual" classical music of all sorts, both ancient and contemporary—a development classical musicians and record companies have been quick to exploit.

Sixth—and this most of all should have caught Easum's attention, given his interest in the "sound tracks" needed for worship—a great many scores for films that feature high drama, serious feeling, or intense introspection still use music that draws primarily on classical idioms. A whole array of recent movies, even popular ones, use music indebted to classical traditions. The music John Williams has composed for the immensely popular *Star Wars* series of George Lucas often sounds like something one might expect from Sergei Prokofiev or Gustav Holst. And much of Howard Shore's music for the immensely popular *Lord of the Rings* has a real affinity with the work of the British composer Malcolm Arnold (who also composed film scores himself). One could also mention John Corigliano's largely classical score for *The Red Violin*, the contemporary classical music for Terrence Malick's much-discussed war movie *The Thin Red Line*, the equally fascinating and contemporary sound tracks for the morally complex films of Krzysztof Kieslowski, and Ennio Morricone's score for *The Mission*, or even Danny Elfman's scores for the more dramatic moments in the *Batman* series, not to mention music for "period" films such as the crowd-pleasing *Shakespeare in Love*. The list could go on indefinitely.

The variety and ubiquity of film music closely allied to classical styles should be sufficient to suggest that not only is "classical" music still very much alive, though evolving; it is also enormously varied, itself—and in fact more varied than one would ever guess on the basis of the so-called classical music typically heard in churches. The historical and cultural evidence seems to indicate that, instead of being the dinosaur some consultants to churches judge it to be, what we term classical music has, over the centuries, been very much a phoenix, albeit an evolving phoenix, consumed by cultural fire in one form only to be resurrected in another.

Clearly, before judging which kinds of music are culturally relevant—and, more important, relevant to the transformation of values appropriate to Christian culture and growth—it is important to attain a theologically adequate and aesthetically informed picture of the musical options. I would argue that, out of those many legitimate options, the Euro-American classical tradition remains among the most varied, profound, and adaptable, and perhaps in ways churches have yet to imagine.

But there is a larger issue here than simply whether classical music per se is still "culturally relevant" and thus of use to churches. It is that the range of "culturally relevant" music in general is altogether more diverse than many promoters of church vitality recognize. In fact, given what we have just observed regarding classical music, it would be surprising if the candidates among popular styles were not, themselves, more varied than we are usually urged to believe. In his book *Virtual Faith: The Irreverent Spiritual Quest of Generation X*, Tom Beaudoin argues convincingly that theological ambiguity and an acute awareness of suffering are central to those forms of faith and culture most characteristic of the members of "Generation X" (born between the early 1960s and the late 1970s).[7] It is his observation that Generation Xers (of whom he is one) often seek out forms of contemplative spirituality, albeit eclectic and heterodox, and would frequently prefer *more* silence in church services than less. These are things church consultants and others ignore when they prescribe a steady diet of peppy music for the younger generations of the church and when they suppose the Gospel message itself needs no reinterpretation, only a new package.

If all churches interested in survival and growth followed the advice being urged on them by those pushing hardest for "cultural relevance"—and many churches are doing just that—Christian churches would be put in the ironic position of refusing to make use of music as serious (or exalted) as what one can still hear on a regular basis in the movie theater, on television and radio, in the opera house, symphony hall, and (indeed) the local restaurant. That would be, in no small part, because the churches would have misunderstood their cultural situation. Still more, it would be because they would have defined their mission primarily in terms of misplaced marketing values—values that, if followed consistently, would seriously undervalue the spiritually transformative potential of challenging artistry (both "classical" and vernacular), and that would surely have had Jesus popularize his image and simplify his message before it was too late. Similar misunderstandings can be found in common assumptions about the viability of simply "packaging" a sacred message in an appealing secular style.

From Sacred to Secular and Back

We have already noted that Protestants and other Christians have made wide use of secular sources for their hymn tunes and religious music. J. S. Bach borrowed from his secular cantatas and harpsichord concerti when composing his sacred works, including his *B Minor Mass*. Martin Luther, moreover, has been credited with saying, and acting as though, he did not want the devil to have all the good tunes.[8] Yet secular and popular music was not the only sort Luther wanted to raid. He was openly jealous of "the fine music and songs" and "precious melodies" the Catholics got to use at Masses for the dead, and thought it would "be a pity to let them perish."[9] In fact, he said, the pope's followers in general possess "a lot of splendid, beautiful songs and music, especially in cathedral and parish churches" that he thought ought to be divested of "idolatrous, lifeless, and foolish texts" and reused for the sake of their beauty.[10] For that matter, Luther also expressed admiration for the Roman Church's "beautiful services, gorgeous cathedrals, and splendid cloisters."[11] He was hardly the advocate of strictly casual and vernacular styles.

John Calvin, for his part, was extremely cautious about the music he sanctioned for use in worship, which he thought should exhibit moderation, gravity, and majesty. Martin Luther and, later, John Wesley (1703–91) could both be very particular about the specific tunes they wanted to use with hymn texts. John Wesley (more often than his brother Charles) ordinarily designated which tunes he judged to be suitable. And, contrary to popular misconceptions today, neither the Wesleys nor Luther would, in fact, have wanted to sanction the free and direct use of music from bars and brothels.[12]

Now, why might any Christian theologian, pastor, or musician want to make such discriminations? It is doubtful that such people would, if they thought music provides nothing more than a "package" for the Gospel message, and one that is adequate as long as it is appealing. But that is not what any of the major Reformers thought, or a good many of their successors either, even though most were sure some secular music could legitimately be borrowed and adapted for religious purposes.

It seems evident that Christians today likewise need to be thinking more carefully and deeply about sacred and secular in the realm of music. Art, and certainly musical art, may have a special religious calling; because art, more than most other things, tends to come from the heart and go to the heart—to paraphrase what Beethoven said of his *Missa Solemnis*. But perhaps not all art is meant to touch the heart, let alone the soul; and perhaps even the music that touches the heart does so in quite different ways. A clever piano sonata Mozart composed in his head is not likely to be perceived as any more religious or "spiritual" than David Hume's wittily composed theory of taste, although the one is artistic and the other is philosophical. However justified

Karl Barth's conviction may have been that Mozart's ostensibly secular music is possibly even more significant, religiously, than his Masses, a lover of Mozart's music may "adore" Cherubino's adolescent and flirtatious songs in the *Marriage of Figaro* without needing to regard them as even remotely religious, let alone as generally well suited for worship. As for the Masses themselves, reservations about their more operatic traits have been expressed by a great many clergy and musicians from Mozart's time to the present—the religious admiration of Barth and Hans Küng notwithstanding.[13] One does not have to believe certain styles of music are inherently religious in order to be convinced that some kinds of music are more suitable for worship in general than are other kinds. In our own day, the pianist and musicologist Charles Rosen has articulated a number of cogent reasons (whether or not one agrees with them) for regarding the classical style, proper, of Haydn, Mozart, and Beethoven as peculiarly handicapped in the realm of sacred music.[14] In Rosen's view, those composers wisely departed from the more strictly "classical" conventions to become more "archaic" in style (modal, contrapuntal) when writing their most serious church music—Haydn's oratorio *The Creation*, for instance, or Mozart's *Requiem* and *Mass in C Minor*, or Beethoven's *Missa Solemnis*.

There is also good reason to believe, in any case, that some musical styles are more flexible than others. Both baroque music and African American Gospel music have roots within the churches as well as within secular settings, permitting composers and performers in these idioms to make relatively minor stylistic adjustments that will readily put into play the appropriate range of associations, thoughts, and feelings. Often, with such adaptable styles, a change in the performance context is enough to serve that purpose.

That cannot be said regarding certain other music, which today may be designed and adapted primarily to do such things as create highly cerebral conundrums (in the case of some avant-garde classical works) or energize sporting events, entertain at parties, reduce stress, or enhance bedroom desires. As Martha Bayles argues in her book *Hole in our Soul: The Loss of Beauty and Meaning in American Popular Music*, early rock 'n' roll, for all its undeniable sexual energy, originated out of a milieu deeply influenced by a white Pentecostalism that borrowed African American musical styles (mainly rhythm and blues) while remaining defensively segregated. Elvis Presley, Jerry Lee Lewis, and Little Richard all grew up in the Pentecostal church and sometimes made highly conflicted, guilt-ridden alterations of its music. But,

Bayles argues, a multitude of influences—not least the impulses of artistic modernism—conspired to push moral and religious associations and tensions out of much subsequent popular music. Her claim may be overstated, but it finds a certain amount of agreement among popular musicians themselves.[15]

In fact, some musical styles, far from being flexible or neutral, seem quite specialized in character—something made exceptionally clear in the following passage from a novel by Robertson Davies entitled *The Cunning Man* (1994). Describing his first encounter with plainsong (chant) at St. Aidan's Church, the narrator says:

> At first I did not know what it was. At intervals the eight men in the chancel choir, or sometimes Dwyer alone, would utter what sounded like speech of a special eloquence, every word clearly to be heard, but observing a discipline that was musical, in that there was no hint of anything that was colloquial, but not like any music I had met with in my, by this time, fairly good acquaintance with music. My idea of church music at its highest was Bach, but Bach at his most reverent is still intended for performance. This was music addressed to God, not as performance, but as the most intimate and devout communication. It was a form of speech fit for the ear of the Highest.[16]

Gregorian chant would serve poorly for purposes of inebriated celebration; by the same token, the latest Ricky Martin hit would serve poorly for purposes of meditative prayer.

Thus, in response to any uncritical willingness to adopt for worship whatever music people favor in their radio listening, one might ask: Is it possible musicians in our notably secular era have become especially adept at shaping music to specifically erotic, recreational, and commercial purposes? If so, might it not be the case that regularly bending those sorts of music to the ends of worship would be rather like regularly choosing to praise or thank God in the tone of voice one would ordinarily use to order a pizza or to cheer a touchdown—or perhaps even to make the most casual sort of love?

No doubt part of the meaning we hear in a given kind of music is "socially constructed," which raises the possibility that an alteration in the construct will alter completely how the music sounds. Simon Frith makes such an argument, in effect, when he proposes that "cultural ideology," rather than anything within the music or its beat, produces most of the sexual and bodily associations of rock 'n' roll; but despite his elaborate and brilliant defense of that claim, it is surely too clever by at least half.[17] Nothing one can do will convert Gregorian chant into a style as bodily and erotic in its center as various kinds of rock; nor can rock be made to sound as contemplative or as ethereal as chant, though it can indeed take on an aura of ecstasy.

The whole question of meaning in music (whether sacred or secular) is of course extraordinarily elusive, and in many ways a matter of intuitions we cannot fully explain. Nonetheless, music does mean, as the literary and cultural critic George Steiner insists:

> It is brimful of meanings which will not translate into logical structures or verbal expression . . . Music is at once cerebral in the highest degree—I repeat that the energies and form-relations in the playing of a quartet, in the interactions of voice and instrument are among the most complex events known to man—and it is at the same time somatic, carnal and a searching out of resonances in our bodies at levels deeper than will or consciousness.[18]

Indeed, Steiner says, because of the virtually sacramental "real presence" of its meaning, music has "celebrated the mystery of intuitions of transcendence."[19]

Although Steiner is prone to talk about the powers of music as such, apart from specific cultural mediations and cultural conventions, it may be best to see particular sorts of music as having a range of possible nonverbal meanings that verbal language and cultural context can then shape and construe in more specific ways.[20] One can then distinguish, by and large, between religious music most appropriate for the inner sanctuary (to use the place name both literally and figuratively), and what is best for the nave of the church, or for the courtyard, recreational hall, or concert stage. One can fittingly choose to use religious music in any of these settings; but its character and purpose will shift accordingly, with convention playing a part in shaping those choices.

Coming back to the question of sacred and secular styles, none of this means that worship services should never make use of rock, or perhaps even heavy metal and "grunge." One scholarly interpreter and performer of heavy metal, for instance, argues that this notoriously "diabolical" genre of music can be converted into a credible and creative force with a Christian evangelistic message. Thus, according to Robert Walser, the Christian heavy metal band Stryper uses heavy metal to communicate "experiences of power and transcendent freedom" in which a new sort of meaning emerges from the sounds and gestures that begin to serve as religious metaphors: "The power is God's; the transcendent freedom represents the rewards of Christianity; the intensity is that of religious experience. . . . Stryper presents Christianity as an exciting, youth-oriented alternative."[21]

That said, it must also be said that, because religious meanings cannot simply be imposed on every sort of musical medium regardless of its style, considerable musical and liturgical experimentation could be required to find out which forms of rock and pop permit or invite stretching for religious purposes. Christians probably need musical "laboratories" involving both clergy and musicians.

In the meantime, people for whom rock, pop, and Broadway musicals are nothing like their native language for serious celebration and for soul-searching expression cannot be expected to worship freely and often in a worship atmosphere dominated by such musical styles. For such people (perhaps still the majority of Christians), an identifiably sacred style can mark a difference that allows them to regard some music as specially consecrated for enjoyment "in God." They will resonate with Edward Farley's observation that, at present:

> To attend the typical Protestant Sunday morning worship service is to experience something odd, something like a charade. . . . Lacking is a sense of the terrible mystery of God, which sets language atremble and silences facile chattiness. . . . If the seraphim assumed this Sunday morning mood, they would be addressing God not as "holy, holy, holy" but as "nice, nice, nice."[22]

Similar observations are made from time to time on the Catholic side as well.

No doubt some of the worship services that have undergone renovation through popular and casual idioms were not, to begin with, so awe-filled as they were awful: bland, stiff, and stifled. Furthermore, it is important to be pluralistic enough to recognize Christianity knows more than one sacred manner of approaching God. In the interests of ecumenical taste, for instance, we could note that, whereas most Javanese Christians address God using only the most formal personal pronouns reserved for someone of higher status, the Amharic-speaking people of Ethiopia use only the most intimate personal pronouns for the same purpose. As they see the matter, God already knows our hearts, motives, and intentions and is therefore too intimately acquainted with us to require (or be flattered by) formal modes of address.[23] Each approach has its theological reasons; and in fact a good many cultures figure out ways to address God both formally and informally, though in different media and contexts.

Nevertheless, if the medium of religious practice and expression is not only predominantly casual in style but also artistically "flimsy" (a complaint lodged by Kathleen Norris),[24] or perhaps even kitsch (which is not to say worthless, or equally cheap in everyone's ears and eyes), then one must ask: What sort of God are worshipers envisioning as they sing or look or move? To what sort of life and growth do they suppose they are being called? The possibility that a relatively casual and unchallenging style might be all there is to a given community's worship life or musical language is bound to be deflating to those whose call to discipleship causes them to yearn for something more by way of aesthetic formation and development.

As for the uncritical religious adoption of "secular" styles themselves, there is no denying that the act of giving ordinary, secular-sounding expression to extraordinary reality can work miracles, transforming the ordinary and secular into something sacred. Nevertheless, marrying Gospel insights and liturgical actions to a musical or linguistic medium originally secular in sound and purpose is an art in itself. Carelessly done, it can inadvertently convert the sacred into something quite ordinary.

Testing Christian Taste: Twelve Premises

Mindful that in *Dancing with Dinosaurs* William Easum helpfully spells out twelve of his underlying assumptions, let me conclude by setting forth twelve assumptions I hope could fruitfully guide discussions of aesthetic taste as they arise in the next stage of religious, and specifically Christian, development in relation to the arts. I regard them as assumptions or premises rather than as goals; but one could also look on them as habits of mind useful for exercising Christian taste in healthy ways. By calling them assumptions I do not mean they do not require support, but only that such points cannot immediately be argued from the ground up when matters of Christian taste are in dispute. These twelve assumptions, or premises, are intended to help guide the fruitful exercise of Christian taste in the practice of Christian music today.

(1) There are many kinds of good taste, and many kinds of good religious art and music. In view of cultural diversity, it would be extremely odd if that were not true.

(2) Not all kinds of good art and music are equally good for worship, let alone for every tradition or faith community. In terms of worship, therefore, it is not enough that a work or style of art be likeable; it must also be appropriate.

(3) There are various appropriately Christian modes of mediating religious experience artistically—from radically transcendent to radically immanent in a sense of the holy; from exuberantly abundant to starkly minimal in means; from prophetic to pastoral in tone; from instructive to meditative in aim.

(4) Every era and cultural context tends to develop new forms of good sacred music and art, which to begin with often seem secular.

(5) Because every musical/aesthetic style calls for a particular kind of attunement, no one person can possibly be competent to make equally discerning judgments about every kind of music. Yet almost everyone is inclined to assume or act otherwise. That impulse is related to the sin of pride.

(6) It is an act of Christian love to learn to appreciate or at least respect what others value in a particular style or work they cherish in worship or in the rest of life. That is different, however, from personally liking every form of commendable art, which is impossible and unnecessary.

(7) Disagreements over taste in religious music (or any other art) can be healthy and productive; but they touch on sensitive matters and often reflect or embody religious differences as well as aesthetic ones.

(8) The reasons why an aesthetic work or style is good or bad, weak or strong (and in what circumstances), can never be expressed fully in words; yet they can often be pointed out through comparative—and repeated—looking and listening.

(9) Aesthetic judgments begin with, and owe special consideration to, the community or tradition to which a given style or work is indigenous or most familiar. But they seldom end there; and they cannot, if the style or work is to invite the attention of a wide range of people over a period of time.

(10) The overall evaluation of any art used in worship needs to be a joint effort among clergy, congregation, and trained artists and musicians, taking into account not only the aesthetic qualities of the art itself but also the larger requirements and contours of worship that should at once respond to and orient the particular work of art or music.

(11) While relative accessibility is imperative for most church art, the church also needs art—including "classic" art of various kinds—

that continually challenges and solicits spiritual and theological growth in the aesthetic dimension. This is art the Christian can grow into but seldom out of.

(12) Almost every artistic style enjoyed and valued by a particular group over a long period of time and for a wide range of purposes has religious potential. That is because life typically finds various and surprising ways of turning religious. As Augustine said, our hearts are restless until they rest in God.

Notes

1. Excerpted and adapted from *Good Taste, Bad Taste, and Christian Taste: Aesthetics in Religious Life* (New York: Oxford University Press, 2000), in part as printed in the *Christian Century* (Sept. 13–20, 2000), by permission of Oxford University Press.

2. Ibid., 37. See also Frank Burch Brown, "Enjoyment and Discernment in the Music of Worship," *Theology Today* 58 (October 2001) 342–58.

3. Charles Trueheart, "Next Church," *Atlantic Monthly* (August 1996) 37–58; quotation on 50.

4. William Easum, *Dancing with Dinosaurs: Ministry in a Hostile and Hurting World* (Nashville: Abingdon, 1993) 81.

5. "Life in the Fast Lane," an interview with Wayne Marshall, *BBC Music Magazine* (July 1998) 24–8; quotation on 28.

6. I have not attempted to recreate the drift of Taylor's seriously playful "virtual discussion" of the "irreducible ambiguity" of fashion, surface, skin, postmodern signs, and the like in *Hiding* (Chicago: University of Chicago Press, 1997) 210, 211.

7. Tom Beaudoin, *Virtual Faith: The Irreverent Spiritual Question of Generation X* (San Francisco: Jossey-Bass, 1998). For observations on the restless spirituality of the older, "Baby Boomer" generation, see Wade Clark Roof, *Spiritual Marketplace: Baby Boomers and the Remaking of American Religion* (Princeton: Princeton University Press, 1999).

8. Friedrich Blume, *Protestant Church Music* (New York: W. W. Norton, 1974) 30.

9. See Martin Luther, "Preface to the Burial Hymns" (1542); *Luther's Works*, vol. 53, ed. Ulrich S. Leupold; general ed. Helmut T. Lehmann (Philadelphia: Fortress, 1965) 327.

10. Ibid., 327–8.

11. Ibid., 327.

12. See Blume, *Protestant Church Music*, esp. p. 29ff.; Quentin Faulkner, *Wiser Than Despair: The Evolution of Ideas in the Relationship of Music and the Christian Church* (Westport, CT: Greenwood, 1996); and Paul Westermeyer, *Te Deum: The Church and Music* (Minneapolis: Fortress, 1998) 205–16.

13. See Hans Küng, *Mozart: Traces of Transcendence*, trans. John Bowden (Grand Rapids, MI: Eerdmans, 1993).

14. Charles Rosen, *The Classical Style: Haydn, Mozart, Beethoven*, 1971; rpt. ed. (New York: Norton, 1972) 366–75.

15. Martha Bayles, *Hole in our Soul: The Loss of Beauty and Meaning in American Popular Music* (Chicago: University of Chicago Press, 1994); see especially the chapter "Rock 'n' Rollers or Holy Rollers?" 127–42.

16. Robertson Davies, *The Cunning Man* (Toronto: McClelland & Stewart, 1994) 146–7. My thanks to William C. James for calling my attention to this passage.

17. Simon Frith, "Rhythm: Race, Sex, and the Body," in his book *Performing Rites: On the Value of Popular Music* (Cambridge, MA: Harvard University Press, 1996) 123–44.

18. George Steiner, *Real Presences* (Chicago: University of Chicago Press, 1989) 217.

19. Ibid., 218.

20. For more on matters of music and meaning, see Joseph P. Swain, *Musical Languages* (New York: W. W. Norton, 1997); Stephen Davies, *Musical Meaning and Expression* (Ithaca, NY: Cornell University Press, 1994); Aaron Ridley, *Music, Value, and the Passions* (Ithaca, NY: Cornell University Press, 1995); Robert S. Hatten, *Musical Meaning in Beethoven: Markedness, Correlation, and Interpretation* (Bloomington: Indiana University Press, 1994); Peter Kivy, *Sound and Semblance: Reflections on Musical Representation* (Princeton, NJ: Princeton University Press, 1984); Leonard Meyer, *Music, the Arts, and Ideas* (Chicago: University of Chicago Press, 1967); Leonard Meyer, *Emotion and Meaning in Music* (Chicago: University of Chicago Press, 1956); Peter J. Martin, *Sounds and Society: Themes in the Sociology of Music* (Manchester: Manchester University Press, 1995). For the aesthetics of music and religious meaning in particular, see Albert L. Blackwell, *The Sacred in Music* (Louisville: Westminster/John Knox, 1999); Clyde J. Steckel, "How Can Music Have Theological Significance?" in Jon Michael Spencer, ed., *Theomusicology* (Durham, NC: Duke University Press, 1994) 35; Edward Rothstein, *Emblems of Mind: The Inner Life of Music and Mathematics*; and Jeremy Begbie, *Theology, Music and Time* (Cambridge: Cambridge University Press, 2000).

21. Robert Walser, *Running with the Devil: Power, Gender, and Madness in Heavy Metal Music* (Hanover, MA: Wesleyan University Press/University Press of New England, 1993) 55.

22. Edward Farley, "A Missing Presence," *Christian Century* (March 18–25, 1998) 276.

23. I am paraphrasing observations passed on to me by my colleague Mick Smith, who has worked extensively among the peoples referred to.

24. Kathleen Norris, "Sinatra in the Bell Tower," *Christian Century* (March 18–25, 1998) 301.

11

Using Music
from Other Cultures in Worship
A Conversation with Mary K. Oyer

Fine Art and Functional Art

Charlotte: Mary, as we begin our conversation, I thought you might help us think about the difference between the music of our own culture and the music of other cultures. You were trained at the University of Michigan, one of the fine music schools in the United States. How did your classical training in the Western tradition help you to understand the music of other cultures?

Mary: I think the classical training has helped me to listen more intently. The basic training of a college music student, such as taking dictation, listening, analyzing music does help one to sharpen the capacity to hear any music. Even though the category of analysis may be Western, one can eventually learn other ways of analyzing.

Charlotte: Just as we must learn one spoken language before learning a second language, so it is with learning a musical language. It is knowing the one language that enables us then to move to another.

Mary: Yes. Perhaps by comparison we feel/intuit our way into another culture. Through that process I've had to repudiate some of my earlier absolutes. For example, I had always assumed that in a good performance the pitch needs to be accurate. I changed my views on this point. By listening to African traditional music, I came to realize that, although precision of pitch is vital for the combination of pitches in Western harmonic music, it is not a high priority in some African cultures. I understood this when I studied a one-string fiddle in Ghana. Salisu, the Ghanaian musician tried to teach me a song about birds eating millet in a field. I recorded his playing the first day. It began

The next day his playing sounded

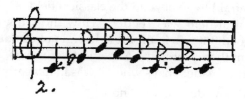

When I recorded the following day, it was still another combination

And a fourth time it was close to this

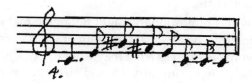

My very Western question to him was, "Which one is right?" His immediate answer was, "Yes." I realized that the basic shape was right for all of them. Incidentally, I learned something also about asking questions.

Charlotte: This is a helpful example of the musical differences between our culture and other cultures. Accurate pitch is certainly a musical value we believe is important.

Mary: But it is not necessarily important in another culture. What are the values then? I think knowing one's own culture is very important for being able to hear what's important in another.

Charlotte: Do you think that classical musicians' training gets in the way of understanding folk music, and conversely, that those who come from a strong folk background find their folk music gets in the way of their understanding classical music? Is it difficult to move between the worlds?

Mary: Well, I can only speak to the classical side, because I didn't begin in the folk music field. I imagine that's true, but certainly it was true for me that I was afraid to go beyond the classical field. At the time, in my mind the classical field was "better." How did we know what was good? It was good if it was in the art field and not useful. In the Dewey Decimal System there were Fine Arts and Useful Arts. And there was quite a distinction made. That's where I was in my early days.

Charlotte: And how do you see it now?

Mary: It's much vaguer in terms of the extremes. The extremes should come into the center. I believe I'm a little more interested in the side that has a function, especially in church music. In the music of the church, you must care about the function. I think one of the reasons musicians have not developed a strong interest in hymns is that they are small and functional. Actually, they're like gems. The really good ones are remarkable pieces of art, I think. But that isn't the usual point of view.

Charlotte: Is that because we equate quality with complexity?

Mary: I think that's true.

Charlotte: Poets and philosophers might not agree that complexity is necessary for quality. They seek a minimum of words, wanting to find a few, precise words to express what they want to say. Is it possible that musicians in the church, similarly, should strive for straightforward music that is finely composed?

Mary: Perhaps. There is some baggage that comes along with looking at a hymn. In addition to the music, you are dealing with what the denomination is saying makes an acceptable hymn, and what kinds of politics and relationships affect decisions about hymns.

Charlotte: Musically, or textually, or both?

Mary: Both, but also the function of the hymn, how it is used. I know that when I was in Africa, going every other year and then staying two years now and then, I played a lot of cello. I played in the orchestra, and then I came home to work on the hymnal. The orchestral musicians were horrified. They said, "On a hymnal? Why a hymnal?" Of course, these were post-Christian people. They could see no relationship between playing the cello and working on the hymnal. And I feel that in academic settings in the U.S., to some extent, it is much better to play the cello than to get involved in hymns, even in a church-related college.

Charlotte: Do you think that comes from inside the church itself or that it is the influence of the academy?

Mary: It is probably the influence of the academy, which would rather not be encumbered with function. The church approaches art differently. It expects the arts to function within the larger framework of worship. So the academy and the church take different approaches to the arts.

Charlotte: Has that always been the case? There are many composers in prior periods of music history who wrote both secular and sacred music, serious and popular music, complex and simple music, as a matter of course. For example, the Brahms late piano pieces are, in some ways, rather spare and simple in contrast to his earlier works. Yet these piano pieces, as you were describing hymns earlier, are absolute jewels. There are no extraneous notes—every note has a precise reason for being in the score, similar to how hymns are written.

Mary: I think there is a lot of variation from one period to another and one composer to another. For example, in the Renaissance and Reformation in England, composers like Tallis and Tye, and then Gibbons, were interested in madrigals and motets and Masses and hymns. They all contributed to all of these fields. They had broad compositional interests. In contrast, I'm not sure that the nineteenth-century classical musicians necessarily would have wanted to claim the hymn writers. I think the people who wrote hymn tunes were quite different from the people who wrote symphonies. In that time the big, expansive musical forms seemed to be more important. And, of course, if you write something big, something on a monumental level, you have a different kind of work. Michelangelo worked with big things, as did Beethoven. Beethoven wrote some short pieces, but not very many. It was the large musical forms that interested him. And Wagner, as you know, used truly massive structures for his composition. So we take little portions from their large works and make hymns. When I first started teaching here [at Goshen College], those were the hymns I thought were the best. It was an "arty" point of view. A work is best if one of the great masters writes it! And now, I think it's better if somebody like Claude Goudimel or Louis Bourgeois writes a hymn tune for the Calvinist movement, or Thomas Tallis for the English service. I think the really good hymns were written by composers who valued what can be done with a piece of music for congregational use.

Charlotte: In other words, music that was written expressly to be in the service of liturgy.

Mary: Yes, that's right.

Charlotte: . . . . not music borrowed from the masters of the classical tradition, with the purpose of dignifying the service.

Mary: Right. Exactly. I remember when, early in my career, I went out from Goshen College to speak in churches. I went with my mentor, Walter Yoder, a really wonderful man. We would speak about hymns and sing with congregations. I remember giving a talk several times, entitled, "What Do We Get from the Masters?" That's not where Mennonites were at all. But I knew that, and I was trying to make an apology for the classics. I would say, "This music is good," and I could give reasons why it was good. But now I think my efforts were misplaced.

Charlotte: And yet, those masters that you studied undoubtedly shaped your understanding of what music is.

Mary: Oh yes, yes. I wouldn't give up the classic study. I would give up the narrowness of it as I perceived it, my narrowness.

Music in the Service of the Liturgy

Charlotte: You have said that you think the best church music starts with a composer who understands the function, and works from the context back to the music, rather than making good music fit the context. Can you expand a little bit on that?

Mary: Well, I could probably illustrate. I think Orlando Gibbons is one of the really outstanding composers of the early seventeenth century. In 1623 George Wither broke the law by publishing a hymnbook that included more than psalms. The hymnbook included other parts of the Bible, and Gibbons wrote remarkable tunes to accompany the texts. He wrote them for the English church as he knew it, a church acquainted with madrigals and ayres. Many American churches now reduce the interesting rhythms to a simple skeleton because they have not cultivated singing of irregular rhythms in congregations. But Gibbons' technique is not just taking a little piece out of a larger work, as we do with the tune HYMN TO JOY from Beethoven's Ninth Symphony. That particular hymn works pretty well, actually, but I came to realize, while working on the *Mennonite Hymnal*, that excerpts from larger works are not necessarily the greatest hymn tunes. I remember singing "Come My Soul, Thou Must Be Waking" to a tune from a Haydn symphony. I thought it was great when I was young, and it had a strong influence on me. It is good music, but it does not have the authenticity of a hymn tune that Gibbons first wrote for a hymn.

Or Vaughan Williams. Vaughan Williams is a bit different because he had assessed the borderlines between what a congregation dared to do and what the choir and the organ should do. He said in the introduction to *The English Hymnal* in 1906, "The congregation must *always* sing the melody and the *melody* only."[1] And so he wrote music that we now sing in parts, but it is music really meant for unison singing with organ accompaniment. It is instrumental in conception. But he was writing music directly for use in the Anglican Church which he knew. And then he revived some English folk music. Vaughan Williams really gave folk song a kind of blessing, "This is okay to use," by making folk music adapt to a Christian text.

Charlotte: Is there something about folk music that makes it more singable for a general population?

Mary: I think that is part of the ethnic side. It differs from one ethnic group to another. The Indonesians from Java, for example, like half steps. One of my students who came from Sumatra wrote a tune that fit his church for "O Worship the King." Half steps stick out all over. It goes like this:[2]

O Worship the King
(Indonesian: Hai mari sembah)

nya - nyi - kan syu - kur de - ngan ber - ge - mar.
ca - ha - ya te - rang i - tu ju - bah - Nya.
O grate - ful - ly sing God's power and God's love.
whose robe is the light, whose can - o - py space.
al - might - y, your power has found - ed of old.

Pe - ri - sai u - mat - Nya, Yang Ma - ha - e - sa,
Ge - mu - ruh sua - ra - Nya di a - wan ke - lam,
Our Shield and De - fend - er, the An - cient of Days,
Whose char - iots of wrath the deep thun - der - clouds form,
Es - tab - lished it fast by a change - less de - cree,

mu - li - a na - ma - Nya, takh - ta - Nya me - gah.
ber - ja - lan - lah Di - a di ba - dai ken - cang.
pa - vil - ioned in splen - dor and gird - ed with praise.
and dark is God's path on the wings of the storm.
and round it has cast, like a man - tle, the sea.

Words: Robert Grant (1779–1838), United Kingdom; tr. Yamuger
Music: MEDAN; Daud Kosasih, Indonesia

Charlotte: We would say that's not very singable. But it was singable for that culture.

Mary: And so many Chinese and African tunes, among those of many cultures, are pentatonic. Well, that Indonesian tune was pentatonic too, but it had a different set of five notes. Many pentatonic tunes have no half steps. And there are many, many groups who use that kind of a folk song, African American as well as African and Chinese.

Charlotte: So context can determine what works, what is good and what is helpful in worship? It can depend on the particular location and what is already in the ears of people who will sing the music?

Mary: Yes, yes. What oral knowledge people bring is what they hear in their first year of life. I think those early years of hearing determine what's ethnic for them. When a group gravitates toward a particular set of musical details that separate that group from the neighbors, from the people on the other side of the world, ethnic music is born.

From the Familiar to the New: Lessons from Dunblane

Charlotte: If you were going to urge hymnody in a new, creative direction, what kind of direction do you think it could go that would be fresh, and yet fit the function?

Mary: Poetic meters and accent in texts affect us, usually subconsciously. Beginning with Wesley, in English hymnody, the exploration of different poetic meters made a tremendous difference. By the time you get to Brian Wren, you can find adjacent phrases of 11 and 4 syllables, and all kinds of other metrical structures that have moved very far from the three basic psalm meters of common meter (8.6.8.6.), long meter (8.8.8.8.), and short meter (6.6.8.6.), and their doubles. The shape of the poem in metrical terms gives freshness, even when it's quite irregular, like the hymn, "He Is the Way."[3]

He Is the Way
NEW DANCE P.M.

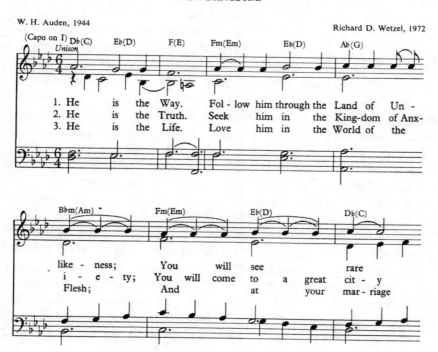

W. H. Auden, 1944

Richard D. Wetzel, 1972

1. He is the Way. Fol - low him through the Land of Un -
2. He is the Truth. Seek him in the King-dom of Anx-
3. He is the Life. Love him in the World of the

like - ness; You will see rare
i - e - ty; You will come to a great cit - y
Flesh; And at your mar - riage

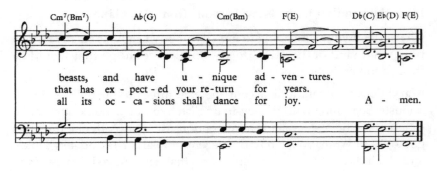

The first verse is 4.10.12, the second 4.11.18, and the third 4.8.14. Maybe this is no longer a hymn, but W. H. Auden meant it to be sung at the end of his Christmas oratorio, *For the Time Being*, in 1949.

In addition to expanding metrical schemes, some recent hymn writers are treating rhyme freely, even omitting it as an essential element of the poetry. Rhyme in most hymns helps to group phrases and relate them in varied ways. But a modern poet, like W. H. Auden in the example above, may choose a more open-ended effect by rejecting rhyme altogether.

In terms of new music, I suppose there is need to explore beyond the next-related keys (adding or removing one sharp or flat) in order to match what's happening in the rest of the music world. What is possible? I have a Mennonite friend, J. Harold Moyer, who has written some very good hymn tunes. His tune, FAITH, for "I Sought the Lord" is used in a number of hymnals. He says that it is much harder to write a hymn tune than a larger musical work. He has written a symphony, but he says it's harder to write a hymn that works. He has a good understanding of the function of a hymn, and how a good hymn can draw people in. Then they can sing more than just a warmed-over nineteenth-century piece, one that already sounds dated. For a more contemporary sound one could move beyond major and minor in pitch and explore more challenging rhythms.

In terms of imagery, there certainly are images of God that go beyond the traditional, images that would fit our culture, fit our time. I think the appropriateness to the culture does not mean that I want to sing about mushroom clouds. I don't really want to. But there should be some imagery that pushes the language beyond what we already have. Lots of hymns are submitted for a hymnal that are just terribly warmed over. They are supposed to be new, but they sound very familiar.

Charlotte: Does a new hymn start with the text?

Mary: Often.

Charlotte: Then the music responds to illumine that text.

Mary: Yes.The music does illumine the text, but its role goes beyond that of being a vehicle for the words. The reverse may be true as well: the text may enable the tune to "speak" as the dominant element. For example, varied musical settings of the *Kyrie Eleison* will elicit quite differing responses to that text. The intensity of the lamenting or pleading quality could cover a wide range of emotions and place emphasis on the music.

Charlotte: I find that with some more recent hymns, Jane Parker Huber's hymns for example, that I'll sing them and then feel that there is too much text to absorb in one singing. They need time for reflection.

Mary: Yes. And she generally uses familiar tunes, so the words fit more traditional notions of rhythm and rhyme. Writing at about the same time were Brian Wren, Fred Pratt Green, Carl Daw, Fred Kaan, and Thomas Troeger, who often pushed the traditional limits of texts with fruitful results.

Charlotte: Were they working more closely with musicians? Were they primarily using existing tunes as well?

Mary: Perhaps they did both at times. But they are good poets, I think. It takes imagination to find the right words, the words that really spark the imagination, and cause us to say, "I hadn't thought of that, but it's just right."

An interesting period of experimental hymn writing happened during the 1960s, a time period when I was in Scotland working on a new Mennonite hymnal. Erik Routley was organizing meetings at Dunblane, Scotland, where he and Wren did some of their first hymns. They would write pieces individually and critique them in the group. The result was a small paperback book, *Dunblane Praises*.

Charlotte: They worked collaboratively?

Mary: Yes. It was an interesting, very heady time. I had gone to Scotland just then to study with Routley for a year. (Sidney Carter was there too, though he didn't meet with the Dunblane group. He wrote the text, "I Danced in the Morning when the World was Begun" using a borrowed tune in that case, but he wrote some very good tunes of his own as well.) I think the '60s were a remarkable era when new texts and tunes emerged. Some of them were probably unusable, but they pushed the boundaries of what could be said in a hymn.

Sometimes such textual experimentation causes trouble in knowing how to use the piece. It is a bit like the difficulty of using a non-Western piece in worship. It has to be placed very well or it doesn't work.

Charlotte: Did published collections of songs result from the Dunblane meetings?

Mary: Yes, two small volumes of *Dunblane Praises*. The texts are complex and difficult. But they are interesting along with the melody and the musical accompaniment. One example is "Christ, Burning Past All Suns:"[4]

2. Christ, holding
   atoms in one
   loom of light and power
   to weave creation's life:
   Man, moulding
   rocket, gun,
   turns creation sour,
   plots dissolving strife.

3. Christ, festive
   in gay bird,
   rush of river flood,
   joy on lovers' part:
   Youth, restive,
   seek new word,
   beat of life in blood,
   chill of death in heart.

4. Christ, humble
   on our side,
   snatching death's grim keys,
   ending Satan's scope:
   We gamble
   on our guide,
   inch our gains of peace,
   work a work of hope.

The contrast between God and humanity was present in all stanzas. (Incidentally, the texts are full of the masculine gender. In the '60s, gender was not such an issue as it came to be later.)

Often the music ended indecisively, pointing back to the beginning. The melodies might have a very wide range, much wider leaps than usual. I think "Christ, Burning Past All Suns" is quite a nice one, but I've never seen it printed in any hymnal.

Charlotte: Did the Dunblane hymns find their way into mainstream use?

Mary: Very few did. I believe people could not sing them with ease. They were probably too difficult for congregational use.

Charlotte: The wide range of "Christ, Burning" would make it unsingable for many.

Mary: Another example is from *Dunblane Praises*, No 2, "Lord, We Are Blind," with words by David Edge and music by Peter Cutts, who is still writing.[5] His tune BRIDEGROOM appears in a number of hymnals.

2. Lord, we are blind; the world around
   confuses us, although we see.
   In Christ the pattern is refound;
   he sets us free.

3. Lord, we are blind; our sight, our life
   by our own efforts cannot be.
   Spit on our clay and touch our eyes;*
   we would serve Thee.

*This is the text authorized by David Edge. Unauthorized text that actually appeared in *Dunblane Praises* was "Touch thou our eyes and give us sight."

And again, this one points back to the beginning. I think that's quite nice. And then Peter Cutts sets a text about the city by Erik Routley.[6] This in most hymnals now, so the text works in today's world.

1. All who love and serve your city,
   all who bear its daily stress,
   all who cry for peace and justice,
   all who curse and all who bless.

2. In your day of loss and sorrow,
   in your day of helpless strife,
   honour, peace and love retreating,
   seek the Lord, who is your life.

3. In your day of wealth and plenty,
   wasted work and wasted play,
   call to mind the word of Jesus,
   'Work ye yet while it is day.'

4. For all days are days of judgment,
   and the Lord is waiting still,
   drawing near to men who spurn him,
   offering peace from Calvary's hill.

5. Risen Lord, shall yet the city
   be the city of despair?
   Come to-day, our Judge, our Glory,
   be its name, 'The Lord is there!'

Then you'd want to look at "God Came, Body and Blood" by Peter Youngson.

1. God came,
    Body and blood,
    Body and blood,
    Into His earth.
 Herod faced it,
    Made his own mind up,
    Made his own mind up,
    "Kill Him at birth."

REFRAIN: Break the body, spill the blood!
        Break the body, spill the blood!
            "Kill Him at birth."

2. Christ came
    Saying "I am,"
    Saying "I am,"
    Was it a lie?
 Caiaphas faced Him,
    Made his own mind up,
    Made his own mind up,
    "Blasphemers must die."

                REFRAIN

3. Christ stood,
    "I am the truth."
    "I am the truth."
    They heard him say.
 Pilate heard Him,
    Washed his own hands clean,
    Washed his own hands clean,
    "Take Him away."   REFRAIN

4. Christ hung,
    Nailed out to die,
    Nailed out to die,
    "Father, forgive!"
 Everyone mocked Him,
    Buried their feelings,
    Buried their feelings,
    "Don't let Him live." REFRAIN

5. Christ rose,
    Showing his scars,
    Showing His scars,
    "Give Him His right."
 We obedient,
    Eat at His table,
    Eat at His table,
    Live in His might.   REFRAIN

It turns out to be triumphant at the end. But one may have a hard time getting a congregation to sing "Break the body, spill the blood." It's so vivid. And that's the way many of these texts are. But it was a fascinating direction in hymnody, I think.

Charlotte: So were theologians, those trained in theology, writing these?

Mary: The writers were from all kinds of backgrounds. They were theologians, they were musicians, sometimes it would be a priest musician, like Erik Routley, a Congregational minister and a fine musician.

There was such a need for this work. The first half of the twentieth century produced rather dull hymnody. We hardly sing any of the hymns written at that time any more. They often referenced "brotherhood of man" and "fatherhood of God." Many social Gospel texts sounded dated. We needed something new.

Charlotte: Do you think the importance of these meetings wasn't so much that the resulting texts and music were important, but that the meetings spawned later hymns that turned out to be valuable?

Mary: Yes.

Charlotte: So it was important to do this work, not as an end in itself, but because it allowed hymn writers to take steps forward into new music.

Forward from Dunblane

Mary: It didn't happen only in Dunblane. That was the first such event I am aware of, except for Sidney Carter's songs. But it was happening in the U.S.A., too.

In 1963 the Lutherans published *Songs for Today*[8] for use in Bible study. As with most of these paperback hymnbooks, the manuscript notation is difficult to read. But they offered fresh ideas. They often used music of familiar ballads and folk songs with biblical words to fit their purposes for Bible study. The "Ballad of Holy History," for example, had nineteen or twenty verses. It gave a way of singing through the whole story of God's acts in history.

Charlotte: A concise version of the Bible sung in nineteen or twenty verses![9] It is clear from the introduction to *Songs for Today* that the book was a utilitarian experiment in the use of music to carry religious content:

> Probably this book cannot please all; but it will stir from apathy. If the music is rejected, the gospel is not harmed. If it is seen as a bridge to the treasures of the church, present and future, it has served its purpose. And, if occasionally a song has strength enough to survive this present time, God's will be done. Charles Wesley wrote a multitude of hymns which have not remained, but the writing was worth it for the several which are perennial.[10]

Mary: In the same collection is a Latvian melody, "By the Babylonian Waters," a setting of Psalm 137. The Lord's Prayer (Our Father) is set in Caribbean style. These songs are not all great music and poetry in and of themselves. But this little book is important both for its support of their experiment in Bible study, and its contribution to future collections.

Charlotte: I see that "O Jesus Christ, May Grateful Hymns Be Rising" was included the *Lutheran Book of Worship*[11] and "By the Babylonian Rivers" in the supplement *With One Voice*.[12]

Mary: Yes, and into other books. The World Council of Churches borrowed from the Lutherans in their 1966 book called *Risk: New Hymns for a New Day*.[13] Isn't it interesting they called it "Risk"? In the introduction a statement is made that there is a risk the songs might be seen as an ends in themselves, making a sort of permanent hymnal. Rather, the editor wanted the songs to be tried, and thrown away if necessary. That really was a revelation to me, that there are disposable pieces which can be valuable. The book began with a melody from Thailand. Then the Sri Lankan hymn writer D. T. Niles brought Sri Lankan tunes to the church. *Risk* includes Sidney Carter's "Every Star Shall Sing a Carol." That's such an interesting one because it reflects on the implications of space travel on hymns. Quite a number of Sidney Carter's songs were included, among them, one for Good Friday titled "Friday Morning." Here is the first stanza and refrain:

> "It was on a Friday morning and they took me from the cell,
> And I saw they had a carpenter to crucify as well.
> You can blame it onto Pilate, you can blame it on the Jews,
> You can blame it on the devil, it's God I accuse.
> Refrain: It's God they ought to crucify instead of you and me,
> I said to the Carpenter a-hanging on the tree."[14]

Charlotte: Wow! That is a text no one could fall asleep singing. It is difficult to understand on a first encounter.

Mary: And it is a text that would be difficult to sing many times because it is so startling. It is a kind of protest song, don't you think? Some of Carter's texts like this one use irony. Irony is hard to grasp. Does irony belong in hymns? The cross-cultural experience raises that kind of question.

Risk also used familiar texts with new musical styles. Here is an example of "O Come, O Come, Emmanuel" whose ancient text is supported by a calypso rhythm, as <u>1</u> 2 3, <u>4</u> 5 6, <u>7</u> 8, in a Caribbean or African style.[15]

Charlotte: But the rhythm of the tune is very straight. It's just the accompaniment that is different.

Mary: Yes, and that may tell us something. It's often true with the contemporary praise songs that the tune may be very singable, but the accompaniment changes it completely. And maybe that takes it in a direction that makes sense for congregational use. It definitely makes it a unison rather than four-part song.

O COME, O COME, EMMANUEL

Tune: James Minchin
Text: 18th Century trans. T.A.L.

New Music at Work in the Liturgy

Charlotte: Can you explain your epiphany about throw-away music? Does it have a role, and should it have a role in the music of the church?

Mary: Yes, I think throw-away music has a role. It gives people ideas that hymns printed in a book are not necessarily there forever. Sometimes a composer will write something for a given occasion and then expect that it belongs in a hymnal. We faced that so much when we worked on both Mennonite hymnbooks. It is not a common understanding that a hymn, once written, isn't meant to last forever. Otherwise, we wouldn't have any changes. We'd do like the Amish and sing the same hymns that were sung in the sixteenth century with no changes except those that occur naturally over the years in a oral society.

Charlotte: Why is it important to have new music, instead of just finding something good and doing it again and again from generation to generation?

Mary: I believe we need both the hymns that have earned a permanent place in our church life as well as those we want to test. I found a section in *Trouble at the Table*, a book on worship by Thomas Troeger and Carol Doran helpful in this respect.[16] (They in turn give credit to the Dutch theologian Edward Schillebeeckx for the model they describe.) They suggest thinking of the historical aspect of worship as three concentric circles revolving around a single axis. The central core, which they call "structural," consists of those practices which are essential to a congregation—the heart of its beliefs and rituals. The outer circle, "ephemeral," draws in new elements which are not yet tested for their enduring qualities. Between the inner and outer circles is the "conjunctural" circle, which can participate in both or either the structural or ephemeral, in the pull toward the center or the releasing of intensity toward the edge.[17]

If we view hymns with this model, we can recognize those hymns which speak for the congregation most honestly and are central to its worship life. We can welcome new hymns that bring vitality for the moment, or perhaps for a longer time. If a new hymn works, it may move to the more stable conjectural position, or even to the center. And some of the favorites outlive their usefulness and move out of the core. If we recognize the fluid character of our hymn choices—always changing if our church life in dynamic—we need not be threatened by change.

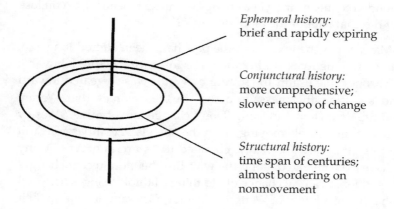

Ephemeral history: brief and rapidly expiring

Conjunctural history: more comprehensive; slower tempo of change

Structural history: time span of centuries; almost bordering on nonmovement

Charlotte: Perhaps change in music is a metaphor for the evolving Christian life. The Christian life has to be constantly relived, re-created, renewed. Theology changes. So it would be natural for hymnody and the ways of expressing Christianity and theology in music to change.

Mary: Yes, that seems to be another way of stating the flux in the repertoire that is used. Somehow it seems to give more freedom to accept change.

Charlotte: What makes for the enduring hymns that either stay for generations, or are revived after a period of disuse? Are there any common characteristics for these texts and music?

Mary: I guess I've changed my convictions about what is good by exploring the hymns of other cultures. I can't judge what's good in another culture. But you're not necessarily asking about another culture. But even in my culture, I suppose there are things that wear well, things you miss when they're left out of a hymnal, that have functioned in important ways in worship. For instance, I miss "Eternal Father When to Thee, Beyond All Worlds by Faith I Soar." We sang it often in my congregation. Of course, it was removed from the most recent hymnal because it used the word "Father" in the first line, even though the next stanza includes the "Son," and then the "Spirit," and finally the "Trinity." That hymn was about the imminence and transcendence of God. And I miss it. The tune may not be great, but it functioned well in my childhood, and later, until the language became a problem. This brought both necessary and disruptive change. One cannot help but feel torn about some of these losses.

Charlotte: What can be done with a text that no longer means what it was intended to mean, and yet a change of the text means that you lose some of the character of the piece of music?

Mary: Many times the texts from the past have been altered long ago, and have had long lives of alteration. For instance, "Before Jehovah's Awful Throne," the Psalm 100 setting by Watts, was so geared toward England shouting the message across to the colonies that Wesley changed the Watts text, but said, "Don't change any of mine." Wesley talked about the bowels moving, as in the bowels of compassion. You couldn't say that now! So it was changed to "Mercies move." Many things have been changed along the way. But the more recent changes were so sudden, a radical change of old things. I think changes occurred in the shaping of a hymn of Watts and Wesley, for example, within their generations. They changed by 1780 when John Wesley made a collection of hymns. That was within the lifespan of these people. That seems different from seeing those things change now. But, of course, they don't mean the same thing. For example, "worm," as in "for such a worm as I," in "Alas, and did my Savior bleed" doesn't mean the same thing as it did in Watts' day. We can hardly use it now.

Charlotte: In some ways we have a multicultural environment in our U.S. churches.

Mary: Yes. Every time we sing a song in church a cross-cultural element is present. It's both historical and geographic. We move back into history and across the globe.

Charlotte: Do you think at this point in your life that you're a good predictor of hymns that will last, those that will work for a long period of time?

Mary: No. Oh, I suppose, things that I like immediately I probably think will last, but I may be wrong. After working on two hymnals, I'm convinced that the things I thought might be great don't necessarily work in the congregation.

What about Quality?

Charlotte: Have you changed your mind about what makes for greatness, or has following the use of those hymns you thought were great changed your mind?

Mary: Probably both. I know I've changed my mind. I was brought up to think, for example, that Gospel hymns were just not right for us to sing. But when we take a whole category of songs—I suppose, like contemporary Christian—and say that they are all bad, we create problems. I was brought up never to sing Gospel songs. If we did, it was with regret. That made it difficult to work on a hymnal where I knew we had to have some Gospel songs. I finally understood that I needed to change. But in those days, in the 1960s, our compiling committee isolated the Gospel songs in a section of their own in the hymnal.

Charlotte: You could box in the Gospel songs so they would not contaminate the rest.

Mary: That's exactly what happened. We put them into a section of their own. And so, I would notice that after a few years that the Gospel songs part of the hymnal would be soiled in some churches and pure white in others. But as time went on I learned to like Gospel songs, in part because I recognized how valuable they were to individuals I knew and to whole congregations. In addition, my research into the background of hymns—the context for writing, the author's complete text, and the original form of the music—interested me, opened my mind, and helped break down my prejudices. When I found a Gospel song after a long search, it was like discovering a friend.

Gospel songs often have good melodies, and interesting rhythm. Many of them are in dactylic or anapestic poetic meter instead of iambic or trochaic, and they just roll on. For example, consider the texts of "When Peace Like a River Attendeth My Way," "Great Is Thy

Faithfulness," and "Softly and Tenderly Jesus Is Calling." The use of new poetic meters encouraged the use of compound musical meters such as 6/8, 9/8, and 12/8. The result was added variety in hymnody.

Charlotte: I was surprised to learn, when attending a hymn sing only a few years ago at Goshen College, that the students really like the Gospel songs. At the very end of the hymn sing when the leader took requests, there were overwhelming numbers who requested "Wonderful Grace of Jesus." That is what we used to sing when I was in high school! I would have thought this generation of students would think "Wonderful Grace of Jesus" was very, very dated. But the college students like it so much—it is the song they request whenever they have a chance.

Mary: Probably because they sang it in their homes. If it is what they sang when they were young, it comes back with pleasure.

Charlotte: And now it starts a new generation of people singing.

Mary: Yes. That happened all along, though we tried not to sing Gospel songs when I first was teaching. We were trying to shape the students' education in a direction we chose for them. We did not ask them, "What would you like to sing?" We just dictated their musical taste.

Charlotte: You gave them what was good for them?

Mary: What we *thought* was good for them. We were the dictators of the musical taste—a position I now find quite unattractive.

Charlotte: What is in between being the dictator of style and taste, on the one hand, and saying on the other hand, "If you like it, it's good"? What constitutes music that is worthy? What keeps us singing?

Mary: The music has to have substance of some kind. It has to be singable. It has to work in the congregation. I'm not so sure that I feel as much the need for new music as the need for new ways of singing. Our hymnals give us no help with the duration of the notes: How long shall we hold them? We tend to sing all our hymns with the same durations and with the same kind of voice. Are we approaching our music with our eyes rather than our ears? I think we could hear the spirit of a piece if we didn't look at the notes so much. For example, a leader could say that we're going to sing "Let our gladness have no end," in a spirited way, or simply introduce it by singing a phrase or two in a suitable style.

Charlotte: I like your point that the written pages are a poor representation of the sounds we should really hear. There is another world that exists beyond that printed page. How do we transcend the page into that beautiful world?

Mary: And how do we create respect for that other world, because the oral learning is not valued by our literate culture.

Charlotte: When we are trained as classical musicians, part of our training is to sit at the feet of musicians who have interpreted musical texts, and we learn what is beyond the page. We learn how to move from the printed page into sound from those who have experience and wisdom in doing that. Then at some point we also learn how to listen inside ourselves to hear what begs to be given to the music. Is this similar to how oral learning is viewed in other cultures?

Mary: The oral world is perhaps even more important for people who do not read music, but rather sing what they hear. But their music has not been respected just as oral history is often not respected.

Charlotte: The suspicion is that if it is not written, it may not have value.

Mary: And that it may not be true. Alex Haley's book *Roots* was discredited by a number of historians who said the sources could not be verified. If the sources come from people . . .

Charlotte: . . . they're not reliable.

Mary: The oral world must be respected so that we catch what is beyond written notes. Written notation is simply an aid.

Crossing Cultures

Charlotte: What happened when you first began to cross cultures? What did you discover?

Mary: Well, I saw, for example, that the sounds of traditional instruments of Africa were new to me. They were seldom sustained and were often fleeting, whether plucking metal keys mounted on resonating wood or playing a fiddle by plucking the strings. You don't play a bowed instrument in the traditional ways I was taught for the cello. Very little sound is produced with that method. In Uganda, the bow plays something like a continuous tremolo of a Western stringed instrument. So the tone quality differs from Western to African cultures, and within cultures in Africa rattles and shakers are always present. What is considered beautiful in tone quality is very different.

I noticed also that my conviction that every piece must have a climax was challenged when I heard African pieces. I couldn't find a climax in African music. Then I began to realize that there may not be one. I'd ask my African friends, and they'd say, "Well, if you understood the words you might get it." But in Western music with words, both words and music tend to reach a climax together.

Charlotte: So the focus of the African music was not the destination, but rather the journey?

Mary: The journey is one of cyclical motion, repetition, a little pattern just going on and on and on, but with no apparent arrival.

In my early days of teaching I purposely chose art works with a clear climax or focus in order to illustrate one of the principles of organization found in the related arts (along with unity, repetition, variety, and balance). Climax seemed to be grounded in ancient Grecian thought. When Aristotle talked about drama in his *Poetics,* he pointed to a beginning, middle, and end. The plot developed organically toward a climax and then subsided. As I tried to make sense of the seeming lack of climax in African music, I found an analogy to a river helpful. In Western music we follow the river from its source to its climax as it reaches the sea. Smetana's program work *The Moldau,* has such a continuous growth and crescendo. In African music we sit on the bank and watch the river flow by. It does have a beginning and ending, but we see its continuous, dependable flow.

These differences seem to me to stem from different perceptions of time. The Western world focuses on the present and the future; we live much of our time in the future. The traditional African world values the present and especially the rich past, incorporating the ancestors. I have found little writing about the subject of time and climax in African music, but one ethnomusicologist, Ruth M. Stone,[18] described community music-making in Liberia, where she had grown up with the people and the language. As the music for a given gathering progressed, various groups within the community made their musical contributions; but when the spirits of the ancestors arrived, the music reached its height. That explanation interests me very much, but I cannot recognize the coming of the ancestors.

Charlotte: Is that because it's not within your cultural framework to understand?

Mary: Yes. My Western mind creates barriers to thinking the spirits could actually come.

Charlotte: Is the music louder, more exuberant?

Mary: No, I suspect that something happens among the people, when all the forces of music and dance combine. I assume that they recognize something is going on, even if I am unaware.

Charlotte: How did you go about learning about African music?

Mary: I learned the most about the pattern and shape of African music by actually trying to play and sing traditional songs. I took lessons on the mbira, a box or board base on which lamellae, or metal keys, are strapped. Kizza, my teacher, gave me brief patterns on the keys and a few phrases to sing. I was grateful for this minimum of materials because, though they looked simple, the playing and singing were far outside my experience. But as it became easier I began to wonder about the continuous repetition that could go on for many minutes, so I asked him what I considered an obvious question, "How do I know when to stop?" It was so Western a question that he was baffled by it. He finally offered, "Stop when you want to." "Stop when you are tired." "Stop when you want to tune." "Stop when someone pays you and you want to put the money away." The continuous repetitions finally helped me to experience a bit of another dimension of time, completely new to me.

Charlotte: What about the idea of climax in Asian music?

Mary: I'm not sure. I have not lived there long enough to generalize. Much of what I hear in Taiwan is Western. I'm trying to think of the zither playing I've heard. We have a student who plays wonderful things on the zither. So often Asian traditional music is related to nature. Its titles suggest cherry blossoms or the tree in bloom, or the stream, with water dripping or flowing.

Charlotte: Which would not necessarily indicate a climax.

Mary: No. I hear it as a continuous flowing. What strikes me about the Asian music I know, in addition, is that their melodies are so richly ornamented. And in contrast to the outward energy of African music, Asian music often pulls inward and makes room for reflection.

Charlotte: What did you find when you began to compare our church music with that of other cultures?

Mary: When I first listened to Africans singing hymns, I was very much troubled by the predominance of Western styles and the loss of the unique character of African traditional music. As I listened carefully, however, I noticed ways in which they contextualized, that is, adapted to their local style, in order to own their songs. For example, in a rousing singing of "Stand Up, Stand Up for Jesus" in Accra, Ghana, I heard a wonderful complexity of simultaneous lines of drumming along with a typical gong rhythm, sounded with claps as well as a metal gong. They used four-part harmonies, but the overwhelming effect was rhythmic.

When missionaries first came, they often took hymns from their own culture and presented them as "Christian." The first truly indigenous African Christian hymn of which I am aware was the "Great Hymn" of the South African leader, Ntsikana, in the early nineteenth century. Although its images and musical style grew directly out of its Xhosa culture, the missionaries could not accept it, probably because they could not understand it; so it went underground for more than 150 years. It would have been hard for any Westerner to understand the shape of the music, which was far from a Western form. It repeated one descending phrase throughout the entire hymn, for the refrain as well as the verses; Western hymns tend to balance upward and downward motion in a melody.

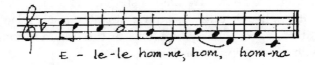

It was probably accompanied by the musical bow with which percussive sounds were much more important than pitches. We can speculate, from the oral tradition that exists today, that a variety of complex rhythms appeared from one performance to another. One which was recorded in our time, for example, moves in this lively rhythm:

So Ntsikana's Xhosa people were left with learning British hymns whose imagery and musical style were foreign to them.

At the Mennonite World Conference in Bulawayo, Zimbabwe, in August 2003, we sang a number of songs from the Brethren in Christ repertory. Although the norm for singing hymns seemed to be the four-part and unaccompanied style of southern Africa, one song recurred so often that it proved to be the informal theme song for the week. This is the way I heard it, although rhythms differed from one performance to another:

They sang in four parts, but drummers added a typically African element, a grouping of two pulses against three. Not only did the congregation clap, often reinforcing the two-against-three rhythm, but they acted out the verse, "We ran and ran everywhere; we turned and turned everywhere; we searched and searched everywhere. There is no one like him." It was close to dance in a church where dance was not usual. They brought this otherwise international pop song style into their own traditional world. The enthusiasm for joining the body with the mind in worship was palpable.

Charlotte: Does the West contextualize the singing of non-Western songs?

Mary: Yes. Thirty years ago, as Westerners began to publish cross-cultural hymns in their hymnals, the editors contextualized by writing down hymns that were originally oral and often did not fit a foreign notation. Then they added three parts to every melody so that songs looked like typical Western hymns. This has changed. Now they present single melodies with a possible percussion accompaniment or other suitable performance suggestions. This practice looks deceivingly simple, but it reminds us to consult authentic sources, either people or recordings, to learn the sound of a cross-cultural hymn.

I suppose I have a double standard. I am happy, on the one hand, to see Africans, who lost something of their own culture when they accepted Christianity, now contextualize as they use hymns from the outside. In doing so, they are recovering some of the uniqueness of their view of the world. On the other hand, I hope that Westerners, who have been free to choose what and how they sing in worship, will move into the unknown field of understanding the African modes of worship rather than altering the new to their level of comfort.

Incorporating Music of Other Cultures

Charlotte: Could we think about function of music in worship now? Is there a point at which we embrace our own culture, and the music we know, in order to go deeper rather than broader? What is the value of incorporating the music of another culture into our own?

Mary: Well, for me, it's learning other ways to know and experience God in worship. That's a humbling experience, I believe, and especially for Americans. We often think everything we do is better than others. I want to understand what is beautiful to those in cultures other than our own.

Charlotte: And do you find that helps to understand your own?

Mary: Yes. Other cultures open my ears to more possibilities of sound, and help me to recognize greater variety of approaches to my own music. I notice that some Western hymns call for more rhythmic energy of the sort that I hear in Africa, and others have the inwardness and meditative character of Asia.

Charlotte: How can other-culture music be introduced into worship without its being received as merely novel, or entertaining?

Mary: Ethnic music may be, at first, novel and exotic and entertaining. That's inevitable. Its novelty may actually lure us into trying to learn it. But its function is not to be novel. I think a hymn has to be placed appropriately so that its function is clear. That's really very important.

And if we want to move our congregation beyond its usual comfort level, we need to begin with small steps. We can search for an appropriate occasion for using just one cross-cultural hymn. For example, at a time when the congregation needs to lament, a *Kyrie Eleison* from another culture may be appropriate. The concept of praying for mercy is familiar, so the congregation could catch the intensity of the prayer through a Russian Orthodox tune:[19]

Kyrie eleison
ORTHODOX KYRIE

Ky - ri-e e - lei - son.* Ky - ri-e e - lei - son.

Ky - ri-e e - le - i - son.

Translation: Lord, have mercy.

Text: Greek litany
Music: Russian Orthodox liturgy

. . . . . one from Ghana:[20]

Greek Ky - ri-e e - le - i - son. Ky - ri-e e - le - i - son.
English Lord,_____ have mer - cy. Lord,_____ have mer - cy.

Note: Lower voices may hum.

Ky - ri-e e - le - i - son. Ky - ri-e e - le - i - son.
Lord,_____ have mer - cy. Lord,_____ have mer - cy.

Text: Early Greek liturgy
Music: Dinah Reindorf (b. 20th cent.), Ghana; arr. *Sing! A New Creation*

. . . or one from Pakistan:[21]

Have Mercy on Us, LORD
(Urdhu: Khudaayaa, raeham kar)

(♩=88)

1,3.Khu - daa - yaa rae - ham kar, Khu - daa - yaa rae - ham,
(1,3.Have mer - cy on us, LORD, have mer - cy on us.

o = <u>ching chap</u>, finger cymbals

Words: Traditional, Pakistan
Music: *KHUDAAYAA*; R. F. Liberius, Pakistan

The experience would offer the possibility of connecting effectively with the religious worldview of another culture.

We could also approach the complexities of a cross-cultural hymn gradually. We can begin examining the character of the music. In "Come, Lord Jesus Christ"[22] from Bangladesh the melody moves predominantly downward, unlike many Western hymn tunes. It does not use chords because its character is best revealed in the ornaments that slide upward into the adjacent note. The only instrument suggested is the *ching chap*, two small cymbals or bells, whose reverberation calls for intensity of listening. Perhaps one should begin with the undecorated melody. The melody begins on *mi*, which the congregation could hum quietly and sustain as a drone throughout the piece as the leader sings the undecorated melody. Then the slides and *ching chap* could be

Come, Lord Jesus Christ

(Bengali: Esho hae Probhu)

E - sho hae Pro - bhu Tu - mi dho - ra yee - sho,
Come, O Je - sus Christ, make your dwell- ing with us.

Am - ra ro - ey - chi ja - gro - to.
We shall be watch - ful through the night;

Bho - rer - a shaye mo - ra ja - gro - to,
we'll wait with hope for your Day to dawn.

Muk - ti - da - ta tu - mi dho - ra yee - sho.
Come, set us free, all our trust is in you;

E - sho hae Pro - bhu Tu - mi dho - ra yee - sho.
now, O Je - sus Christ, make your dwell- ing with us.

Words and Music: Bart Shaha   o = ching chap

added, and eventually members of the congregation could be invited to sing either the drone or the melody.

Another example comes from the Methodist church in Nigeria, "Jesus, We Want to Meet."[23] It has a refrain, "on this thy holy day," which is all the congregation needs to sing. The rhythm throughout alternates by the measure between 3/4 and 6/8. The people could clap this rhythm first, or tap on their legs for the more timid person. Then half the group could clap three beats for each measure while the other half claps two beats. Finally, one person could add the important west and central African gong rhythm which covers twelve beats for each two measures: we could treat this as **1** 2 **3** 4 **5 6** | 7 **8** 9 **10** 11 **12** | (accents on bold), which Africans

Jesus, we want to meet

Irregular

1 Je - sus, we want to meet on this thy
2 We kneel in awe and fear on this thy
3 Thy bless - ing, Lord, we seek on this thy
4 Our minds we ded - i - cate on this thy

ho - ly day. We gath - er 'round thy throne
ho - ly day, pray God to teach us here
ho - ly day. Give joy of thy vic - to - ry
ho - ly day, heart and soul con - se - crate

on this thy ho - ly day. Thou art our
on this thy ho - ly day. Save us and
on this thy ho - ly day. Through grace a - lone
on this thy ho - ly day. Ho - ly Spir - it,

heav'n - ly friend, hear our prayers as they as - cend.
cleanse our hearts, lead and guide our acts of praise,
are we saved. In thy flock may we be found.
make us whole. Bless the ser - mon in this place,

Look in - to our hearts and minds to - day, on this thy ho - ly day.
and our faith from seed to flow - er raise, on this thy ho - ly day.
Let the mind of Christ a - bide in us on this thy ho - ly day.
and as we go, lead us, Lord; we shall be thine ev - er - more.

* The rhythm pattern spans two measures, or the equivalent of 12 eighth notes:

LO KON KO LO KON KON KO

Text: A. T. Olajide Olude; tr. Biodun Adebesin, versified by Austin C. Lovelace

Music: Nigerian melody; adapted by A. T. Olajide Olude

would count using syllables the LO KON KO LO (see example). It is the rhythm the composer suggested, and with it we clearly cross into another culture. If we were to add harmonies to the melody, as was done when first published, we would be contextualizing and Westernizing it.

Charlotte: How did your Mennonite heritage allow you to experience other cultures?

Mary: In working on a hymnal all through the 1960s, I discovered that I had to deal with the different cultures within my own congregation that I would not have acknowledged before. The Gospel song culture, African American culture, the German Chorale culture—what is good within each? The "good hymn" became not what I preferred, but what makes for an effective, nourishing congregational hymn. It is less absolute than I believed earlier.

Mennonites meet in a world conference every six years. I was asked in 1978 to lead singing at the Mennonite World Conference in Wichita, Kansas. This was the first time that we had a book with songs from five continents. It was a heady experience to try these hymns with the help of a choir for leading the congregation. We had to find out from national delegates what was the appropriate sound for each culture. The congregation was very lively. They were responsive to trying this music with the people who represented these different cultures. That made a very profound impact on me, and my cross-cultural education advanced.

Over the years I visited a number of Mennonite, as well as other missionaries, who offered me valuable insights into the cultures where they lived. They were continually dealing with what it means to cross cultures, and I began to see the complexity of their work in a new light. Although they dealt with many kinds of cultural and religious issues, some of them were very sensitive to the particulars of music for the church. I was in Africa shortly after Vatican II of 1964 opened the way for indigenous musical practices in the Catholic Church, and I was fortunate to witness the process of change among both Catholics and Protestants during the 1970s and '80s.

Charlotte: While studying Western music history chronologically, we begin with the single lines of Gregorian chant, moving to polyphony, and then on to increasingly more complex music, based on the written texts that survive. Since my college years, I have learned that oral music had complexity beyond one line long before Gregorian chant was sung.

Mary: We don't have the oral history of these ancient times. But one can guess from recordings of hunters and gatherers today, like the

Baka and other Pygmy groups of central Africa and the San (Bushmen) of Botswana, that oral music has been more complex than Westerners have generally thought. As soon as we try to notate it, we oversimplify because we are using a system of writing that does not fit the sounds.

Charlotte: Certainly your African experience would indicate that is true, or Bartok's experiences in Eastern Europe would as well.

Charlotte: Do all cultures take seriously the passing of music traditions from one generation to another?

Mary: I don't know. I am aware, however, that Gambia and Zimbabwe are two countries in Africa where a few families of musicians carry musical traditions from generation to generation. This would be true of drummers, too, in cultures where families taught the drumming techniques for generation after generation. In Gambia, I studied the kora, a twenty-one-stringed instrument. There were four families in Gambia that played it. I studied with a man whose son chose not to learn the instrument. The father tried to teach on television and in schools. It was very sad that after hundreds of years the generational line was broken. The secret societies and the educators of the age groups have helped to carry on the traditions. Traditional society took seriously the education of the young. But perhaps a breakdown is inevitable. Traditional life disintegrates as people move to cities.

Music as a Means of Understanding and Building Community

Charlotte: What is unique in the cultural context of the church that we should keep in mind as we study its music?

Mary: Well, I believe that the corporate aspect is most important. Church means community. We are talking about "we" even when singing "I." For example, when an African American congregation sings "Sometimes I feel like a motherless child," "I" means "we" because everyone is feeling like a motherless child. Singing in a group means to sing "we." And the corporate group is more important than the individual. So in order to understand how to choose music appropriately, I think we have to think about what is possible for a particular group of people. We make judgments about what we use because of the group rather than because of individual tastes.

Charlotte: What value does the music of other cultures have to our religious experience?

Mary: I think it broadens our experience, but then, why is it important to have a broader experience? I guess that is a given for me. It's better to have a broader than a narrow religious experience because it deepens our own faith and helps us to understand a wider view of faith than we would otherwise know. It opens our spirits, I think, to new possibilities, to new senses, to gaining information and experience in different ways.

Charlotte: Some have said that new developments in theology will come out of artistic experience. What better way to do that than to understand the one art that we know and that has always been associated with our faith, that is, our music. How better can we develop our own faith than by understanding how music has affected other cultures, to see our own in contrast, and to open our eyes and ears in new ways of experiencing God through music of other Christians?

Mary: You have put that well. I might add that, in these times when we have an urgent need to understand rather than fear people who differ from us, singing the strangers' songs offers an attractive possibility for creating peace amid our differences.

Notes

1. *The English Hymnal* (Oxford: Oxford University Press, 1906) xiii.
2. *Sound the Bamboo* (Tainan, Taiwan: Taiwan Presbyterian Church Press, 1990; 2000) 24.
3. *The Worshipbook* (Philadelphia: The Westminster Press, 1975) 413.
4. *Dunblane Praises No. 1* (Dunblane, Perthshire: Scottish Churches' House, Consultation on Music, 1964) No. 2.
5. *Dunblane Praises No. 2* (Dunblane, Perthshire: Scottish Churches' House, Consultation on Music, 1967) No. 3.
6. Ibid., No. 4.
7. Ibid., No. 16.
8. John Ylvisaker (music) and Ewald Bash (text), ed., *Songs for Today* (Minneapolis: Youth Department of the American Lutheran Church, 1963).
9. Ibid., 26–9.
10. Ibid., 3.
11. *Lutheran Book of Worship* (Minneapolis: Augsburg Publishing House, 1978) 427.
12. *With One Voice* (Minneapolis: Augsburg Fortress, 1995) 656.
13. *Risk: New Hymns for a New Day*, vol. II, no. 3 (Geneva, Switzerland: Youth Departments of the World Council of Churches and World Council of Christian Education, 1966).
14. Ibid., 19.
15. Ibid., 22.
16. Carol Doran and Thomas H. Troeger, *Trouble at the Table: Gathering the Tribes for Worship* (Nashville: Abingdon Press, 1992) 119–23.
17. Ibid., 119.

18. Ruth M. Stone, *Let the Inside Be Sweet: The Interpretation of Music Event among the Kpelle of Liberia* (Bloomington: Indiana University Press, 1982).

19. *Hymnal: A Worship Book*, 144.

20. *Sing! A New Creation* (Grand Rapids, MI: CRC Publications, 2001) 50.

21. *Sound the Bamboo*, 120.

22. Ibid., 8.

23. *Hymnal: A Worship Book*, 10.

12

Choosing Music for Worship

Charlotte Kroeker

Introduction

According to a 2002 survey of Protestant and Catholic churches in Indiana, the most difficult task of those responsible for planning worship was choosing music. Conflict over the kind of music to be chosen, who made those choices, and who offered the music adversely affects one of the major events in the life of a church, that of the community gathered for worship.[1] Indeed, it is much easier to speak theoretically than it is to participate in shaping the music practices of a real congregation. Music does not become truly problematic until we deal with the music itself in context. Attempting an essay about choosing music may seem foolhardy; yet, in the end, surely what matters is the practice of music in liturgy, yes? So in response to the concerns voiced nearly a century ago in the opening quotation of Robert Bridges from the introductory section of this book, concerns equally valid today, how can we think creatively about making musical choices that result in effective worship?

Simone Weil (1909–43), an early twentieth-century philosopher, saw beauty as an incarnation of God, and the arts (art, poetry, music) or anything we deem precious (love, justice, tradition, religious ceremony) as a bridge or "opening" for our souls to God.[2] Fr. Joseph Gelineau, a Roman Catholic priest in France who has given us much wisdom about music in liturgy, says music gives meaning to worship by its service to the worshiping congregation, inviting them to greater faith, hope, and love of the mystery of Jesus Christ.[3] Erik Routley (1917–82), a Congregational minister and musician from Britain who influenced much of twentieth-century hymnody, suggests that the music of worship should point to the death and resurrection of Christ, lead worshipers to a greater maturity in Christ, and spur the congregation to the building of God's kingdom.[4] Given that these are worthy goals for music in worship, how can this standard be reached in practice?

Just as the texts of the liturgy and the Scriptures help us choose with care the sermons we preach and the words or prayers we offer for worship, so effective worship and prayer also depend on the choice of music—the choice of texts we sing as well as the music that accompanies those texts, the coherence of the way the text and music fit together in dialogue, and how both together fit the action of the liturgy. In addition, the music must "fit" the congregation, so that it can be an effective vehicle for encouraging worship and prayer, or, perhaps, an appropriate response to a liturgical action that has just occurred.

How can we move from an appreciation of the role of music in enhancing worship to effective liturgy itself, given all the challenges involved? We will be guided here by three principles suggested earlier by Nicholas Wolterstorff, and a fourth that follows naturally from the first three: (1) The music should be aesthetically excellent. (2) The style of the music should be fitting to its placement in the liturgy. (3) The character of the music should fit the liturgical action, should fit the theologically correct understanding of that action, and it should be clear what that action is.[5] To these three principles, I add a fourth: (4) The context for liturgy is important, and, therefore, any musical choice must be based upon the awareness, knowledge, and experience of the congregation who will participate in the worship, and the environment in which the service will take place (day, season, circumstance, place).

In addressing these issues it is necessary to identify the nature of the music to which these principles pertain. That is no easy task. Some music is easily traced to an ethnic source (such as "Jesu, Jesu, Fill Us with Your Love," from Ghanaian origins) and some music has origins in the Western tradition (such as "Praise to the Lord, the Almighty," or music from the Taizé Community). Other music we use may originate in one tradition while being used primarily in another. Our music for worship is shared so prolifically that it is often difficult to find its denominational "home." Or, the music in question might be chant, which "belongs" to us all. Regardless of origin, the ecumenical music repertoire that is common to most English-speaking, Christian worship practice is the focus of this discussion. As ethnomusicologist Michael Hawn would remind us: "Singing global song is most effective in congregational settings where the musical traditions of a particular faith heritage are vibrant."[6] It is my intent to address the music with a faith heritage primarily in the Western tradition, although that will of necessity include music of other origins that has come to be included in the canon of music commonly used in English-speaking faith traditions.

Aesthetic Excellence

Aesthetic excellence in music is not easily determined in a postmodern age, and perhaps it is even more difficult to determine what counts as excellence for the music of the church. There are so many factors that come into play in any such judgment. Those who study ethnomusicology have defined it as "the division of musicology in which special emphasis is given to the study of music in its cultural context; the anthropology of music."[7] If we extrapolate from this definition, it could be argued that the music in any one congregation becomes their "ethnic" music for that context, and that excellence in that context is determined by looking at that music alone. Yet, much of the music sung or played in churches of the early part of the twenty-first century is common to churches within denominations, and also between denominations, including the music of most Protestants and, since Vatican II, Catholics. An ecumenism is apparent in the music of the Christian church, just as a lectionary and basic Christian doctrines are shared across denominations. So questions of excellence arise beyond the confines of any one congregation, and beyond the music originating in the United States and Europe as well. How can we develop discernment for excellence within this body of music?

A formally trained musician in Western traditions is likely to use fairly recognizable criteria to discern the quality of a piece of music. Is the melody a good one? Does the piece of music have contour, using harmonic and melodic tension and release, building dynamically and musically to a climax and subsiding? Does it combine elements of variety and sameness? As a whole, is it musically coherent? Does the harmony flow naturally, and does it adequately support any melody present? Has the piece survived the test of time? These are a few questions one could ask about any piece of music, regardless of its complexity.

For the purposes of this discussion, we will assume quality is not equated with complexity. Indeed, a simple piece of music, when well crafted, can be excellent. As Father Gelineau noted: "Simple music is not the same as poor music, and accessible music is not the same as banal music."[8]

But even if the criteria for excellence can be agreed upon, a piece of music for worship requires additional criteria beyond quality. For example, if its function is for congregational singing, does it have a melody that is singable for the average congregant? Is the text meaningful and theologically congruent within the faith tradition where it will be used? In addition, do the text and music work well together, each adding meaning to the other? Does it serve a helpful purpose in illumining the core ideas of a particular liturgy? Is it possible for the piece to be rendered effectively, given the musical ability of the musician in leadership and the congregation? Questions of quality may be a beginning point, but they are certainly not the only criteria to be considered, and perhaps not even the definitive criteria.

Fittingness of Style as to Placement in the Liturgy

Regardless of whether a worship service is "liturgical" or "nonliturgical," there is a pattern or plan for that worship. This implies that some music will be more effective at certain places than others. The right choice of music for a specific location in the liturgy can enhance or carry the liturgical meaning; conversely, the wrong choice may interrupt or distract the worshiper from the progression of the worship. For example, consider the location for the Agnus Dei, just before Communion. The text for the Agnus Dei gives us the nature and meaning of the moment:

> *Agnus Dei, qui tollis peccata mundi, Miserere nobis.*
> Lamb of God, who takes away the sin of the world, Have mercy on us.

It is a serious moment. The text is a plea for mercy (and later, for peace) from the Lamb of God, who has the power to take away our sins, as well as the sins of the entire world. Music chosen to accompany this text could either open us to experience the mystery of the moment, or it could trivialize it. How have composers met this challenge, and what does history have to tell us about the nature of appropriate music for this ageless text? Though there are countless settings of this text throughout history, here are four examples composed in three different time periods, and all are in use today. The first is a John Merbecke setting from the sixteenth century found in the Episcopal *Hymnal 1982* for the Rite I Mass.[9]

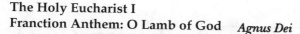

The Holy Eucharist I
Franction Anthem: O Lamb of God   *Agnus Dei*

Setting: John Merbecke (1518?–1585?); adapt. *Hymnal 1982*

This is clearly a piece intended for congregational use, with the melody in stepwise motion, and encompassing little more than a five-note range. The simplicity of the music and its rhythm seem appropriate to the text. The music and the text are bonded, with one note for each syllable of text. Nothing is startling, nothing detracts from the serious moment in the liturgy, and the straightforward setting allows congregational participation without worry about "performance." If the text is uttered, the music almost sings itself.

A second example, the "Agnus Dei" from the *Mass in B Minor* by J. S. Bach gives us a very different setting from the baroque period.[10] Note the plaintive, troubled sense of the piece. The simple scoring is for strings only (instruments sometimes thought to most resemble the human voice), and the contralto solo is in a minor key, perhaps signifying the personal nature of the plea. The melody is chromatic, making for a complex harmonic structure. The prayer is hardly perfunctory,

nor is the music, yet it is straightforward. The complex nature of the melody line does not lend itself to congregational singing, but the complexity of the music can certainly add meaning to the text for those who hear it sung.

A third example is found in *With One Voice*, the 1995 "extension" of the *Lutheran Book of Worship*, where we find a contemporary example of the Agnus Dei:[11]

Daniel Kallman (b. 1956)

The piece is intended for congregational participation, as is the Merbecke. The range of the melody is small, and the melody moves primarily by stepwise motion. Variety is achieved by transposing the second repetition of the text up a minor third, from the key of A to the key of C. The exact transposition makes it easy for the congregation to sing, as the intervals remain the same even though the pitch is higher. The third repetition returns to the original key. In both this piece and the Merbecke example, the text and the music are closely linked. There is nothing in the music to take away from the solemnity of the moment in the liturgy or the text. Instead, the music enhances and augments the depth of the liturgical moment.

A fourth, and another contemporary example, is Richard Proulx's "Agnus Dei" from *A Community Mass*:[12]

Note the use of the minor key, the plaintive nature of the melody, the close alliteration of text with the rhythm of the music. Again, the music is very singable on first encounter, and the simplicity of the setting enhances the solemnity of the moment.

What these examples have in common is straightforward, uncomplicated music. (The Bach is complex without being complicated; simple rhythms flow with the text.) A contrasting style or character of music to these examples would have a different effect. A syncopated rhythm, or otherwise complicated musical characteristics, would draw attention to the unique qualities of the music rather than allowing the flow of the liturgical text to occur. Or, if the congregation were asked to sing the "Agnus Dei" from the *Mass in B Minor*, all but very capable musicians would be consumed with the task of trying to sing the music rather than being able to concentrate on the liturgical moment, the action of the liturgy, and the meaning of the text. The accompaniments for the above examples are simple. If they were scored for a band, for example, or had busy organ accompaniments, the straightforward character of the music might likewise be lost. The dominance of the instrumental accompaniment would supersede the action of the liturgy.

Fit of Music and Theology to the Action of the Liturgy

A common but erroneous assumption, prevailing among musicians and theologians alike, is that good music training is good training for church music. A closely related assumption is that sacred art music belongs in the worship service because of its excellent quality. But as Wolterstorff says so eloquently in the first chapter of this book:

> At no point should the liturgy be halted so as to enable the choir to sing a religious anthem or a soloist to render special religious music. Mind you, I have no objection to concerts of religious music. Quite the contrary: my own life has been wonderfully enriched by attendance at such concerts. But the divine liturgy is not the occasion for concerts of religious music. Religious music may or may not be liturgically appropriate music.[13]

A good musician knows very well how to choose and perform quality music. In addition to these competencies, a good church musician knows what music is appropriate for worship, where it belongs in the liturgy, how it should be offered in order to fit the liturgical action, and how it will lead the congregation into worship and prayer.

Wolterstorff's term "fittingness" is appropriate here. The choice of music for a particular use in worship should "fit" its purpose for that use. And the nature of the way it is offered by the person/instrument offering it should "fit" the action of the liturgy at that point. But what determines "fit"? There are not likely to be hard and fast rules here, but the combined wisdom and knowledge of a good theologian, a skillful church musician, and thoughtful lay congregants, all of whom are intent on the building of sung liturgical prayer, are a strong basis for decision-making. Sensitivity to the moment from those who understand the liturgical function, who know how to choose an excellent piece of music, and who have an understanding of the abilities and perspective of the congregation will usually yield an appropriate choice.

Awareness of Context in Musical Choice

Good musical choices are dependent upon the context in which the music will function. Each service, each congregation, each day and season in the life of the church bring unique characteristics that can determine whether a musical choice is effective. Music can be aesthetically excellent and theologically sound, but still be a very wrong choice for a particular place and time. Rather than offering specific guidelines, perhaps the following questions and considerations might lead to answers that result in wise choices:

1. Is congregational singing important for worship, as compared to a passive listening to the music? If so (and I hope so!), then the

melodies must be singable, and a repertoire of singable music can and should be developed over time that serves as a basis for building a worship service. New music can be introduced, with care, building on what is known.

2. What are the singing capabilities of the congregation, both in the degree of difficulty they can handle, and their awareness of musical style, and what repertoire is already familiar to them? How much can they be stretched to incorporate new music on any one occasion, and how can that be done so as not to interrupt the flow of the liturgy? How can the new build upon the known?

3. How does each individual piece of music contribute to the coherence of the whole? Just as a piece of good music has coherence within itself, so a service needs musical coherence from beginning to end.

4. What are the musical traditions in this congregation? Each congregation has developed certain traditions over time. Whether or not they are worthy of being continued, those traditions must be known, and changed only with great care.

5. The function of the music must be considered for the choice to work liturgically. Consider these questions: Does the processional hymn bring the worshiper comfortably into the worshiping experience? Is the music intended for the ritual part of the Mass? If so, can the singing be almost effortless in order for the singer's concentration to be on the eucharistic moment? How could the reading of the gospel be enhanced by a thought-provoking text in the hymn that precedes the reading? Is the offertory music better if provided by the choir or instrumentalist(s), so that hymnals and bulletins are not competing with offering receptacles? What is the best choice for Communion, when a familiar tune and text (or cantor/response) may be helpful to parishioners who want to sing while waiting to receive? Is the recessional hymn text a summary of the service theme, a companion to a tune that can be whistled or hummed on the way to the car, all the while reminiscent of the text?

6. What are the educational opportunities offered by the music? Can the choir or soloists "teach" the congregation a new piece of music, perhaps by singing the first stanza or two? Do the texts of the music reinforce or explicate the theological themes of the Scriptures and the sermon in a different way than the spoken word might? Is it possible for children to learn hymns and litur-

gical music of their faith that will continue to serve them well as adults?

7. How can the musical gifts of the congregation be used in ways that help them develop those gifts, whether it be as a child learning an instrument or as an adult who has studied for years? How can we, by using the gifts of the congregation first, create music that is truly ours? Can we provide circumstances for choirs to sing more beautifully, for soloists to develop their technique and repertoire, for gifted younger members to consider a calling to a vocation in the music of the church? How can we incorporate gifted musicians from outside the church in meaningful ways from time to time?

8. When does grace supersede excellence and expertise? Granted, we can agree that offering our best musical gifts to God is the goal. But are there times when even higher values may prevail? For example, Gus, a valued and lifelong choir member, has a hearing problem that causes him to sing slightly off pitch at times. Gus stays. Ruth slows the choir procession because walking is becoming difficult for her. We wait. An amateur composer in the parish writes a piece of music for the church. We find a way to use it. A distraught granddaughter asks that her grandfather's favorite song, otherwise theologically inappropriate, be included in his memorial service. We find a way to use it, but unobtrusively.

Concluding Reflections on the Contributions of Music and Theology to Liturgy

Addressing church music in an interdisciplinary mode is subject to the same potential pitfalls present when different disciplines are combined. Ideally, mastery of these disciplines is required; in this case, music and theology. If mastery of all is not possible, at least mastery of the most relevant discipline is required, together with a way of working competently with the other. The methodologies for theology, music, and liturgy are very different, and our current situation in the music of the church makes us sharply aware of the difficulties that may arise when theology and music come together in the context of liturgy. Add to this the implementation of the music in a congregation that may be largely unversed in either theology or music, and it is no surprise that we should encounter difficulties.

Perhaps we can take a lesson from the fields of science and religion, where controversy is not in short supply, and where progress has been made in bringing two very different methodologies from discrete fields into fruitful interaction with one another. Ian Barbour,[14] in his 1997 book *Religion and Science: Historical and Contemporary Issues*, distinguishes four different ways in which the relations of religion and science tend to be viewed.[15] The two contexts are, of course, quite different. The function of music and theology working together is expected to culminate in enhanced liturgy, itself a well-defined activity with its own norms. Science and religion on the other hand can often remain autonomous without having to make a contribution to yet another entity. Nevertheless, some comparisons are helpful. Barbour's fourfold division can give us some insights for answering the question: In what ways do music and theology characteristically relate as they attempt to contribute to liturgy?

1. **Conflict**. This way of thinking would place the two disciplines at odds with each other when a liturgy is being planned, each operating coherently within itself but in conflict with the other discipline. Certainly what has been described as the "worship wars" could reflect this model. In these "wars" some issues seem to recur frequently, such as: pastoral concerns collide with music quality concerns; pragmatic concerns contend with theological ones; style preferences dictate choice rather than theological or musical awareness. Often, no apparent resolution is possible that respects the natures of both theology and music, and both the musician and pastor feel they must constantly battle for the integrity of their discipline.

2. **Independence.** This manner of relating the two assumes no difficulty in either theology or music accepting the other, because each operates in its own sphere. God would be seen as working in each sphere differently and independently, with no need to make the two spheres relate to each other. In this case the pastor would make decisions involving theology, the musician those concerning music, and the congregation would be free to choose a church that best met their needs for worship. The independence of those making the choices does not imply mutual respect, it is hardly necessary to add.

3. **Dialogue.** In this case, each side agrees to respect the other, to talk together about their differences, and to acknowledge the

distinct ways God works in each, perhaps even finding that God is at work when the two coexist. If consonance occurs between the two in such a case, however, it may seem almost an accident. The two sides talk to each other but do not really influence one another to any marked extent. In such a case, one can be grateful on those occasions when theology and music combine to make a powerful and effective liturgy.

4. **Integration.** But there is a further possibility, one that involves dialogue but goes beyond it, with a view to achieving a real harmony in the liturgy, to which both fully contribute, each in its own way. This would seem the obvious ideal; the fact that it is not more often achieved, that the three prior modes of relating are as common as they are, testifies to the difficulty in achieving this ideal.[16]

These are not the only ways in which one might view the relationship between music and theology in the context of liturgical practice. Since our focus in this book is on the music, we might probe the role music itself is expected to play in the planning of the liturgy. Here the options might be ones similar to those suggested by Calvin Johansson.[17]

1. **Aesthetic:** Some would maintain that the more effective the music of the liturgy is in aesthetic terms, the more effectively it will serve to make God known. Just as we might contemplate a magnificent seascape and understand something about God in nature, so we can experience God by hearing a piece of sacred music from the fine art repertoire. What guides the choice of music for the liturgy in this case would be the same criteria that would govern choice when music is considered as a fine art. The criteria are internal to the world of music and reflect the special needs of liturgy only in that the music is somehow considered to be religious.

2. **Experiential:** Here the focus is not primarily on the aesthetic quality of the music but rather on its effectiveness in evoking religious *experience*. The choice of music is governed by how the music *functions* as religious experience. It might do so simply as a consequence of association: one has heard the music often enough in a liturgical context that hearing it tends to foster an experience of a broadly religious sort. Or the quality of the music itself, its solemnity perhaps, or its reflective nature, might evoke the sort of emotions characteristically regarded as religious.

Johansson would likely refer to this way of categorizing music as *pragmatic*.[18] The appropriateness of the music would be determined by function, by whether it does what it is intended to do, that is, to create or enhance religious experience.

3. **Integrated:** Here the theme of integration would once more seem to serve as the appropriate ideal, as it did earlier. While the aesthetic qualities of the music and its effectiveness in evoking religious experience are both evidently important in their own right, they have to be integrated into a larger, coherent whole. Johansson calls this "Biblical Counterpoint," drawing on the musical term that refers to the interplay of two or more independent lines of music that work together harmoniously.[19] This way of thinking about the role music should play in the life of the church would weigh theological and liturgical considerations when making musical choices. There would be different voices in this dialogue, each with a right to be heard, each with something to learn from the others. The goal is a simple one: effective worship. But orchestrating the elements in the counterpoint is far from simple. It is, however, a goal eminently worth striving for.

We make choices about music in liturgy best when we use all the elements at our disposal—all we know about music, about theology, and the nature of the community and context. Granted, we may not know enough about how music works in liturgy to draw definitive conclusions or to formulate rules about choosing music. But this is art, not science. And we may get it right one time only to fail the next. Or our choices may be right for some people and occasions, but not for others.

Just as well, perhaps. Our yearnings help us recognize that, despite our best efforts, we are not really in charge. It is God present with us in the choosing; it is to God we offer the music we make. Just as each new day can be lived with fresh awareness of God's presence, so each new liturgy, each piece of music we offer, can be given in partnership with each other and with God. It is God's work, not ours alone. And if we are in the "place just right"—as the text to accompany the Shaker tune "Simple Gifts" would remind us—we perhaps will be moved through our music, in the words of Father Gelineau, to greater faith, hope, and love of the mystery of Jesus Christ.

Notes

1. Unpublished study that was part of a larger project, "Empowering Congregational Music: Linking Thought and Practice," funded by the Lilly Endowment, spring 2002.

2. Dorothy Tuck McFarland, *Simone Weil* (New York: F. Ungar Publishing Company, 1983).

3. Charles S. Pottie, s.j., *A More Profound Alleluia! Gelineau and Routley on Music in Christian Worship* (Washington, D.C.: The Pastoral Press, 1984) 26–7.

4. Ibid., 61.

5. Nicholas Wolterstorff, in the seminar, "Liturgy, the Arts, and the Practice of Christian Worship," Calvin College, summer 2002.

6. C. Michael Hawn, "Singing with the Faithful of Every Time and Place," in *Reformed Liturgy and Music* (Louisville: Joint Office of Worship of the United Presbyterian Church, U.S.A., and the Presbyterian Church, U.S., in cooperation with the Presbyterian Association of Musicians, vol. 23, no. 1) 17.

7. Helen Myers, ed., *Ethnomusicology: An Introduction* (New York: W. W. Norton, 1992) 3.

8. Joseph Gelineau, *Liturgical Assembly, Liturgical Song* (Portland, OR: Pastoral Press, 2003) 61.

9. John Merbecke, "Fraction Anthem: O Lamb of God," in *The Hymnal 1982* (New York: The Church Hymnal Corporation, 1985) S157.

10. J. S. Bach, "Agnus Dei" from *Mass in B Minor, BWV 232* (Valley Forge, PA: Barenreiter-Verlag/European American Music, 1955) 233.

11. *With One Voice: A Lutheran Resource for Worship.* "Lamb of God" from Setting Four, *Light of Christ,* for Holy Communion (Minneapolis: Augsburg Fortress, 1995) 25.

12. Richard Proulx, "Agnus Dei," from *A Community Mass* in *Worship: A Hymnal and Service Book for Roman Catholics* (Chicago: GIA Publications, Inc., 2001) 255.

13. Nicholas Wolterstorff, this volume, p. 12.

14. Ian Barbour is retired from Carleton College, where he was professor of physics and professor of religion, and is a recent recipient of a major award from the John Templeton Foundation for work in science and religion.

15. Ian Barbour, *Religion and Science: Historical and Contemporary Issues* (San Francisco: HarperSanFrancisco, 1997) 245–7.

16. I am indebted to Ernan McMullin, professor emeritus of philosophy, University of Notre Dame, for articulating the Barbour categories in ways helpful to understanding how theology and music can relate in the context of the liturgy.

17. Calvin Johansson is recently retired as professor of music at Evangel College in Springfield, Missouri, where he has also served as a musician in an Episcopal church.

18. Calvin M. Johansson, *Music and Ministry: A Biblical Counterpoint* (Peabody, MA: Hendrickson Publishers, Inc., 1998) 4–6.

19. Ibid., 7.

Contributors

Wilma Ann Bailey is associate professor of Hebrew and Aramaic scripture at Christian Theological Seminary in Indianapolis. She has also held faculty positions at Messiah and Goshen Colleges. Her degrees are from Vanderbilt (PH.D. and M.A.), Associated Mennonite Biblical Seminaries (M.DIV.), and Hunter/Lehman College (B.S.), with additional study at Northwestern University, and the University of Haifa. She is the author of numerous scholarly journal articles and book reviews, as well as a frequent contributor to interdisciplinary journals and denominational publications.

Frank Burch Brown is Frederick Doyle Kershner Professor of Religion and the Arts at Christian Theological Seminary in Indianapolis. He is author of four books, including *Religious Aesthetics* (Princeton University Press, 1989) and *Good Taste, Bad Taste, and Christian Taste: Aesthetics in Religious Life* (Oxford University Press, 2000). He is currently editing the seven-hundred-page *Oxford Handbook of Religion and the Arts*. A composer with twenty commissioned works to his credit, he also directs degree programs in music and the arts for CTS. He was a visiting fellow in the Faculty of Divinity at Cambridge University in 2000 and the inaugural Henry Luce Visiting Professor of Theology and Art at St. John's University School of Theology-Seminary in 2003. He has lectured widely, having given multimedia presentations at academic institutions such as Oxford, Cambridge, Yale, University of Chicago, Northwestern, Union Theological Seminary (NYC), and seventy others.

Linda J. Clark, professor emeritus of sacred music at Boston University School of Theology, is the author of over thirty articles and three books, including *Music in Churches: Nourishing Your Congregation's Musical Life* (The Alban Institute, 1994) and [with Joanne Swenson and Mark Stamm] *How We Seek God Together* (The Alban Institute, 2000). Her latest book details the results of a research project on the relationship between musical style and religious identity. She is currently working with colleagues at the University of Notre Dame on a research project on planning in worship. She is also the director of music at Grace Episcopal Church in Newton, Massachusetts. Dr. Clark's advanced degrees are from the University of Wisconsin, Madison, and Union Theological Seminary.

Michael Driscoll is professor of theology at the University of Notre Dame where he teaches courses in liturgy and theology. After graduating from Carroll College, he received degrees at the University of Paris-Sorbonne (PH.D.), the Institut Catholique de Paris (S.T.D.), Sant' Anselmo, Rome (S.T.L.), and the Pontificia Università Gregoriana, Rome (S.T.B.). He was ordained presbyter for the Diocese of Helena in 1977. He has served as both president and vice-president of the North American Academy of Liturgy. Author of numerous scholarly and denominational articles, he is a member of the Council of the *Societas Liturgica*.

C. Michael Hawn is professor of church music at Perkins School of Theology, Southern Methodist University, where he has taught since 1992. He has also been a professor in two Baptist seminaries and has directed church music in congregations in Kentucky, Georgia, North Carolina, and Texas. He has received several grants for the study of worship and music in Africa, Asia, and Latin America. Professor Hawn is the author of over eighty articles and several books. Most recently his publications include a collection of global songs entitled *Halle, Halle: We Sing the World Round* (Garland, TX: Choristers Guild, 1999) and two books on global music and cross-cultural worship: *Gather into One: Praying and Singing Globally* (Grand Rapids, MI: Wm. B. Eerdmans, 2003) and *One Bread, One Body: Exploring Cultural Diversity in Worship* (Bethesda, MD: The Alban Institute, 2003).

Ordained in 1980 as a priest of the Archdiocese of St. Paul-Minneapolis, Minnesota, **Fr. Jan Michael Joncas** serves as associate professor of theology and Catholic studies at the University of St. Thomas in St. Paul, Minnesota. He holds degrees in English from the (then) College of St. Thomas in St. Paul, Minnesota, and in liturgical studies from the University of Notre Dame, Notre Dame, Indiana, and the Pontificio Istituto Liturgico of the Ateneo S. Anselmo in Rome. He has served as a parochial vicar, a campus minister, and a parochial administrator (pastor). He is the author of three books and over one hundred articles and reviews in journals such as *Worship, Ecclesia Orans*, and *Questions*

Liturgiques. He is composer and arranger of over two hundred pieces of liturgical music.

Mary Oyer, D.M.A., is professor emerita at Goshen College in Indiana. She was trained in music literature and related arts, and performance practices (cello) at the University of Michigan. After some years as a college music professor, she built upon her broad training to do research into the music of other cultures. Her journey as a Christian and her work in hymnal research led her to explore the music of diverse cultures. Guiding force for two different Mennonite hymnals, Dr. Oyer is a frequent clinician and song leader for hymn festivals across the U.S. and Canada.

Bert Polman is a professor of music at Redeemer University College in Ancaster, Ontario, Canada, as well as a church organist, hymnologist, and workshop leader at worship conferences. He is the primary author of the *Psalter Hymnal Handbook* (1998) and has served on the editorial committees of five hymnals: *Psalter Hymnal* (1987); *The Worshiping Church, a Hymnal* (1990); *Songs for LIFE* (1994); *Amazing Grace: Hymn Texts for Devotional Use* (1994); and *Sing! A New Creation* (2001). He is currently working on a book-length study of musical settings of the *Magnificat*. His degrees are from Dordt College (B.A.) and the University of Minnesota (M.A., PH.D.).

Don E. Saliers teaches at Emory University where he holds the Wm. R. Cannon Distinguished Professorship in Theology and Worship, and directs the MSM Program. Educated at Ohio Wesleyan, Yale and Cambridge Universities, he has served as president of the Society for the Study of Christian Spirituality and the North American Academy of Liturgy, having held teaching positions at Yale Divinity School and St. John's University, Collegeville. Well known in ecumenical circles, he received the Berakah Award in 1992 for his contributions to liturgical reform and renewal. Among recent publications are *Worship Come to Its Senses, Worship as Theology: Foretaste of Glory Divine*, and in 2004 with his daughter, Emily, *A Song to Sing, A Life to Live*.

Joanne M. Swenson holds the M.DIV., TH.M. and TH.D. degrees from Harvard University, where she was a North American Fund Fellow. A philosophical theologian, she focuses on congregational aesthetics as a way of introducing laypeople to the otherwise-problematic notion of reconstructing an inadequate concept of God. She has taught at Pacific Lutheran University and Oregon State University, is ordained in the United Church of Christ, and an active member of both a progressive

U.C.C. congregation and an evangelical Presbyterian church—a stimulating contrast of styles and theologies.

John D. Witvliet is director of the Calvin Institute of Christian Worship and serves as associate professor of worship, theology, and music at Calvin College and Calvin Theological Seminary. A graduate of Calvin College, Dr. Witvliet holds graduate degrees in theology from Calvin Theology Seminary, in choral music from the University of Illinois, and the PH.D. in liturgical studies and theology from the University of Notre Dame. He is the author of *Worship Seeking Understanding: Windows into Christian Practice* (Baker Academic, 2003), coeditor of *Worship in Medieval and Early Modern Europe: Change and Continuity in Religious Practice* (University of Notre Dame Press, 2004), and editor of *A Child Shall Lead: Children in Worship* (Choristers Guild, 1999). He serves as editor for two books series, the "Calvin Institute of Christian Worship Liturgical Studies Series" (Eerdmans) and "Vital Worship, Healthy Congregations" (Alban Institute), as well as coeditor, with Pearl Shangkuan, of the Calvin Institute of Christian Worship Music Series (GIA).

Nicholas Wolterstorff is Noah Porter Professor Emeritus of Philosophical Theology, and Fellow of Berkeley College, at Yale University. He is a graduate of Calvin College, and received his PH.D. in philosophy from Harvard in 1956. After teaching for thirty years at Calvin, he joined the Divinity School at Yale, where he was also adjunct professor in the Philosophy Department and in the Religious Studies Department. He has been president of the American Philosophical Association (Central Division) and of the Society of Christian Philosophers. He has given the Wilde Lectures at Oxford University, the Gifford Lectures at St Andrews University, and the Stone Lectures at Princeton Seminary. In addition to Calvin and Yale, he has taught at the University of Michigan, the University of Texas, The University of Notre Dame, Princeton University, and the Free University of Amsterdam. His most recent publications are *Divine Discourse* (Cambridge 1995), *John Locke and the Ethics of Belief* (Cambridge 1996), *Thomas Reid and the Story of Epistemology* (Cambridge 2001), *Educating for Life* (Baker 2002), and *Educating for Shalom: Essays on Christian Higher Education* (Eerdmans 2004). Earlier publications were *Art in Action* (Eerdmans 1980) and *Works and Worlds of Art* (Oxford 1980). He is currently working on a book that he has tentatively titled *Justice: Divine and Human*.

Index